HANSARD SOCIETY SERIES IN POLITICS AND GOVERNMENT

Series Editor
F. F. Ridley

HANSARD SOCIETY SERIES IN POLITICS AND GOVERNMENT

Edited by
F. F. Ridley

1. THE QUANGO DEBATE, edited with David Wilson

2. BRITISH GOVERNMENT AND POLITICS SINCE 1945: CHANGES IN PERSPECTIVES, edited with Michael Rush

3. SLEAZE: POLITICIANS, PRIVATE INTERESTS AND PUBLIC REACTION, edited with Alan Doig

4. WOMEN IN POLITICS, edited with Joni Lovenduski and Pippa Norris

5. UNDER THE SCOTT-LIGHT: BRITISH GOVERNMENT SEEN THROUGH THE SCOTT REPORT, edited with Brian Thompson

6. BRITAIN VOTES 1997, edited with Pippa Norris and Neil T. Gavin

7. PROTEST POLITICS: CAUSE GROUPS AND CAMPAIGNS, edited with Grant Jordan

The Hansard Society Series in Politics and Government brings to the wider public the debates and analyses of important issues first discussed in the pages of its journal, *Parliamentary Affairs*

Protest Politics:
Cause Groups and Campaigns

Edited by
F. F. Ridley and Grant Jordan

Series Editor
F. F. Ridley

OXFORD UNIVERSITY PRESS
in association with
THE HANSARD SOCIETY FOR
PARLIAMENTARY GOVERNMENT

Oxford University Press, Clarendon Street, Oxford OX2 6DP
Oxford New York
Athens Auckland Bangkok Bombay
Calcutta Cape Town Dar es Salaam Delhi
Florence Hong Kong Istanbul Karachi
Kuala Lumpur Madras Madrid Melbourne
Mexico City Nairobi Paris Singapore
Taipei Tokyo Toronto
and associated companies in
Berlin Ibadan

Oxford is a trade mark of Oxford University Press

Published in the United States
by Oxford University Press Inc., New York

© Oxford University Press, 1998

First published in Parliamentary Affairs, 1998
New as paperback, 1998

A catalogue for this book is available from the British Library

Library of Congress Cataloging in Publication Data
(Data available)

ISBN 0–19–922374–2

Printed in Great Britain
by Headley Brothers Limited, The Invicta Press,
Ashford, Kent and London

CONTENTS

PREFACE   1
by F. F. RIDLEY

INTRODUCTION   6
by GRANT JORDAN

GUN CONTROL AND SNOWDROP   21
by STUART THOMSON, LARA STANCICH AND LISA DICKSON

CALF EXPORTS AT BRIGHTLINGSEA   37
by RHODA McLEOD

SECOND RUNWAY AT MANCHESTER   50
by STEVEN GRIGGS, DAVID HOWARTH AND BRIAN JACOBS

OPPOSITION TO ROAD-BUILDING   62
by BRIAN DOHERTY

NUCLEAR POWER AT DRURIDGE BAY   76
by ROB BAGGOTT

BRENT SPAR, ATLANTIC OIL AND GREENPEACE   89
by LYNN G. BENNIE

PESTICIDES, SHEEP DIPS AND SCIENCE   103
by ALAN GREER

NUCLEAR WEAPONS AND CND   116
by PAUL BYRNE

REPRESENTING WOMEN IN SCOTLAND   127
by ALICE BROWN

THE PRO-LIFE MOVEMENT   137
by MELVYN D. READ

DEFENDING ANIMAL RIGHTS   150
by ROBERT GARNER

EUROPE, GOLDSMITH AND THE REFERENDUM PARTY   162
by NEIL CARTER, MARK EVANS, KEITH ALDERMAN AND SIMON GORHAM

INDEX   178

CONTRIBUTORS TO THIS VOLUME

Keith Alderman is Senior Lecturer in Politics at the University of York.

Rob Baggott is Reader in Public Policy, De Montfort University, Leicester.

Lynn G. Bennie is Lecturer in Politics, University of Aberdeen.

Alice Brown is Professor of Politics, University of Edinburgh.

Paul Byrne is Senior Lecturer in Politics, Loughborough University.

Neil Carter is Lecturer in Politics, University of York.

Lisa Dickson is Lecturer in Law, University of Kent at Canterbury.

Brian Doherty is Lecturer in Politics, Keele University.

Mark Evans is Lecturer in Politics, University of York.

Robert Garner is Lecturer in Politics, University of Leicester.

Simon Gorham was a postgraduate student in Politics at the University of York.

Alan Greer is Senior Lecturer in Politics, University of the West of England, Bristol.

Steven Griggs is Lecturer in Public Policy, Staffordshire University, Stoke-on-Trent.

David Howarth is Lecturer in Politics, Staffordshire University, Stoke-on-Trent.

Brian Jacobs is Reader in Public Policy , Staffordshire University, Stoke-on-Trent.

Grant Jordan is Professor of Politics, University of Aberdeen.

Rhoda McLeod is a Researcher in Sociology at the University of Aberdeen.

Melvyn Read is Lecturer in Politics, Queen's University, Belfast.

Lara Stancich is an honorary Research Fellow, Public Administration and Law, Robert Gordon University, Stirling.

Stuart Thomson is a Researcher in Politics at the University of Aberdeen.

Cover photograph by Ben Curtis

PREFACE
Crusaders and Politicians

BY F.F. RIDLEY

FOR most, politics is a complicated business and all but the highlights boring as well. The highlights are about people in politics, human interest, too often scandals, rather than the machinery of the political system. Television producers and newspaper editors reflect this. What is remembered, thus what made a personal impact at the time, is pictures with elements of drama or touching our emotions: some election night constituency declarations, flowers for Princess Diana outside Buckingham Palace, the soft brown eyes of calves on their journey to slaughter abroad, 'Swampy' as David cocking-a-snook at developers' Goliath excavators. Often such memories relate to campaigns outside the run of established politics, involving people who would be offended if described as politicians.

The contributions to this volume cover a variety of causes and a range of strategies, linked by the fact that they fell outside the established political system (meaning Westminster model: representative government, parties, elections, Parliament, and Whitehall model: organised interests, pressure groups and the Executive). The selection is wide as the Contents page shows: campaigns against private ownership of guns, against environmental damage through roads and runways, against dangerous pesticides, against oil pollution of the ocean, against nuclear weapons, against nuclear power stations, against live calf exports, against further European integration.

Action campaigns are often triggered off by something that has just happened or is just about to happen (against something as focus) and may be less readily mounted to promote longer-term improvements (thus spontaneous protest about threatened reductions in single parent and disability allowances). Of course, that is not the whole story: the women's rights movement is ongoing. In any event, the cases studied in this volume cover campaigns organised differently, engaging supporters differently, relating to government differently, and fitting differently into society.

One interest of the present case studies lies in reminding readers of events they may have seen on television or read about in the press not so long ago (though what seems not so long ago probably varies with age). They fill in the stories, explain the organisation and background, for example, and contextualise the events—making better sense of contemporary history. The contributions are also intended as pegs for discussion of the political system and the policy process, as political science material.

Contributors express opinions, moral and political, and refer to political science theories as they analyse the significance of the movements they describe. They do not, however, let conceptual frameworks dominate the stories as so much political science research does. The hope is that readers will move through the volume from one contribution to the next as chapters in a book, interested in all, rather than read only a selected piece relevant to a specialised research assignment. That links with another intention of this volume. Singularly or separately, the accounts may be used as case studies to which readers can bring their own (or their teachers') theories, or from which, as researchers, they can develop theory. In this respect Grant Jordan's opening piece is very helpful: it overviews relevant theory, adds comments, introduces ideas and draws attention to illustrations later in the volume.

In *The Times* (7.3.98) the weekend of writing this Preface, there was an article headed 'Tree crusader claims moral high ground'. It opened: 'Her view is astounding. Her winter has been terrifying. Her lavatory is a bucket on a rope. Julia "Butterfly" Hill has spent the past 86 days perched on a plywood platform 180ft. up in the branches of an ancient redwood tree. Her object is to save the 1,000-year-old giant from logging, but at times her chief worry has been how to stay alive. As the worst storms in memory pounded the northern Californian coast last month, she wrapped herself in a torn tarpaulin, clung to the swaying branches and prayed.'

Seen to occupy the moral high ground, though not always so adventurously, are a good number of cause groups and campaigners—when compared to career politicians, establishment figures or industrialists. Martin Bell, the knight in a white suit, against Neil Hamilton (Hamilton, to be fair, not representative of MPs but Bell was nevertheless seen as whiter than most); mourners for Princess Diana when the Queen (or probably palace officials) would not fly a flag half-mast at the Palace; ordinary people stirred to protest against animal suffering imposed by agribusiness; defenders of the fox against hunters in fancy dress, raising a glass (champagne?) before cantering off for a day's sport (little to do with culling vermin, a task otherwise left to low-paid workers). The moral characteristic of many protest movements is that they have no personal interest to promote, no material gain from the outcome—unlike their opponents, altruism is common.

Of course, that is not always the case. The Not In My Back Yard element in protest can also be seen on occasion: local residents fighting a proposed runway, noisy and likely to reduce house values, for example—though interestingly some developed a wider environmental concern through their participation. The great Countryside Rally, a quarter of a million in London to protest against threats to centuries-old ways of rural life by ignorant townies, had interests to protect: their sport for a start, large tracts of often unfarmed land that walkers would like to ramble on occasionally, and of course house values protected by Green Belts that others might want to build on. But see *The Sunday Times* (8.3.98) the weekend of writing. Under the heading 'Countryside crusaders offer green belt to developers', it tells of a farmer who lit one of the beacons that signalled the march (not that much marching was done) but who was selling farmland for a housing estate, and of a foxhunt master who had sold his parents' riding school to developers. A voting-strength demonstration but not one likely to win great moral respect.

There is probably a lesson about the society we live in here. Pursuit of self-interest appears to dominate. Indeed, an international survey just published claims that the British, from childhood onwards, now rate material interests more highly than anything (including family life) and outstrip other Europeans in this respect. The result, of course, may be that latent emotions, if touched on a national scale, can bring unexpected disarray to our socio-political order (the Princess Diana case a portent?). Mr Blair, backing away from support of anti-bloodsports legislation in the face of a mass rally of hostile future voters, may one day regret disregarding the quieter but much larger number of people that opinion polls show opposed to such sports. The Snowdrop story surely has some lessons.

Equally important for the public appeal of several campaigns is the courage of their activists. Some eco-warriors risked their lives up trees and under ground at Twyford Down and on Manchester's second runway site. Many more endured considerable discomfort to make their point, not to mention encounters with less than gentle private security forces. The same is true of Greenpeace crusades, even if their organisation (and there is far more organisation here than 'Swampy' and friends had) saw much of what was done as media stunts. But just as notable were the 'good ladies' of Brightlingsea (a term probably acceptable to the respectable, elderly demonstrators formed in days before political correctness), outraged by the uncaring transport of live calves through their small town. It must have needed great courage to break with upbringing and stand in the road as they did, and in doing so they earned a respect that professional politicians should envy.

That brings one to another point about causes and campaigns. A possible title for this volume was Politics Without Parties—and indeed it is the well-chosen title of Grant Jordan's opening contribution. Some of the campaigns in this volume worked outside parties because their cause did not fit into party programmes or because the campaigners did not wish to become party activists, but since their goal was legislation they nevertheless set out to influence Parliament. The Countryside Rally presented itself as a show of strength of future voters, lobbying Parliament to kill an expected Private Member's Bill and later passed its membership list to the Conservative Party. The Snowdrop campaign also needed to influence MPs. It started as a hoped-for million signature petition to Parliament calling for legislation to ban private ownership of firearms. From this, however, grew a much wider purpose of arousing public awareness and creating a climate of opinion MPs could not ignore. Despite some help from MPs, it kept its distance from parliamentary politics.

The most obvious example of a single-issue campaign entering the political system in the Westminster-model sense is found in the last contribution to this volume: Goldsmith's Referendum Party at the 1997 general election. There never was a hope of seats—the intention was to persuade candidates of other parties to take an anti-Europe stance in order to avoid losing votes. Even in this case, the anti-system character of the project deserves mention: Referendum Party candidates, if elected, promised to resign if they got a referendum—and many of them, in the unlikely event of election, would have been as out of place in the system as the early Poujadistes, barkeepers and small shopowners, in the French parliament.

Other campaigns are further removed from politics. They act directly against their opponents. The second Manchester Runway Campaign was directed against Manchester Airport and, after failing at the public inquiry, against its contractors. Some try to disrupt business by direct action (blocking work for example) or bring indirect pressure on business (promoting customer boycotts for example)—Greenpeace against oil companies, the Druridge Bay campaigners against a power company. Here one sees another possible title for this column: Politics Without Politicians.

Cause groups are often described as outsiders that do not fit into the established system of interest organisations/pressure groups which, with government, constitute the networks of policy-making. They are excluded because they have no ongoing concern with a set of material interests, no clientele that can be defined in such terms, and often no permanent organisation either. But they may also be outsiders by choice. This can be a tactical choice, as suggested above (e.g. to mobilise support that crosses socio-economic divisions as well as party-political lines). It can also be a tactical choice to avoid being tarred with the brush of politics, since a political colouring is more likely to lose than win supporters.

Politicians stand low in public esteem in Britain and elsewhere. Opinion polls place them among the least trusted professions. This is not the place to discuss the reasons: policy failures, parliamentary slanging matches, scandals of one sort or another and so on. Politicians are also seen as unresponsive to public demands where these do not fit their own political needs. A final quotation from the weekend's press, *The Sunday Times* (8.3.98) claimed that a person described as 'head of Labour's parliamentary party' 'has recommended that MPs stop holding open advice surgeries for their constituents and concentrate on "real work" instead'. Real work presumably means in Westminster, in Whitehall and in the party.

Of course, most MPs still do their best for constituents and most will listen to approaches from cause groups, sympathising or not on personal as much as on party basis. The point, however, is that much of the public sees politicians as careerists, which, to be fair to MPs, they have to be these days. Protestors, on the other hand, are not career politicians, nor, in most cases, career protestors. Even those who seem to engage continuously in protest campaigns (unlike the one-off Brightlingsea or Druridge Bay residents) cannot be described as careerists if that means 'one intent on personal advancement' (OED). Few are employed in permanent organisations that make protest campaigns a central part of their activity — and even for those pay prospects are limited. Collaboration between the representatives of protest groups and officials representing other institutions thus has its difficulties: protestors do not necessarily want to become like those they deal with in politics, government and industry (perhaps remembering what happened to the pigs in *Animal Farm*).

In the end, however, if a democratic political system is to survive, it has to find a place for cause groups and protest campaigns. Widening policy networks is suggested in several contributions, in environmental planning and pesticides control for example. More generally, decision-making structures need to recognise that cause groups now mobilise as many people as interest groups. While cause groups are likely to be more volatile, thus hard to integrate in an institutionalised network, their supporters may show unexpectedly strong emotions, displacing expected behaviour patterns and disrupting established ways of government — as did the Crusades many centuries ago. Political science is addressed to political scientists but the contents of this volume concern all citizens. Are the cases described warnings of more serious storms to come? Do we need to think about organising ourselves more effectively to take account of the cause groups and protest movements that fall outside the politics of parties?

Special issues of Parliamentary Affairs and volumes in the Hansard Society Series in Politics and Government cover topics of contemporary concern (recently *Britain Votes 1997*, *Parliaments and Publics*, *Under the Scott-light*, *Women in Politics*, *Sleaze*, *The Quango Debate*). Readers may sympathise with all, some or none of the causes covered here. Our intention is neither to persuade readers to join a crusade nor to warn them against crusaders. The point is that single-cause movements are here to stay. Their campaigns need to be studied, their role integrated in any analysis of British government and politics (with other examples, any democracy), just as parties and pressure groups are. By and large, textbooks do not yet to so adequately. This volume may help fill a gap.

INTRODUCTION
Politics Without Parties: A Growing Trend?

BY GRANT JORDAN

TWO related conventional wisdoms have emerged in recent years. The first is that political parties are no longer important instruments of public participation. This belief flourished in America in the 1980s and has been reinvented in other countries. For example, Cigler and Loomis noted as trends of the time, 'a great proliferation of interest groups since the early 1960s' and 'the continuing decline of (US) political parties' abilities to perform key electoral and policy-related activities'.[1] An increase in interest group activity is part of the second conventional wisdom: that popular protest (both organised by interest groups and more spontaneous) has increased in the frequency and significance of its occurrence. Thus Peter Gundelach has asserted that, 'In Western Europe, as in the United States, the relatively stable social and political life of the 1950s and early 1960s was replaced by social unrest, political protest, and social movements during the late 1960s and 1970s'.[2] Citing Offe, he argued that an old style of politics centred on consumption and material progress had been replaced by 'new politics' which stressed issues of personal autonomy and identity. In the US, Charles Euchner, citing an address by Vaclav Havel, has referred to 'anti-politics' and 'extraordinary politics' as other synonyms for this notion that politics by protest had evolved as a response to 'demosclerosis'. He claimed, 'Protest and other forms of outsider politics had come to play a central role in setting the agenda for national and local politics'.[3] Cigler and Loomis in their 1991 edition could, without the need for qualification, note that in America, 'a participation revolution has occurred ... as large numbers of citizens have become active in an ever increasing number of protest groups, citizen's organisations, and special interest groups'.

This collection of contributions covers both group-orchestrated activity and more spontaneous mobilisation of protest. These are different phenomena, and in a sense ad hoc protest can be seen a challenge both to party membership and to that sort of traditional interest group activity which used protest as a selective weapon. While some protests claim, as an ideological merit, to be 'leaderless', is this rhetoric rather than description? The description of the Snowdrop campaign by Thomson et al., which pursued gun control shows the almost inevitable need for organisation in successful protest.

Is this a 'new politics'? Characterising the phenomenon

That all protest has not been orchestrated through formal and organised groups has encouraged use of the 'social movement' term. McFarland gave examples of social movements that included women's movement, environmentalism, consumerism. While conceding that it was difficult to define, he suggested that the term 'is characterised by activity directed to changing institutions and behaviours of importance to society' and had a mode of political expression 'often consisting of unconventional tactics and behaviours, such as civil disobedience, organising demonstrations, breaking up into small groups for the purpose of "consciousness raising", and even the threat or actual use of violence'.[4] It is claimed by Inglehart and others that protest is more likely by individuals who have post-material values.[5] One of the contributors here, Paul Byrne, has set out a vigorous version of the new social movement case in *Social Movements in Britain* in which he, too, draws attention to the possibility that over recent years hundreds of thousands of people in Britain have become engaged in a new kind of politics. He has identified a distinct trend of people showing less enthusiasm for the main parties and more interest in 'single-issue' politics'. However, he concedes that one of the distinctive features of social movements is their 'nebulous nature'. The added benefit of the social movement perspective is questioned in Jordan and Maloney.[6] That there is protest is not necessarily confirmation of new social movements as protest exists without the associated developments implicit in New Social Movement analysis. Protest can occur without the deep lifestyle changes and the fundamental rejection of the conventional political system of that interpretation. Byrne is reluctant to extend the social movement label to Greenpeace because it lacks the egalitarian instinct among supporters: it is very much based on a distinction between the activists and the financial supporters who are often otherwise passive.[7]

Some of the more spectacular examples of protest in the 1990s were essentially counters to the previous protests on issues such as the banning of fox hunts. On 1 March 1998, there was a march in London foreshadowed by the lighting of 5,500 beacons across the country—all under the slogan 'Let the Country Voice be Heard'. This protest was organised by the Countryside Alliance which itself was a federation of the British Field Sports Society, the Countryside Movement and the Countryside Business Group. Organisations supporting included the National Farmers' Union, the Royal Agricultural Society of England, National Cattle Association, British Equestrian Trade Association, National Federation of Young Farmers, Clay Pigeon Association, the Worshipful Company of Gunmakers, the Country Landowners' Association, Scottish Landowners' Federation, British Horse Society, British Horse Racing Board, The Jockey Club, National Trainers' Federation, Thoroughbred Breeders' Association, The National Game Dealers'

Association, National Association of Registered Gamedealers (Ireland), FACE (Federation des Associations de Chasseurs del Union Européenne), The Trout and Salmon Association, the Point to Point Owners and Riders Association, the British Falconers' Club, Essex Young Farmers, The Worshipful Company of Saddlers, British Association for Shooting and Conservation, British Equine Veterinary Association, the British Show Jumping Association, Timber Growers' Association, and the British Agricultural and Garden Machinery Association. The march claimed 284,000 participants and was highly organised, with 29 special trains chartered, 46 extended train services and 2,033 buses. It was certainly spectacular protest but not, it appears, well captured and described by the new social movement approach. Surely social movements have neither Chief Executives nor Chief Press Officers? This was about interest groups demonstrating their support and potential muscle. The Countryside Movement was financially guaranteed by the Duke of Westminster through a £1.3 m loan. The march was perhaps initiated by an opposition to the banning of hunting but it also exploited an inconsistent parcel of other rural concerns such as the government's handling of BSE in cattle, closing of rural schools, building in rural areas, lack of access for walkers. Ultimately, this was a strange variant of protest as the participants were not so much seeking to overturn the status quo but to preserve it. It did not have the sort of 'lack of personal comfort' that characterised anti-poll tax and anti nuclear weapons protest: more party that partisan. The similarities between this 'street protest' and that described by Rhoda McLeod in connection with live animal exports are few.

Earlier, in July 1997 there was an impressive (perhaps 100,000 in attendance) pro-field sports rally in Hyde Park. In early 1998 there were numerous protests at Anglesey and in south west Scotland about the entry of non-British beef into the country: four thousand Scottish farmers lobbied ministers in Edinburgh. In February farmers surrounded the Gold West bakery in Heywood which was McDonald's biggest supplier: McDonalds, which had at one stage had banned all British beef, agreed to increase its purchases of British beef to 80% and to promote 'the great British burger'. Farmers also targeted Heinz. The distribution centres of retailers were systematically disrupted until assistance in promoting British beef was agreed. The *Sunday Times* (8.2.98) concluded 'Where once taking to the streets was the preserve of the French—who used to infuriate British farmers by their blockades—now British farmers have discovered the power of protest.' The organiser of the Countryside March claimed it in the *Daily Telegraph* (22.6.95) as 'the biggest voluntary movement of people in this country since D-Day'. He argued that 'One of the things politicians hate is big numbers of single-issue voters because you can't buy them off with anything else.' (However, governments might well look to the contrary pointers of opinion polls in seeking measures of public concern.)

Moreover, the Labour government refused to directly confront the countryside challenge, arguing that it too shared many of the concerns. Though ministers were divided on the matter at least one reaction was to incorporate it as a 'celebration of the countryside'.

An issue is whether the protest events reported in the contributions to this volume match the behaviours indicated by the term social movement. Are the sorts of protest discussed in fact social movements or better understood in the interest group paradigm? Dalton, like McFarland, records that for many observers 'new social movements' including women's groups and the peace movement, are 'the new political style of advanced industrial democracies'. He says 'These movements also supposedly follow a decentralised structure and participatory style of decision making that differs from the neo-corporatist style of European interest groups. Theory holds that these new movements are changing the style of interest representation, placing greater reliance on protests and unconventional political activities.'[8] In some interpretations, the social movement is a sort of pre-institutionalised protest that will increasingly conform to interest group characteristics as it becomes incorporated in the political system. Others see social movements as being forces that provide new ideas for the more established parties and groups. As a result of the imprecision of the social movement term, Byrne advocates a protest movement concept to allow for the fact that the Campaign for Nuclear Disarmament does not have the organisational structure (or lack of it) that seems a prerequisite for a social movement.

Social movements are usually seen as mobilising constituencies not otherwise represented. They are also seen as outsiders challenging the status quo. But it is far from clear whether the primarily sociological term 'social movement' is an analytical concept distinct from the sort of interest group that has been used in political science. There is a tendency to relabel any group using non-conventional strategies and tactics as social movements. Burstein and his colleagues note that as used by significant sources in the literature (Gamson and Tilly), once a movement begins to succeed — by mobilising its constituency or gaining formal representation — it ceases to be a movement.[9]

The breadth of meaning covered by the term 'protest' means that very different activities are within the focus of the collection. Burstein et al identify non-institutionalised tactics that are not part of the formal political process and are intended to be disruptive. As Trevor Smith pointed out, at one extreme political violence that is unambiguously outside the law is a form of protest.[10] This is a very different phenomenon from peaceful protest, but in chaotic situations any definitional line can be crossed in an unpremeditated way: some would claim that certain forms of direct action (e.g. hindering the entry of lorries carrying beef into the country) — even if tolerated by the police — are still technically illegal. Because behaviours do not quite fit received concepts, there is a continual process of innovation to try better to relate practices to terms. Above Byrne's idea of the to protest movement is introduced. Another useful term suggested by Yael Yishai is the interest party. This label she applied to political organisations combining some characteristics of both political parties and interest groups.[11] Not only does the Referendum Party described by Carter and his colleagues fit this general pattern, in the firearms campaign both sides of the controversy came near to fielding candidates in the 1997 general election (in 1998 there was also speculation about a countryside party contesting the European elections against candidates who wished to ban hunting).

The decline of party and rise of non-party activities are connected by some commentators, so that the phenomenon of party atrophy is seen as being caused by the diversion of energy and resources to single-issue campaigns rather than to the broad-church parties. In this view, members of the public recognise that they secure a better return on their participatory investment by acting through specialist organisations that match their particular concerns, rather than through parties that are reluctant to identify with narrow causes for fear of upsetting other sections of their party constituency. Campaigns and groups are seen as better catering for intensely held views than do catch-all parties that try to offend few potential supporters and often avoid the controversial. In this interpretation, political parties are too much coalitions aimed at centrist opinion to be satisfactory for the well-informed and well-motivated public concerned about particular elements of the political menu. For example, as Robert Garner shows, major political parties are loathe to be too clearly be associated with something controversial: there are electoral costs (and costs in internal cohesion) in too clear a position. Those committed to narrow agendas are seen as better targeting their efforts through single issue groups. This may not be terribly novel. Almond and Verba, in their cross national study of participation in 1963 suggested that political parties are really not where members of the public look when they wish to be involved in decision making — 'relatively few citizens think of them as the first place where support may be enlisted for attempts to influence government'.

This party weakness seems to open the door to a more participatory, group-based politics where people are active in specific organisations with which they agree. Many see this sort of participation as allowing a closer connection between the active public and political outcomes. Seyd and Whiteley have drawn attention to 'alternative forms of participation that include single-issue pressure groups, and new social movements ... They provide a more rewarding type of political participation for many people than membership of a political party'.[12] Dalton has argued that 'citizen groups are transforming the nature of contemporary democratic politics'.[13] A key topic of study since Barnes, Kasse et al.,'s *Political Action* in 1979 is whether this sort of 'unconventional political activity' was complementary to, or a rejection of, normal political participation.

Getting a sense of scale

Generally, the increase in this sort of politics is asserted rather than documented. Size is a matter of interpretation. Is a Campaign for Nuclear Disarmament support of 40,000 large—or can one say it is a very small proportion of the electorate? In fact, the largest battalions that are regularly cited as part of contemporary large-scale participation are different from, and on a different scale than, those where the individuals involved personally engage in protest. In particular, one notes that tables of membership of selected voluntary organisations are dominated by the National Trust with 2,189,000 (1993) and the Royal Society for the Protection of Birds 1,000,000 (1997). Such group memberships are aggregated to compile a population of those active on the environment—though many of those involved may be neither very environmentally aware nor willing to act politically in other than very low cost ways. As the contributions here show, some of the high profile protests are based on very small numbers of individuals. Dunleavy's language developed to discriminate variations in interest group behaviour can be adapted to distinguish between low-cost and high-cost strategies of participation for individuals.[14] Applied to individuals this might look something like:

LOW COST ACTIONS

Choosing to read/view political items in media
Talking about political subjects in the family
Talking in public places about politics
Voting
Signing petitions
Consumer boycott
Attending political meeting
Giving financial contribution to party or cause
Regular financial support to party or cause
Strike over pay or conditions
Personally lobbying politicians
Taking part in peaceful demonstrations
Being active in the organisation of a party, protest or group
Direct action

HIGH COST ACTIONS

The higher the cost of the action the much smaller the scale of involvement. The argument about the large scale of protest often rests on counting in activity that is scarcely political by subsuming activity such as the annual subscription to a campaigning group that may be

1. Protest (%)

Attended protest meeting	14.6
Organised petition	8.0
Signed petition	63.3
Blocked traffic	1.1
Protest march	5.2
Political strike	6.5
Physical boycott	4.3
Physical force	0.2

scarcely political in its content. Moreover, the so-called membership of bodies such as Greenpeace may express financial support with no internal rights to participate in the organisation to policy making. As recorded in Byrne's contribution here, even the Campaign for Nuclear Disarmament—for long regarded as the definitive protest movement—now has a membership that is largely passive.

By 1992 Parry, Moyser and Day, in *Political Participation and Democracy in Britain*, were able to argue with confidence that 'protest has become firmly established as part of the array of actions citizens might consider using to make themselves heard'. They found that while 5.2% of the British public claimed to have engaged in fund-raising for a party, protest activity seemed higher (Table 1).

If one looks at Greenpeace support (recorded in *Social Trends* 1995, Table 11.4), then among the 410,000 'members' relatively few will be active in protest but, arguably, among those active in demonstrations few will not be financial supporters. Giving of time is probably more costly for most than giving financially, yet, paradoxically, for some of those participating the activity is a reward rather than a cost. While there seems to have been a marginal increase in willingness to protest in recent years, the figures are still low in absolute terms. Borre's work on 'Scope of Government Beliefs and Political Support' shows that in Britain in 1990, 33% of the public were prepared to tolerate protest (the figure in 1985 had been 29%). However, further analysis of the data showed that the toleration of protest appeared to be linked to the level of satisfaction with the government. Only 20% of those who were near to the government's position in terms of policy sanctioned protest, but 52% of those who were far from the government in policy terms did so.[15] Though tolerating protest is a different from protesting, it does suggest that protest may be linked to governmental popularity. In one sense this is a truism, but it does suggest there will always be an element in the public from which protest might be anticipated.

Miller, Timpson and Lessnoff found that there was a gap between support by the public for the principle of protest and its application. While there were only 16% against the principle, 73% would ban a disruptive religious parade. Their data showed that taking part in non-electoral politics was a minority activity (except for the 70% signing a petition): 25 % claimed to have been involved in a community action group; 13% had engaged in a demonstration, picket, march or protest meeting, while only 3% had taken part in a political campaign (other than an election).[16]

How much of an increase?

If at first sight it seems 'there is a lot of it about', this does not mean protest is distinctive for the 1990s. In 1799, Fisher Ames writing in *Russell's Gazette*, Boston, was despairing of 'mobocracy' (as recorded on Paul Gilje's book *The Road To Mobocracy* in 1987). Gilje records a large number of examples of popular disorder in New York City from 1763 to 1834. The contributions in this collection look at protest in Britain in the 1990s. They primarily attempt to supply accounts that help readers wanting to know more about the headlines in that area. However an underlying question is whether there has been an increase in protest? The past in Britain too has its examples. Peter Townsend in his introduction to Michael McCarthy' *Campaigning for the Poor* (1986) noted how, 'The creation of new kinds of pressure groups like Shelter, the Disablement Income Group and the Campaign Against Racial Discrimination, as well as the Child Poverty Action Group, in the mid-1960s, was more than a sign of the times. It was a reaction to what was perceived to be the fraudulent character of British democracy . . . In 1965 the Child Poverty Action Group was formed in the crucible of outrage . . .'

Kriesi, Koopmans et al., have presented important comparative data on protest, but they open by drawing attention to a large peace demonstration in Germany in 1983: so the 1980s can be seen as being stamped by the protest style as validly as the 1990s.[17] If there is an increase, then the start date of the trend can be debated. In 1983, David Marsh edited a very useful collection of case studies on *Pressure Politics* that even then noted a drift towards 'single-issue' politics with radical activists rejecting insider politics — partly for ideological reasons and partly because they would have been denied the status — and trying to influence public and elite opinion. In 1972, Robert Benewick and Trevor Smith published a book of case studies on *Direct Action and Democratic Politics* with contributions such as Peter Hain's 'Direct Action and the Springbok Tours'. A chapter on historical patterns by Victor Kiernan found militant protest had been a regular feature of British political life. The editors noted a wave of political unrest in recent years that had 'inclined the British government in a restrictive direction'. In his conclusion, Smith drew attention to the 'steady decline of the activity of politics as conventionally defined'. The importance of protest depends on its impact as well as its frequency. A catalogue of examples of unsuccessful protest would suggest different conclusions from a picture of policies regularly changed by direct public action. The idea that there has been an increase in protest probably hinges on the fact that there have been some examples of policy change that have been ascribed to protest. Somehow, the more numerous unsuccessful protests are subsumed into an argument that relates to the successful.

Do parties incorporate successful groups?

This introduction started by considering the assertion that political parties are in decline and have been replaced by groups. Another way in which the two can relate is if the parties selectively absorb groups that prove themselves to be successful. There are frequent comments of the type that the Conservative Party turned 'green' to compete with green groups, but there really are few examples, if any, of this sort of issue -recruitment by parties. The Thatcher government certainly repositioned itself over the National Health Service, flirting first with the idea of making it more efficient by increasing private medicine and reducing public spending, then seeking public approval for higher public sector spending on the NHS, but this was not so much stealing a group agenda as realising the political unpopularity of the initial position. Even when causes seem popular, parties seem reluctant to pay the price of offending minorities who may disagree.

From a group perspective, collaboration with established political parties is a political opportunity choice.[18] Dalton quotes the pioneering argument in the 1950s by Heberle that 'in order to enter into political action, social movements must, in the modern era, either organise themselves as a political party or enter into a close relationship with political parties'.[19] In fact, competition with established parties seems more common than integration. However, parties, short of absorption, can try to buy-off protest by concessions, as was the case with the 1998 Countryside March: not coincidentally, there were governmental announcements on policy changes involving rural schools, the financing of the slaughtering of cattle, dropping the idea of banning 'green top' milk, restricting the use of country lanes by lorries, improving bus services and speculation about the creation of a rural affairs ministry.

While in the 1960s and 1970s political science developed the rational choice theme that focused on the free riding by individuals who, it was supposed, would decline to support causes unless there was selective personal and material gain only for those in membership. A counter theoretical tide has since built up that stresses participation as giving its own gratification and that does not see participation as needing to overcome the material cost-benefit calculation as posed in rational choice. Some argument is needed to account for the proliferation of groups and expanded support despite the free rider argument that looked theoretically convincing. A collection of accounts about political action does have to bear in mind the point that for individuals to act is a challenge to the free rider argument.

Protest: the ethical high ground?

There is ambiguity about the optimum type of participation in terms of democratic virtues. Classical participatory theory considered direct involvement of the public in decision making as meritorious, but this was partly because participation was seen as educative for those involved. Participation that was based on prior certainty would not have been seen as so commendable. Protest seems to borrow something of the colour of direct democracy, but participation in pursuit of predetermined and fixed ends is not in the spirit of deliberative participation. Protesting behaviour, particularly when it challenges the rule of law, poses serious problems for democratic theory. While public participation is seen as a good thing, not all participation is of a kind. At least initially one might be inclined to give higher 'demo-cratic' marks for action that is not self-interested: thus action on behalf dumb animals (Not Affecting My Best Interests—NAMBI) is seen as being more commendable than action to stop a motorway from polluting one's own private good (Not In My Back Yard—NIMBY). However, there is not a simple divide between self-interest and the public interest. Rarely do members of the public defend their private interests without consciously or subconsciously assuming that their interests are also those of the wider society. On the other hand, while those without an immediate interest in a matter may not be the direct beneficiaries of any policy defended or changed, they do receive a gratification that is personal and the policy change might well give them greater satisfaction than the general public. One aspect assumed by those who seen protest as a 'good thing' is that the values pursed by the protesters are often endorsed by those judging the protest, but in fact protest need not be for liberal ends: it can run close to vigilante activity.

Protest and political resources

It is trite to say that protest is the political tool of those without better political resources, but the visual image of protest perhaps obscures that obvious truth. A picture of a larger number of active protesters gives an impression of resources that is perhaps misleading. Perversely the weakness of the protesters is in one sense at least useful to them. An angle that the media frequently adopt is support for the underdog. Thus the media can give prominence to some under-resourced causes simply because they are weak. For protest to succeed involves changing perceptions of events, and the media are an important means by which the protesters can do so. As McFarland argued in the chapter cited earlier, 'Demonstrations, consciousness-raising groups and various forms of protest may condition public opinion to look favourably upon a movement's goals'. However, this is not a guaranteed route to success for protesters: the media coverage of anti-motorway protesters or pro-Field Sports demonstrators in 1997 meant that the feel good factor for those participating was reinforced by the sense of solidarity created — but the support for the cause in the wider population might actually have been diminished.

The Brent Spar episode: myth of protest

The *Guardian* (2.6.95) claimed 'Greenpeace has won a stunning, and possibly seminal, victory over Shell UK and the British government . . . A voluntarily funded pressure group (albeit with more members in the UK than the Labour Party and a better balance sheet than the Conservatives) has single-handedly taken on one of the world's great multinationals — often thought to be beyond the reach of national sovereignty — and given it a bloody nose . . . It is no exaggeration to say that environmental politics may never be the same again . . . Greenpeace has demonstrated the awesome political power it can now wield worldwide.' This comment related to what is almost certainly regarded widely as the most important example of effective action in sustaining the new conventional wisdom about the power of protest: the U-turn by Shell UK after the occupation of the Brent Spar oil loading buoy by Greenpeace. Eventually, Shell decided not to dump the structure in the North Atlantic. Lynn Bennie's contribution looks at the events surrounding the Brent Spar protest and she then tracks the protest in succeeding years when the focus of protest moved from the North Sea to the North Atlantic. Her piece reveals above all that success is a very contingent matter: Greenpeace, feted as all powerful, came to be seen again as a actor with mixed success.

The Brent Spar case was subject to much analysis that presented is as a 'defining moment'. The press at the time of Shell's Brent Spar policy change saw the decision as a sign of the growth in a new political agenda based on animal welfare, anti-roads, pro-life. The *Guardian* (22.6.95) saw signs that the future was 'painted green'. Some saw the defeat of Shell and the government as democracy in action. The *Guardian* (21.6.95) said 'Shell did have some arguments on its side . . . even so, its decision to bow to public protests and abandon this decision should be celebrated. People still count. Boycotts can still work. This is as refreshing for democracy as for the North Sea.' A leading article in the *Independent* (21.6.95) was headlined 'Shell's Loss is Democracy's Gain' and said 'Greenpeace deserves the credit for mobilising a political force that we can expect to see grow in power and have an impact on a host of other environmental issues . . . Anyone who feared that the globalisation of business would give international companies carte blanche to act as they pleased should be cheered by what has happened.' The *Daily Mirror* declared 'Victory for the People.'

Hugo Young (*Guardian*, 22.6.95) considered the Brent Spar case as part of a more general trend of the reduction of party politics and the rise of single-issue politics: 'Single-issue work these days makes a stronger appeal. It is pure. It is clear. It is unencumbered by complications. Its virtue is obvious. It also brings widespread benefits to society.' However, Young then identified the drawbacks: such certainty sought a world of clarity that did not exist; such groups exist to make pressure, not to compromise; overlooking what government cannot—the need to broker deals and to act. Others also saw the Brent Spar policy change as a sign of democratic weakness—elected Government could be defeated by single-issue groups An analysis from within Shell argued that 'The real debate—and it is a vital one—centres on the role of emotive, single-issue campaigning in the democratic process, and on how, within a democratically established framework of reasoned discussion, painstaking evaluation, and thoughtful consultation, the best practicable environmental solutions can truly be reached.'

So while at least some commentators see such protest activity as enhancing democratic life (good for the participants and good in subjecting policies to real debate rather than fudge), others see it as a threat to the existing political process. The general case was famously put by President Jimmy Carter in his farewell address to the nation. He put the single interest groups in the frame as the cause of his administration's problems: 'We are increasingly drawn to single-issue groups and special interest organisations to insure that whatever else happens our personal views and our own private interests are protected ... this tends to distort our purpose because the national interest is not always the sum of all our single or special interests' (*New York Times*, 15.1.81). A *Times* leader (22.6.95) argued that the single-issue victory on Brent Spar was bad for democracy. It claimed that so great are the media opportunities for single issue crusades that they are now firmly established in public life. In the same issue William Rees-Mogg supplied the chorus: 'It is a victory for a single—issue pressure group and a defeat for rational environmentalism ... It never pays to appease hysteria.' Tim Eggar, the minister responsible for oil, complained that Shell had given in to what could only be described as blackmail.

However, Brent Spar was not really a good example of single-issue pressure leading to policy change. To an extent, as argued by Lynn Bennie, a myth of popular protest has grown up. This has three components—a myth of the extent to which there was large-scale concern about the issue, a myth about the mechanics of change, and a myth of the role of the public. As part of its regular polling exercises Gallup asks 'What would you say is the most urgent problem facing the country at the present time?' Compared with items such as unemployment, health, law and order, education or cost of living, the environment receives derisory attention. Much the same could be said of other even less successful campaigns covered in this collection: they did not transform broad public opinion. But success should not be measured in too short a time-span. Even if, as Rhoda McLeod shows, the protest against the export of live animals had only partial success, it did build up the background support for animal welfare organisations and increased the visibility of animal welfare in other settings.

The Brent Spar outcome seems far more the product of a chance pattern of factors and long-term pressure for attitudinal change by

Greenpeace than was obvious at the time. The *Guardian* (22.6.95) suggested that Greenpeace could 'push the right media buttons and, with the right political backing, it doesn't take much to make lightening strike in several places at once'. In fact the Greenpeace success may have inoculated the media against a repeat infection. The press were very critical of the group once it had to apologise to Shell for using some faulty data in its campaign. As it has found in other campaigns, it has no push button success formula. If Brent Spar was the result of single-issue politics Greenpeace did not discover a patent protest formula that worked elsewhere.

Some of the press comment in the heat of 1995 perhaps exaggerated the power of the single issue groups. The Greenpeace victory was not an indicator of the irresistible power of environmental groups but was the result of a combination of circumstances that distance the outcome from that obtained by various motorway protesters or the anti-veal campaigns. What, after all, was the reaction of one of the Greenpeace activists on the Brent Spar when they were radioed the news? 'I am speechless. We do not normally win things, do we?' If, as recorded in the *Guardian* (17.6.95), there were 35 boycotts going on in Britain in June 1995, the puzzle is why the Brent Spar example succeeded where others failed. That said, the cases presented here record successes as well as failures, even if success generally depended on other factors as well as the protest and direct action campaigns.

Protest and information

The issue of informed participation underlies this discussion. One argument in favour of consultation with organised interests is that it is a system for developing policies involving those who are affected by them—and who have better knowledge of what is needed than most. However, lurking as a politically incorrect criticism of representative democracy is the idea that the public are under-informed and therefore gullible. Can the public really understand the technical side of European Monetary Union or whatever? When issues such as the Brent Spar issue were no longer discussed in the private world of the original policy communities, the lack of specialist information among the newcomers to the field emerged as a criticism of the policy process. Sincerely, but not thereby necessarily reasonably, the original experts think that any criticism of their preferred solutions are based on ignorance or cranky science. It is then easy for the experts to see the subsequent debates as being a match not on a level playing field: they often continue to believe that if only the issue was treated properly, what they see as the correct solution would be adopted.

To a certain extent of course, protest may well be by a minority better informed than the general public (sometimes even as well informed as the established policy communities). Those with concerns may well pay more attention to the topic. But there is a persistent criticism of those opposing protesters that they themselves have even more information — that the protesters do not understand the rural economy, the scientific evidence or whatever. In the Brent Spar example, the policy community in favour of deep sea disposal thought that part of the biasing of the playing field was the mobilisation of the public onto their patch — the brain-washed tools of a single-issue group rather than democratic participants.

*

The contributions in this collection try to describe some of the most important and/or typical protests recent years. They are intended to allow the reader to judge the effectiveness of protest. (Is it a signal of weakness used by those excluded from better political access?) They do suggest that protest is common, but this might indicate that it is perennial rather than new. However, an implication of seeing the current protest as 'business as usual', rather than some unprecedented transformation of the political system, is that protest as a phenomenon becomes more important not less. Even if it is assumed that protest has always been with us, it might be that recourse to it is getting more common. Partly, one suspects, through the media and repeated examples suggesting protest is normal, the members of the public seem ready to protest as consumers and as citizens whenever they do not find themselves satisfied. Protest in large part is now ordinary politics rather than extraordinary. For consumers fed up with rail services, air passengers refusing to leave delayed aircraft, dissatisfied car owners contacting 'Watchdog' on the television, protest might be a likelier response than the articulation of grievances through political parties — but the commoner such behaviour becomes, the less does it look like the system-transforming expectations of new social movements. Those with points of view to articulate have realised the importance of 'events' in securing press and media coverage: an implicit contract exists whereby if protesters can give the media stories and pictures, then opportunities to air concerns are available. Protest without media coverage is like a mime performance in the dark: possible but fairly pointless. There is clearly no simple pattern of activity, with political parties replaced by action within traditional interest groups or even new social movements; but it may be that if a broad enough interpretation of protest is allowed, then protest is on the increase. However, to be viable this argument has to recognise that it can simply be consumer choice, voting for interest parties and other participation far short of direct action.

1   A. Cigler and B. Loomis (eds), *Interest Group Politics* (CQ Press, 1986 edn), p. 1.
2   In J.W. Van Deth and E. Scarbrough (eds), *The Impact of Values* (Oxford University Press, 1994), p. 412.
3   C. Euchner, *Extraordinary Politics* (Westview Press, 1996).
4   In Cigler and Loomis (1983 edn), p. 338.

5 R. Inglehart, *Culture Shift in Advanced Industrial Society* (Princeton University Press, 1990).

6 G. Jordan and W. Maloney, *The Protest Business?* (Manchester University Press, 1997).

7 P. Byrne, *Social Movements in Britain* (Routledge, 1997) p. 171.

8 R. Dalton, 'Strategies of Partisan Influence' in J.C. Jenkins and B. Klandermans (eds), *The Politics of Social Protest* (UCL Press, 1995), p. 296.

9 P Burstein, R. Einwohner and J. Hollander, 'The Success of Political Movements', in Jenkins and Klandermans, op. cit.

10 R. Benewick and T. Smith, *Direct Action and Democratic Politics* (Allen & Unwin, 1972), p. 305.

11 Y. Yishai, 'The Thin Line Between Groups and Parties in the Israeli Electoral Process', in K. Lawson (ed.), *How Political Parties Work* (Praeger, 1994).

12 P. Seyd and P. Whiteley, *Labour's Grassroots* (Clarendon Press, 1992), p. 204.

13 In Preface, *The Annals*, 528, 1993.

14 P. Dunleavy, *Democracy and Public Choice*, (Wheatsheaf, 1991), p. 20.

15 O. Borre and E. Scarbrough, *The Scope Of Government* (Oxford University Press, 1995).

16 W. Miller, A. Timpson and M. Lessnoff, *Political Culture in Contemporary Britain* (Clarendon Press, 1996).

17 H. Kriesi, R. Koopmans, J.W. Duyvendak and M. Giugni, *New Social Movements in Western Europe* (University of Minnesota Press, 1995).

18 Term introduced by Eisinger, 'The Conditions of Protest Behaviour in American Cities', *American Political Science Review*, 1973.

19 In Jenkins and Klandermans, op. cit., p. 303.

Gun Control and Snowdrop

BY STUART THOMSON, LARA STANCICH AND LISA DICKSON

13 MARCH 1996 witnessed the tragedy of the Dunblane massacre. It was to mobilise unprecedented public support for gun control, in this country, resulting in the swift passage through Parliament of the Firearms (Amendment) Act 1997, under the then Conservative government, and a further tightening of the law under the Labour government elected on 1 May 1997. Until March 1996 the worst single act of mass murder in Britain had been that of the 'Hungerford Massacre' where Michael Ryan killed 16 people in 1987, and although outrage over this particular tragic incident was great, the government response, in terms of legislation, was not. While a review of gun control and licensing was conducted then, the changes advocated and implemented were considered by some not to be sufficiently far-reaching and the feeling was that the government had given way to the pro-gun lobby.

The events in Dunblane that morning in 1996 are well-known. Thomas Hamilton, a licensed gun holder, entered the local primary school shooting a number of rounds at a class of children in the gymnasium. As a result, 16 young pupils and their teacher were killed, with only 13 of the class surviving. The immediate aftermath of the massacre saw the birth of the Snowdrop Appeal, created by a number of concerned families in central Scotland, but not by the parents of the victims. Anne Pearston and a friend of one of the families decided to do something to prevent the reoccurrence of such as event, and in discussions with a member of her yoga class the idea of a petition came into being. The name 'Snowdrop' was adopted because it was the only flower in bloom at the time of the shootings. So Pearston and a few others launched the petition which called for the banning of the private ownership of handguns. Martin O'Neil, Pearston's Labour MP, provided advice on how to set up a parliamentary petition, but a key feature of the appeal in its early stages was its apolitical nature. None of the group had been political in the past and their knowledge of the British political system and political lobbying was minimal. This was a genuine local community group that grew beyond the intentions of its founders.

The first stage began simply with the group setting up a pasting table outside a shopping centre in Stirling with copies of the petition for shoppers to sign. Originally, the Appeal was to be anonymous and unrelated to the families of the victims. 'None of us seek public recognition. We welcome the publicity for the petition's aims so that every British citizen who wants to sign it is able in the short time-scale we have until the summer recess' (Snowdrop Petition press release). Pearston nevertheless rapidly became the public figurehead of the group. Out of respect for the families of the victims, copies of the petition were not sent to the town, though a number of the Dunblane families did sign it. The petition was, however, taken to a string of other Scottish towns, including Edinburgh. The link between the families and the group was cemented when one of the bereaved parents, Dr Mick North, appeared at the launch of the Appeal—the press release noted that 'although not involved in organising the petition, he has shown great personal courage and strength in order to demonstrate his support for its aims'. Dr North also accompanied the campaign to lobby MPs at the Scottish Grand Committee in Inverness. Subsequent to the launch and its support by a number of the families of the victims, the Snowdrop Appeal, in the eyes of the public and the media, became organically linked with the tragedy of Dunblane.

The media adoption of the Appeal, and the subsequent campaign by the *Sunday Mail*, *Sun* and *Sunday Times* amongst other newspapers, ensured that Snowdrop grew from its original intentions. From its inception it sought merely to demonstrate public support for the control of guns by a petition to the government. During 1996 its degree of politicisation grew as the pro-gun lobby mustered arguments against the tightening of gun laws and Members of Parliament came forward to state their position on the issue, with both sides of the argument finding support. The Conservative government set up the Cullen Inquiry into the tragedy and its remit included the current state of legislation relating to the control and licensing of firearms. Politicians began to comment on the situation by indicating how far their personal support would extend in relation to a total ban on guns. The issue, much discussed in the media, moved up the political agenda, and with it climbed support for the increasingly politicised Snowdrop campaign. At one point, the campaign declared its intention to field candidates at the next general election in Conservative-held Scottish seats because of their refusal to support a total handgun ban. This was later modified to a promise of support for Labour, which did support a ban, showing how far the Appeal had changed over time from a group coordinating a petition to an organised, politicised campaign.

This study addresses a number of issues stemming from the Dunblane tragedy. Primarily, it seeks to assess the effects of the Snowdrop Appeal in lobbying for gun control, how the campaign operated at a political level in influencing legislation and how far the resultant legislation reflected its initial demands. Such discussion raises questions concerning the extent to which the demands of a single-issue pressure group reflect societal opinion and how far the perception of either the campaign or the issues involved are manipulated by the media's embrace of the original campaign. The Appeal gained its demands only after a change in the party of government, and also after a change in tactics to a much more aggressive and political approach. This has to be placed into context, and the group was fortunate in other events and actions conspiring to aid their cause.

The campaign

Originally, the Snowdrop Appeal and the parents of Dunblane called for the tightening of gun control and the safe storage of recreational firearms at gun clubs, but the debate soon became polarised with demands for a total ban on handguns. The petition called for changes in the law so that 'all firearms held for recreational purposes for use in authorised sporting clubs be held securely at such clubs with the firing mechanisms removed; the private ownership of handguns be made illegal; certification of all firearms be subject to stricter control'. It neatly summarised the arguments against changing the gun laws and put its response to them. A copy was sent out to every school in mainland Britain by the Scottish Schools Boards for parents to make copies of; it was distributed throughout the organisation of Clackmannan Council and was supported by the Scottish National Party and the National Union of Teachers.

The group itself had no formal organisation, but Anne Pearston became its effective head because of her media-profile. A Snowdrop bank account was held in three joint names. The campaign was largely run by volunteers with little free time because of their family commitments, but that did not appear to hinder activities. One of its first actions was a newspaper advertisement with a tear-off slip that could be sent to Prime Minister John Major calling for a total ban. The question then arises: when did the pressure change and how did the issue became as explosive as it did in so short a period of time?

The events that followed Dunblane ensured that the pressure would increase on Parliament to alter the law relating to gun control. On the 19th March two youths were arrested for the theft of four firearms from a private house in Buckinghamshire. A number of schools in the area were alerted despite a statement by Thames Valley police noting that while charges against the youths were not likely, it was not seeking any other people in connection with the theft. The alert nevertheless heightened the anxiety of many concerning safety, especially in schools, in the wake of Dunblane. The Thames Valley Assistant Chief Constable stated that unarmed plain-clothes officers had attended three local schools in order to reassure teachers, parents and children after news broke of the search for the guns and the youths. While there was no evidence or intelligence to suggest that schools might have been a target, they decided certain schools would be offered whatever protection they deemed necessary.

The reporting of this event and the reaction to it ensured that individual MPs would not remain silent as had been suggested shortly after Dunblane (as a mark of respect for the families of the victims). On the 20 March David Mellor, a former Home Office minister, led demands for radical changes to the existing legislation, commenting that events in Buckinghamshire had once again highlighted the total inadequacy of the existing controls and the need for immediate legislative action. Others, however, disagreed fervently. Michael Colvin, Conservative MP for Romsey and Waterside and captain of the Commons shooting team, was reported to be opposed to a wholesale reform of the law, arguing that it had already been subject to a rigorous review following the Hungerford shootings in 1987. Paddy Ashdown, leader of the Liberal Democrats, called for a rational response but said it was clear that they would have to consider how to control guns better.

Both Conservative and Labour backbenchers demanded early action on the ownership of handguns such as those used by Thomas Hamilton in Dunblane and on the storing of firearms in private homes. These were similar reactions to those after the Hungerford massacre, when reviews of firearm controls banned the keeping of weapons such as those used by Michael Ryan, but little more. After Dunblane the calls for change grew in strength partly as a result of the perceived failure to act adequately then. George Foulkes, Labour MP for Carrick, Cummnock and Doone Valley, said there was a 'growing tide in favour of outlawing handguns' and 'also growing support for handguns, but not shotguns, to be held at gun clubs rather than in private homes'. The debate had quickly shifted from whether there should be changes in the law to what form such changes should take. By the closing weeks of March, according to the *Telegraph* (24.3.96), there was a growing consensus among MPs for new controls, centring on a requirement for two referees instead of one before a gun licence was granted, together with a note from a doctor stating there was no medical or psychological reason why an individual should not hold guns. Party lines began to emerge in what had previously been a non-partisan issue, with Labour pressing for a parliamentary debate, and this was endorsed by George Robertson, shadow Scottish Secretary and a resident of Dunblane. Twenty eight people, including relatives of the victims, went to London to deliver the petition in July. They were received by the Home Secretary and by Tony Blair, while Michael Forsyth arranged the flights from Scotland for the group.

While debate over the extent of reform raged in anticipation of the Cullen Report, the government offered an interim gesture to demonstrate its commitment to firearms control. In an attempt to reduce the number of unauthorised guns, an amnesty was offered from 3 to 30 June. Gun amnesties were not new and this merely suggested a hurried response to public opinion and it did nothing to stem the tide of popular opinion.

Public perception was likely to attribute much of the success in gun control to the Snowdrop Appeal, its public statements, the work of the

Dunblane parents, and, in particular, Ann Pearston, who spearheaded an attempt to force the government's hand by declaring her intention to stand against it in a general election should it fail to implement radical changes in gun control. Conversely, media reporting of the emotive responses of Members of Parliament suggests that the issue was taken to heart by Parliament and changes would have been precipitated in any case. Snowdrop's lack of faith in Parliament was confirmed, however by the fact that although all received a letter, only 37% responded to the petition, with only five Conservatives (*Guardian*, 23.7.96). Views were vociferously expressed, spanning the gamut from advocates of banning all handguns to those who believed that the post-Hungerford reform had been a sufficient response to that tragedy, all that a government could do in a free society. Opponents of a complete ban often raised fears about a 'big brother' state intervening in all aspects of an individual's life. Firearms control was not a new item on the political agenda. Legislative reform had been proposed unsuccessfully the previous year by Terry Lewis (Lab), who had called for a ban on keeping guns on domestic premises and arguably Dunblane acted as the catalyst on an issue about which Parliament was already aware. This suggests that the effect of the Snowdrop Appeal on parliamentary debate and legislation was useful, but not as decisive as may have appeared.

The Cullen Report appeared in September 1996. It was wide-ranging in its scope (covering gun clubs, gun licences, safety in schools, etc.) but very narrow in its recommendations. By that time, however, it had already been overtaken by other events As a result of a Home Affairs Committee's leak (see below) and the ensuing public pressure which continued to favour a ban despite attempts by the gun lobby to present its case, the government had declared itself for the banning of all handguns except those used specifically for sport in secure gun clubs. Together with Labour Party's decision to support a total ban after Ann Pearston's party conference speech, this made the report, which in any case fell short of the campaign's demands, almost irrelevant.

David Marsh has argued that changes in single-issue politics in the 1970s led to a reliance on influencing public opinion rather than parties. This was partly an effort by groups to maintain radical integrity, but it had limited success. Single-issue/ideological groups are generally outsider groups and thus lack the insider, corporatist-style of business interest groups.[1] The Snowdrop campaign is a single-issue group which could be identified as a form of 'condensational symbol', defined as a situation where the issue is so central to the group that negotiation is a kind of moral betrayal, compromising human rights or freedoms. This kind of single issue politics does not lend itself to incremental decision-making, coalition formation, or mutual accommodation.[2] It is usual to associate this with such radical single-issue groups as the pro-life/anti-abortion groups. The Snowdrop campaign was run almost exclusively as a moral appeal and as one unwilling to compromise this moral stance. Speaking at the Labour Party Conference, Ann Pearston made an emotional and uncompromising appeal: 'If there is no ban on handguns, it is sending the clear message that our children are expendable in the name of sport.' She had been invited by shadow Scottish Secretary, George Robertson: Conservatives accused Labour of making Dunblane a partisan matter and refused to invite Pearston themselves— though apparently she was a Conservative voter. Labour subsequently pledged itself to pursue a total ban on the private ownership of handguns. After this position was defeated in the House of Commons in November 1996, as the Conservative government did not support it, the Snowdrop campaign, rather than accept the compromise of a partial ban, vowed to continue its campaign until after the 1997 general election in the hope of a non-Conservative government, bringing in a total ban.

The legislation

The imminence of a general election, with its likelihood of coming close to the first anniversary of the tragedy, not only put the controversial issue of gun control firmly on the political agenda but also placed pressure on the government to have legislation in place before the election, preferably before the anniversary.

In the days following the massacre, party leaders had agreed not to exploit the issue politically, nor to speculate on possible political outcomes. They agreed to await the findings of the Cullen Inquiry. However, consensus broke down some two months before the publication of Lord Cullen's report, with a series of leaks from the House of Commons Select Committee on Home Affairs report of August 1996, 'Possession of Handguns', in which the Conservative-dominated committee concluded that a ban was not necessary (the Labour minority supporting a ban). This created a great deal of controversy for the government. There was some suggestion that the leaks were intended to 'test the water' for the Home Secretary about the possibility of stopping short of a ban (*Sunday Times*, 4.8.96). The tabloid press strongly supported a ban and suggested that the committee's position reflected the weight given to submissions from the Association of Chief Police Officers (the ACPO submission actually favoured a ban of all handguns except .22 single-shot pistols). There was little evidence that the shooting lobby wielded undue direct influence over the committee, as only two members had declared shooting as an interest. And whilst 32 MPs list shooting as a recreation, the suggestion that they may have rebelled against any legislation to ban handguns was rejected. In fact, the only successful 'rebellion' by the pro-gun lobby MPs was to raise the levels of compensation for gun owners. The reaction by the media to the select committee report was characterised by the *Sun*'s attack, which printed the telephone numbers of its Conservative members and suggested that readers might like to ring them to complain about its conclusions. BBC television had a fifty-minute Panorama programme which interviewed the parents of victims who criticised the Select Committee. The government could have been left in doubt as to the depth of feeling over the issue.

Had the leak been intended to test the water for legislation which stopped short of a ban on handguns, its effect was to send a clear signal to the government that the public (in so far as it was represented by the media and opinion polls) would accept no less than a ban. It also appeared to catalyse more direct political action by both anti-gun and pro-gun lobbies. The Snowdrop campaign announced that it would put up candidates in the ten Conservative-held Scottish seats in the general election unless the government obtained a total ban on handguns in Parliament before then. When the campaign dropped the idea of candidates, pledging its support to the Labour Party instead, the Shooters' Rights Association indicated its intention to contest the Stirling seat of Michael Forsyth, Secretary of State for Scotland, which included Dunblane.

Public outcry over the insensitivity of the gun lobby, as well as the arrest and media exposure of certain leading figures in the Shooters' Rights Association, led it to withdraw its intention. In October 1996, a new pro-gun association was launched, the Sportsman's Association of Great Britain and Northern Ireland, partly as an effort to restore some of the credibility lost by 'hot-headed attacks on the Dunblane parents' but also to distance itself from the Shooters Right's Association which was now perceived as extreme. One of its main objectives was to recruit a million members (in response to the Snowdrop campaign's 705,000 signatures) to demonstrate the legitimacy of the gun lobby's voice. It also sought to explore the possibility of fielding candidates in the general election, not with the intention of winning votes, but as a single-issue spoiling manoeuvre.

Whilst single-issue candidates generally obtain a derisory vote, and may have little impact on the national political agenda, they can influence the campaign agenda locally. It remains, however, an expensive and unreliable means of exerting pressure. In the case of Forsyth's Stirling constituency, boundary changes before the general election had reduced his majority to little over 200 so that he could ill afford local difficulties. Whilst the prospect of a Snowdrop candidate might not have threatened his ability to win votes, it may have undermined his reputation, encouraging his personal vote to switch to another party. Many believed, however, that his behaviour after the Dunblane events had strengthened his reputation. Fielding a gun lobby candidate in that constituency on the other hand, would have had little impact on the local political agenda and no positive effects for that gun lobby.

The government's proposal for a partial ban on handguns seemed to satisfy no one. The gun lobby felt that its members were being made to pay for the crime of one man. It remained unmoved by the argument that all guns are dangerous, countering that it is not the gun which commits a crime but the person using it. The anti-gun lobby was not satisfied with a partial ban because legally held weapons could still be misused. Few believed the government was proposing the right solution: the legislation was opposed by the Snowdrop campaigners, the Shooters, the police, and the Dunblane parents.

The measures could be criticised, not just on cost grounds (the high compensation bill), but on how effective they were likely to be in protecting the public. Crimes involving legally-held handguns were dismissed by opponents of a ban; yet Cullen suggested that 'there is a relationship between firearm ownership and firearm-homicide when considered overall', and a Home Office revealed memo between 1992 and 1994 that licensed weapons had been involved in nearly half of all domestic killings by gunfire and in nearly one fifth of all homicidal shootings (the level of debate concerning knives remained low, despite the fact that the largest number of deaths are caused by them). More important to the government and the police was that they should not be implicated in crimes by having licensed the weapons. A new Firearms Act should set out to achieve this, but the argument remained over the possible involvement of legally-held firearms in crime. Any retroactive and piecemeal legislation, such as that suggested by the Conservative government, can always be subject to further alteration, such as the covering of handguns below .22 calibre or shotguns in the event of a further tragedy. There is delicate balance between public safety and the liberty of individuals to own a firearm for a recreational or occupation purpose: for the most part, public opinion appeared to favour the public safety argument.

The Firearms (Amendment) Bill was given Royal Assent on 27 February (and became law on 3 March 1997). The legislation had progressed speedily through Parliament despite several Conservative backbench rebellions and concerted attempts by the House of Lords to dilute its provisions. In summary, the Bill prohibited all handguns other than small-calibre pistols, muzzle-loading guns and signalling apparatus. Exemptions were made for guns used in slaughterhouses, those used for the humane killing of animals, starting guns in sports events and guns acquired before 1946 as a trophy of war. Firearms certificates could be granted for the ownership of small-calibre (.22 or less) pistols as long as they were housed and used in licensed, secure gun clubs. Firearms certificate holders were required to be members of a licensed club. Special permits could be granted by the chief officer of police for the restricted use of small-calibre pistols outside gun clubs (primarily for competitive target shooting). The legislation provided for compensation to gun owners surrendering their prohibited firearms and ammunition. It set out new requirements for the granting, renewal and revocation of firearm certificates, and new requirements for applications for such certificates, with two referees providing a much wider range of information than previously. Greater powers were given to the courts and police concerning the entry and search of premises.

One of the main amendments voted for by the Lords allowed the owners of small calibre weapons to keep their guns at home provided the working parts were stored at gun clubs. This would have substantially altered the focus of the bill. Ninety-one Conservatives supported the Lords' amendment in the Commons but the government ensured its rejection with a majority of 279, courtesy of the overwhelming support of the opposition parties. The option of disabling guns was suggested in the Cullen Report as a matter for consideration; but if this proved impracticable, it had recommended banning possession. In the government's response to the report, storing disassembled firearms was rejected on the grounds that certain guns could not be stored safely, and a commitment was made to banning all those above .22 calibre. The debate over whether to store small-calibre pistols in gun clubs, or to disassemble them and allow the gun owner to store part of the gun at home, centred on whether clubs would pose a greater risk as weapons arsenals—a potential target for terrorists and criminals—or whether the disassembled parts could be easily replaced or substituted, thereby rendering the system difficult to monitor. The government took the view that disassembly would not provide adequate protection or assurance to the public against misuse of a handgun by a club member.

When the legislation was first debated in Parliament, in November 1996, an amendment was introduced by Conservative MP Bob Hughes to ban all handguns rather than just those above .22 calibre. This was comfortably defeated by the government, which had refused a free vote despite great pressure from the Snowdrop campaign, the Dunblane parents, the media and the Opposition. Its refusal was defended on the grounds that government legislation is normally 'whipped'. The Labour Party, having pledged to pursue a total ban on handguns should it win the 1997 general election, supported the government in order to ensure some strengthening of firearm regulation.

The other main amendments proposed by the House of Lords concerned compensation. The Lords voted to compensate dealers and manufacturers for lost trade, at one year's post-tax profit, and to compensate gun clubs and associations which could not survive the imposition of such legislation. Both amendments were rejected in the Commons on the grounds that government cannot accept liability for business losses resulting from legislation aimed at improving public safety. Nevertheless, compensation for the loss of private property is accepted practice in English law and an obligation under the European Convention on Human Rights; dealers and clubs would be compensated in the same way as individuals, for the value of prohibited firearms, ammunition and related accessories.

An amendment voted by the Lords to establish a central, computerised register of all gun licence-holders was accepted. It would include all firearm and shotgun certificate holders, as well as those who have had such certificates refused or revoked. It is not clear why this was not in the original draft of the legislation since it was recommended in the Cullen Report and had been an issue of concern to the police and others for some time. The amendments voted for by the Lords proved to provide further embarrassment to a government which was seen to be reacting to events rather than shaping them.

The media

The role played by the media, in particular the press, was a vital factor in the campaign for tighter gun controls. Media support is very important to the successful outcome of public pressure campaigns. A 1992 survey revealed that a not insignificant proportion of groups regard the media as the most important target (13%, compared to 20% in another 1990 survey), and four out of five groups believe good relations with the media were important, seeking media contact at least once a week (50% contacted the media at least once a day).[3] In many ways, this has led to a professionalisation of group-media relations, with organised public interests employing public relations experts and ex-media personnel; conversely, a group with financial resources and a degree of expertise can be used by the media as experts, even though its advice may be neither impartial nor accurate.

A topical issue often leads the media to the group rather than vice-versa. This was seen in Dunblane, where the Snowdrop campaign was more or less 'adopted' by the press. Such an endorsement of campaigns by the media facilitates and enhances the building up of public support. Grant has also argued that media coverage can reinforce a single-issue campaign by presenting it as a matter of public concern and can assist in moving an issue up the political agenda. A number of questions have been raised over the representativeness, and thus legitimacy, of 'public interest' groups.

While organised public interest groups such as Greenpeace or Friends of the Earth over-represent the middle-class section at the expense of other parts of society,[4] it may be the case that ad hoc, single-issue campaigns, on the other hand, such as public protest against the live export of calves in 1995, or the Snowdrop campaign, mobilise a wider cross-section of the population. Snowdrop, for example, collected around 705,000 signatures for tighter gun control, with a further 450,000 people signing the *Sunday Mail*'s petition calling for handguns to be made illegal. The Police Federation, representing rank-and-file officers, favoured an all-out ban; whilst the Association of Chief Police Officers supported a ban on handguns above .22 calibre and the prohibition of other multi-shot weapons. Many members of the shooting community, whilst opposing prohibition, favoured improved controls over the licensing and storage of firearms. It can be suggested, therefore, that Snowdrop's aims did not simply represent a small and highly vocal proportion of society, but rather that gun control was of great concern to the public as a whole. Nevertheless, media coverage and publicity is ephemeral, and generally has a short attention span.[5] The consistent coverage given to the gun control issue over the year following the Dunblane massacre is in this light remarkable.

The campaign to ban handguns, which was given great impetus by the *Sunday Mail*, and *Scotland on Sunday*, among other newspapers, was not the first campaign to be spearheaded by the media. Baggott cites a number of examples where single-issue campaigns were instigated, or given impetus by the press. They include the thalidomide campaign in the 1960s, undertaken by the *Sunday Times*, and the campaign for restrictions on potentially dangerous dogs, led by a number of tabloids. In this regard, the media can be said to be acting as a pressure participant in itself.[6]

Public campaigns are undertaken mainly by groups lacking influence elsewhere. The traditionally powerful and well-resourced influence of the gun lobby, whose influence was seen after the Hungerford massacre, meant that the anti-gun campaigners stood little chance of achieving their objectives without overwhelming popular support. The role of the media in attaining this was vital. The Snowdrop campaign started out as a simple petition, without funding or sophisticated organisation, and with its organisers intending to remain anonymous. If this had been the case, it might have sunk quietly once its petition had been submitted to the Prime Minister. But not only did the media support make the Snowdrop petition difficult for the government to ignore, it also forced the gun lobby to seek legitimacy in the public arena.

The role and use of the media in single-issue politics is not always benign as the Snowdrop case implies. One may compare the Shell/Greenpeace/Brent Spar and the Snowdrop campaigns. Both mobilised a considerable level of favourable media attention which afforded them the appearance of a high level of public support and an apparent legitimacy. As Lynn Bennie shows Greenpeace, however, provides an example not only of the professionalisation of group-media relations but also one where their of the media backfired. In the wake of the Brent Spar episode, the media was said to have been (mis)led 'by the nose'.

The 1997 election and beyond

The more openly political approach adopted during the 1997 election campaign (including Pearston's recommendation to vote Labour) was an attempt to achieve a change in government and, with it, a handgun ban. Snowdrop had been encouraged to take this position by polls conducted by the Gun Control Network, a London-based anti-gun pressure group, which found that 97% of Labour candidates supported a complete ban, 86% of Liberal Democrat, but only 29% of Conservatives. It was at this time, however, that splits began to appear in the hitherto united front of the Snowdrop campaign. One of the founders claimed that she, and the majority of supporters, wanted the group wound up before the election because it had gained almost all of its objectives and accused Pearston of 'not being able to let go' (*Sunday Times*, 13.4.97); 'Snowdrop used to be a democratic group where we all respected the majority view but now Anne tries to dictate' (*Sunday Times*, 30.3.97). Her example was a free cinema advert in the run-up to the election, with voice-over by Sean Connery, which she had single-handedly decided should go ahead. A poster campaign (a school blackboard with the slogan 'Ban all Handguns' written in a child's handwriting) was also delivered free of cost at 25 poster sites in London, Birmingham and Manchester. Problems concerning when to end the campaign and how the tactics should proceed heightened tensions, but after a meeting with the other founders (two of whom resigned) Pearston decided to maintain the campaign until the general election.

The commitment to banning handguns was in the Queen's Speech at the opening of the new Parliament. The previous day fourteen parents of the victims of Dunblane were welcomed at No.10 Downing Street by Cherie Blair and given a guided tour of the House before meeting Blair, the Home Secretary, Jack Straw, and the Scottish Secretary, Donald Dewar. A bill was given its first reading in Parliament, on 27 May 1997, to ban all handguns, including those .22 calibre and smaller that had been exempted under the previous legislation, as well as revoking the possibility of owners holding their guns on club premises. Labour MPs were promised a free vote. The bill gained its second reading on 11 June 1997 and during the debate Anne McGuire, as MP for Stirling, made an emotional appeal on behalf on the people of Dunblane for the ban. The Conservative Party tabled an amendment, claiming that there was no justification for extending the ban to cover .22 calibre weapons, but this was defeated by 384 votes to 173 (although the SNP, Labour and the Liberal Democrats voted together, six Labour MPs voted with the Conservatives). The second reading was passed with a government majority of 203 before the bill went to the Lords for further debate.

At the same time as the new legislation was being discussed in Parliament, the previous measures were coming into effect so that 116,000 larger calibre pistols were being removed from circulation, as well as 26,000 smaller weapons being handed in (Home Office press release). The new ban would mean a further 40,000 small pistols being removed. The pro-gun movement did attempt to rally forces against the new legislation and a meeting in Trafalgar Square in September 1997 attracted 2,000 people. However, this did not prevent the new law from gaining Royal Assent on 27 November 1997 and coming into force on 26 January 1998. As with the previous law, an amnesty period until the end of February 1998 would allow those wishing to dispose of their weapons to do so and also to claim compensation.

Yet this may not be the end of the story for the anti- and pro-gun groups; the process of legislating against the use of firearms looks set to continue. A fresh review (to begin in 1998) is to consider the laws surrounding the use of rifles, shotguns and air weapons, tighter licensing, age limits, etc. The Prime Minister may believe that the government has repaid its debt to the people of Dunblane, but in answer to Anne McGuire's question whether the government would 'consistently review the procedure and regulatory framework for the ownership of firearms to keep pace with the increasingly sophisticated weaponry in private use', he insisted that the regime would be kept under 'tight scrutiny' (4.2.98).

Reasons for the campaign's success

The Snowdrop campaign was totally successful in achieving its aim. A number of factors aided its cause.

Change of tactics by Snowdrop. Starting as an apolitical, anonymous, unprofessional and amateur grouping, Snowdrop built itself a public profile with a competent leader. The group became involved in day-to-day Westminster politics because of its belief that the Conservative government had not pursued the issue to its logical conclusion, a ban on all handguns. Pearston's ability to combine highly rational argument with emotional appeals moved many potential supporters. The tragedy itself was never used as a tool to gain an emotional reaction, it served merely to draw the empathy of supporters. Her Conservative background meant that she could not be portrayed as a 'loony lefty' by opponents of the group's aims. Her Labour conference speech and non-appearance at the Conservative conference, because she was not invited, along with the threat to stand a candidate against Michael Forsyth in Stirling, and the sharing of a campaign platform at the general election with Labour, and the Liberal Democrats, cemented the group's move to becoming a highly political force.

Tactics of the pro-gun lobby. The pro-gun groups which tried to tackle Snowdrop's appeals were constantly hampered by their own inept performance. The British Shooting Sports Council simply argued against any sort of changes in the law and claimed to be 'opposed to any principle to any restrictions' (*Observer*, 20.10.96) A Newsletter of the National Pistol Association made accusations against John Crozier, whose daughter had been killed in the massacre; the outcry that followed led Sebastian Coe MP to resign his position as honorary president. Pro-handgun letters sent to all MPs were also considered inappropriate. A sign of the desperation of the pro-gun lobby was its proposal to stand a candidate against Forsyth in the election and appeals on the Internet for information that could discredit Snowdrop leaders. Pearston became a target of personal slurs, including claims that she had been a Greenham Common protester, had raised money for the IRA and had a conviction for non-payment of the poll tax. Her reaction that it was better she be attacked than the families of the victims compared favourably to the behaviour of the pro-gun groups. The latter were not aided either by the crass remarks of the Duke of Edinburgh. Despite a fighting fund of £500,000 and use of public relations firms lobbying firms, their campaign was viewed as weak and ineffective. The perceived inaction of government and the aggressive tactics of the pro-gun groups gave Snowdrop a platform on which to build a campaign.

Intervention of traditional party politics. The argument is not that the political parties hijacked the Snowdrop campaign but that they came together to serve common aims. The Labour Party offered support for the banning of handguns before the release of the Cullen Report, thus gaining support from Snowdrop. Pearston's appearance at the Labour Party conference cemented the bond: she was coached by Labour's chief media spokesman; her speech was checked and altered by George Robertson; Mo Mowlam, from the platform, led the applause at the appropriate moments. The attention of the political parties was aided by the precarious position of Michael Forsyth in his Stirling constituency. He followed Snowdrop's line on handguns, and argued the case strongly in Cabinet, but the Conservative government's approach was not as convincing. Dunblane itself was also of significance; it was the home of Shadow Scottish Secretary, George Robertson (it also has the highest concentration of professional people in Scotland, articulate and able to argue their case).

Moral tone. The moral atmosphere in 1996 and 1997 was heightened by events which were exploited by the political parties but also gave credence to the aims of Snowdrop. The Port Arthur massacre in Australia, also involved guns, brought the events in Dunblane back into the minds of the public; and the Australian governments' swift implementation of comprehensive gun control measures compared favourably with the perceived inaction of the British government. A further school attack, this time with a machete, at St. Luke's School in Wolverhampton, raised the issues of security and weapon restrictions. The killing of a headmaster, Philip Lawrence, in London and his widow's subsequent campaign added legitimacy to the moral agenda and made it a political issue. The parties were not afraid to use this moral climate for their own ends. The Labour Party, especially, found it a useful stick with which to beat the Conservative government, presenting itself as new, young, listening to the people and totally unlike the incumbent government.

Role of the media. The influence that the media have on the attitudes of the public has been widely debated and the evidence, either way, is far from conclusive. But what cannot be ignored in the case of Snowdrop is that there was a concerted campaign by many of the tabloids, and some of the broadsheets to pursue the goals of the Snowdrop Appeal. This campaign took place over a period of time, and all the publications concerned did their best to claim that they were influencing the debate. This ensured the subject became a political issue. Opinion polls showed a large majority for banning handguns: 72% in a *Sunday Times*/NOP poll in July 1996; 68% in a MORI poll in October 1997, when some measures had already been implemented. One may suggest that the media used the Snowdrop appeal to sell newspapers, but Snowdrop also used the press in order to gain publicity for its campaign.

Conclusion

The emotion generated by the horror of the Dunblane massacre and the simplicity of the Snowdrop campaign led the media to throw their support behind the campaigners and the Dunblane parents. The Snowdrop case generated coverage in the media which was almost wholly one-sided. The government's desire to rush the legislation on gun control through the statute books added to this lack of serious public debate.

There can be no doubt that the manner in which the gun control issue snowballed to capture both a public and political response makes the Snowdrop campaign stand out amongst single-issue campaigns. A range of factors leading to the partial ban of handguns make it difficult to give it full credit. Nevertheless, it was a catalyst for government action and it is highly questionable whether even a partial ban on handguns would have been attained without the generation of so overwhelming a display of public opinion.

The highlighting of a range of factors contributing both to the development of the Snowdrop campaign and to the development of the legislation serves to illustrate that means alter over time and that single-issue groups, on their own, are unlikely to alter the political agenda radically. Gun control was not entirely absent from the earlier political agenda, but the tragedy which occurred at Dunblane Primary School in March 1996 impelled the issue to the centre of debate. The campaign ensured that gun control remained in the public eye until legislation was passed, and when this was not forthcoming under the Conservative government the group continued its battle until a new government was formed. It is important to note, however, that the campaign itself evolved significantly in the months following the tragedy. Having achieved its original aim, a petition to the government, it was galvanised to further action by the realisation that the issue might simply fade from the public's view. Speculation that a ban on handguns would not be recommended by Lord Cullen, coupled with the report of the Home Affairs Select Committee suggesting that a firearms ban would not be necessary, also encouraged the campaign to continue its pursuit of a total ban on the private ownership of handguns. Endorsement of the campaign by the media and sustained coverage of the gun control issue ensured heightened political awareness of the strength of feeling in favour of a total ban. The Snowdrop Appeal was successful in its aims only after it had changed tactics and the inability of the pro-gun lobby to counter the arguments or the emotion generated—and, of course, only after a Labour victory. Although the Appeal no longer exists, the Gun Control Network has taken on its mantle and is likely to be at the forefront of the debate concerning future legislation.

1   D. Marsh (ed.), Pressure Politics: Interest Groups in Britain (Junction Books, 1983).
2   See M. Hershey and D. West, 'Single Issue Politics: Prolife Groups and the 1980 Senate Campaign' in A. Cigler and B. Loomis (eds), Interest Group Politics (Congressional Quarterly, 1983), p. 34.
3   R. Baggott, Pressure Groups Today (Manchester University Press, 1995), p. 183.
4   For example, G. Jordan and W. Maloney, Protest Business (Manchester University Press, 1997).
5   W. Grant, Pressure Groups, Politics and Democracy in Britain (Harvester Wheatsheaf, 1995), p. 89.
6   See Baggott, op. cit., especially pp. 190–1.

Calf Exports at Brightlingsea

BY RHODA McLEOD

THE export of live animals from the United Kingdom is a legitimate economic trade. It has offended public sensibilities, however, to become one of Britain's highest profile animal welfare campaigns in recent years. In 1995 thousands of people, predominantly from the South and South East of England, took to the streets to register their revulsion at a trade which they perceived as barbaric, immoral and unnecessary. For many, it was to be their initial exposure to, and first personal experience of, protest activities. In November 1997, a petition advocating an end to live exports spearheaded by Compassion in World Farming (CIWF) secured about 800,000 signatures. This was presented to Elliot Morley, minister responsible for animal welfare, by horse-racing commentator Sir Peter O'Sullevan and has been 'hailed as the biggest petition—calling for a live export ban' (*Herald*, 4.11.97). The campaign to ban live exports seems quite distinctive in relation to other animal rights/welfare campaigns because it has at times literally been brought home to members of the general public, as opposed to them having to initiate or manufacture an interest. This observation is particularly relevant to the residents of Brightlingsea, as will be discussed below. The transportation of live farm animals through narrow residential streets played a major part in bringing into public view what was previously hidden. Farm animals had become an urban spectacle.

What follows is an historical and ethnographic exploration of the campaign to ban live exports from Britain. It will focus predominantly on the activities and lobbying capacities of the animal welfare organisation—Compassion in World Farming—since it has played a significant role at a local, national and European level in mobilising people at the grass-roots; has pushed the issue up the media's agenda, as well as up the political agenda; and finally, because it has initiated fundamental legal challenges to European legislation which have a direct bearing on the export trade of live animals. The case study of Brightlingsea provides an opportunity to examine the extent to which the recent protests were a NIMBY (not in my back yard) response. In addition, it provides a context in which to consider the influence of geographical location both on the activity of protesting, since protests do not occur in a spatial vacuum, and on its contribution to bringing the animal into public view.

Background to the export of live animals

The dramatic and high profile protests during 1995 attracted wide-spread media attention, which put places like Shoreham and Brightling-sea on the map. It is important to note however, that there has been ongoing and increasing public concern about the export of live animals since the mid-1950s. According to the Balfour Committee's report, published in April 1957 (Enquiry into the export of live cattle to the Continent for slaughter), the contemporary export market for live animals was established in 1956, when American soldiers based on the Continent were keen to secure a supply of meat from Britain. However, when British slaughterhouses failed to meet standards deemed accept-able by the American Army Veterinary Corps, the wheels had to be set in motion for alternative arrangements. This entailed live British cattle being shipped to Europe and then slaughtered in Dutch abattoirs which had gained American approval. The quality of British cattle was soon appreciated by the Dutch, who jointly imported live animals with the Americans. This turn of events attracted the attention of French buyers, who subsequently purchased British cattle in Rotterdam. Organisations such as the Protection of Livestock for Slaughter Association shadowed such consignments of animals. They unearthed evidence that animals were not receiving food and water during transit and that the majority of exported cattle were slaughtered with the pole-axe, 'a system so cruel that it had been outlawed in Britain since 1933'.[1]

The public became increasingly concerned about such findings, which spurred the British government to inquire further into the trade. This culminated in the Balfour Committee's report. According to the Com-mittee, public anxiety generated by the export trade of live animals revolved around the following issues: the exportation of animals which were unfit to travel; inadequate care and attention before embarking on their journey; long train journeys without food or water after disembar-kation on the Continent; animals were not protected by British legisla-tion relating to the method of slaughtering once they had been exported to the Continent. It declared: 'That there is justification for anxiety on all these grounds. We feel bound to say also that we do not think that all those engaged in this trade have shown themselves to be fully alive to the degree of suffering capable of being caused to animals during transport by land or sea.' It then went on to propose that a carcase trade was not considered feasible at that time but did concede that 'slaughter before export would be desirable'. In effect, this statement takes us to the very heart of the debate. It gives weight to a fundamental observation made by those campaigning to ban live exports, that the trade should be 'on the hook not the hoof'. Their rationale for a meat trade is that animals are subjected to unnecessary suffering during the process of transportation, just to be slaughtered (in most cases) on arrival. Notwithstanding this, the committee recommended: 'The trade should be allowed only to small countries such as Holland or small autonomous territories, where internal transit after disembarkation can only be over short distances and where the government concerned can give satisfactory assurances that the animals will not be allowed to move out of their territory. The method of slaughter must satisfy British requirements, and conditions of lairage and slaughterhouse facilities must be satisfactory.'

Hence, the trade was to continue provided conditions known as the 'Balfour Assurances' were adhered to by the countries importing animals from Britain. These Assurances proposed a maximum journey length of 100km (62 miles) from the destined European port to the abattoir; animals exported from Britain were not to be re-exported from the importing country; animals about to be slaughtered were still to be adequately fed and watered; and prior to slaughter animals had to be stunned electrically or by a captive bolt pistol. The implementation of these Assurances appeared to restore confidence in the trade. The O'Brien Committee Report (Export of Live Animals for Slaughter, published in 1974) noted that the 'acceptance of the Assurances by Continental governments was secured through diplomatic channels. The agreements were not embodied in any formal instrument of ratification or in United Kingdom legislation'. The Assurances were not legally binding, hence no sanctions could be invoked to ensure their compliance. The O'Brien Committee regarded this as a 'serious weakness'.

By the early 1970s a picture was emerging that they were being regularly disregarded. According to Stevenson, in *A Far Cry from Noah*, animals were indeed routinely re-exported and transported over the recommended 100km, as well as being slaughtered without initial stunning. The combination of mounting public pressure calling for an end to live animal exports and the overwhelming evidence provided by e.g. the Royal Society for the Prevention of Cruelty to Animals that the Assurances were being ignored, led the Minister of Agriculture in February 1973 to temporarily stop issuing export licences for sheep for immediate slaughter or for further fattening. This generated unprecedented media interest. In July of the same year, a three-hour parliamentary debate was followed by a vote (285 votes, including 23 Conservatives, to 264) which defeated the Conservative government — the Commons had voted to suspend all live animal exports. The government proposed an independent committee to be chaired by Lord O'Brien to inquire further into the issue. It is worth noting here that at the beginning of 1973 Britain joined the European Community, as a result of which EC Directives were increasingly to influence animal welfare legislation throughout Europe. It has been noted by Peter Stevenson (political and legal director of Compassion in World Farming) that such legislation was little more than a paper exercise, poorly monitored (if at all) and regularly contravened.

In March 1974, the O'Brien Committee published its findings. It concluded: 'Although there have undoubtedly been shortcomings in the past which may, on occasion, have amounted to ill treatment of the animals, we believe that these can be remedied. We do not consider that the degree of stress involved in any one section of the export trade, nor its cumulative effect, is sufficient to justify a permanent ban. On the other hand we believe that the issue of further export licences should continue to be suspended until acceptable and enforceable conditions can be introduced to ensure that the welfare of the animals is safe-guarded with greater certainty.' It advocated the setting up of an export supervisory body incorporating representatives of all those involved in the trade, which would advise the Minister of Agriculture, Fisheries and Food on conditions pertaining to the export trade in live animals for slaughter. This body was to be further supplemented by a small team of inspectors who would investigate any reports of misconduct and make sure that the recommended standards were in practise being upheld. It believed that 'the inspection arrangements would provide a method of ensuring that the conditions laid down for the trade were being satisfactorily implemented at working level and this would answer one of the major criticisms of the existing arrangements that they did not provide for a means of scrutiny and enforcement'. It considered that the move towards European standardisation of animal welfare legislation relating to slaughtering practices and transportation was the most effective way of protecting animals involved in the export trade. The report also states: 'We have been reassured by the discussions which we have had with the European Commission which have reinforced our impression that a growing concern for animal welfare is being translated into practical regulations.'

However, Stevenson suggests that animal welfare organisations 'were deeply disappointed' with the recommendations of the O'Brien Report, as they had hoped that it would adjudicate against the continuation of the export of live animals for slaughter.[2] He also noted that the British Veterinary Association responded by issuing a press statement which reiterated its view that animals should be slaughtered as near as possible to the place of production, as they were concerned that the 'report's proposals did not go far enough and would not be really effective'. Although the report was published in spring 1974, it was not debated by Parliament until January 1975. Following a seven-hour debate (a Labour government having been elected in 1974), there was a pro-government vote (232 to 191) for the resumption of the export in live animals. The export trade commenced immediately. This decision ignored the O'Brien Committee's recommendation that the trade should remain suspended until steps had been taken 'to ensure that the welfare of the animals is safeguarded with greater certainty'. Stevenson argues that the Minister of Agriculture at that time considered the implemen-tation of the O'Brien safeguards to be impractical and had made no attempt to address this issue but focused instead on the EC Directive. This particular piece of legislation required animals to be stunned prior to slaughter. Prioritising the effectiveness of harmonising European animal welfare legislation over the Committee's other recommendations would seem to have been based on the assumption that the legislation would indeed be adhered to. However, as the mechanisms for monitoring the trade were considered unworkable and the necessary safeguards could not be guaranteed, Stevenson suggests that the minister's decision to resume the trade was 'extraordinary'.

Moreover, animal welfare legislation outlined in EC Directives relating to slaughtering practices and international transport (1974 and 1977/81 respectively, which are no longer in force) have been shown (by RSPCA and CIWF investigation teams) to be routinely disregarded. Despite accruing evidence, officials have seemingly turned a blind eye to blatant infringements, and since 1975 the trade continued relentlessly despite continued public protest. It was in response to governmental apathy that animal welfare groups decided to intensify their campaign to ban live exports. CIWF, founded in October 1967 by Peter Roberts, an English dairy farmer, has over the years become a well-established farm animal welfare organisation committed to peaceful campaigning for an end to cruel factory farming systems. The main organisation in Britain appears to have 10,400 supporters (these figures are based on people who have paid their annual subscription) but there are a further 25,000 people who offer financial donations towards its campaigns. In addition to this, many of these donors will write letters to lobby for legislative changes and actively participate in marches or demonstrations. According to its quarterly magazine (*Agscene*, Spring 1991)[3] all new government legislation or Codes of Practice pertaining to farm animal welfare is now sent to it for comment. The campaigning side of the work is overseen by CIWF Ltd, although it is commonly referred to as CIWF. In 1982, the founder established the educational side through a separate charity, the Athene Trust (now called CIWF Trust) because organisations like CIWF which campaign for a change in legislation are denied charity status. In 1992, it expanded by establishing an office in Ireland (when the export of Irish cattle resumed to North Africa and the Middle East) and in 1994 it helped set up Protection Mondiale des Animaux de Ferme—its French equivalent. 1995 saw further reorganisation in response to increasing activities: CIWF Supporters Ltd would predominantly deal with membership and fundraising, while CIWF Ltd would continue with the campaigning side of work.

CIWF's campaign to ban live animal exports intensified in June 1990 when it organised a mass lobby of Parliament. This attracted over 800 CIWF supporters and the backing of 26 animal welfare societies. It enabled many members of the public to express their concerns about the live animal export trade directly to their MPs. The 1990s marked an increased momentum in the campaign to ban such exports. This was to be paralleled by a massive escalation in live animal exports: from 490,000 lambs/sheep and 340,000 calves in 1990 to an estimated 2,000,000 lambs/sheep and 450,000 calves in 1993 (Ministry of Agriculture figures). CIWF was beginning to release video evidence relating to slaughtering practices in Spanish abattoirs and the transportation of animals, including calves destined for the veal crate system in Europe (prohibited in Britain since the beginning of 1990), which illustrated the continued violation of animal welfare legislation. The campaign to ban live exports was gaining the support of many celebrities, such as Penelope Keith, Jilly Cooper, Peter O'Sullevan and Joanna Lumley. This undoubtedly increased media attention. For example, in February 1994, during a press conference to launch a new stage in the campaign, Joanna Lumley said after a video which had shaken her: 'We breed these animals. Their lives and deaths are our responsibility. It is simply unacceptable to treat living creatures in this way.' The event attracted major national newspaper coverage. At that time Granada Television showed a World in Action documentary entitled 'Animal Traffic' apparently seen by 5.8 million viewers. CIWF described it as 'a hard-hitting exposé ... which highlighted the suffering behind the trade'.[4] The campaign to ban live animal exports had now become a high profile media issue.

By raising public awareness, animal welfare organisations play a major role in mobilising the public. They can activate public outrage and harness it to increase lobbying effectiveness. To channel public feeling maximises the pressure that may be exerted on key participants in the trade. For example, in October 1994 two of the main ferry companies, P&O and Stena Link (said to process 90% of the export trade between them) announced that they would no longer ship live animals abroad. It would seem that considerable pressure had been exerted on the ferry companies through letters expressing opposition to the ferries' role in the export trade and threatening to boycott their passenger services. Exporters continued their business by chartering ships and aircraft, which meant that they had to negotiate access to minor seaports and airports. Ironically, this led to an intensification of the campaign culminating in mass protests in places like Shoreham and Brightlingsea. As new sites were identified, 'lightning demonstrations' were organised by CIWF at locations such as Humberside airport, Bournemouth, Coventry, Prestwick, Carlisle, Folkestone, Plymouth and Swansea. Contact members living near to these areas played a crucial role in mobilising local support.

Partial success followed. Several of the airport boards, port authorities and city councils decided that the exporters would not be able to export live animals from their facilities because they were concerned about the scale of disruption that would result from the public demonstrations. In April 1995, however, a High Court decision taken by Lord Justice Simon Brown and Mr Justice Popplewell declared that Dover,

Coventry and Plymouth had no right to surrender to 'mob-rule' and they must allow the trade irrespective of the protests. They also reiterated that the police had sufficient legal powers to deal effectively with disorderly public events, citing the 1986 Public Order Act, and the 1994 Criminal Justice and Public Order Act. Danny Penman, a journalist who covered the protests extensively at the time, raised a fundamental question as to whether animal export is an example of public sensibilities having been offended, resulting in considerable strength of feeling. Irrespective of whether the judges' decision is considered right or wrong, Penman suggests: 'The judges should have shown more sensitivity to the real dilemmas facing the ports and to the moral anger and comparative restraint of the protesters. By their sweeping condemnation of the protests, they have demonstrated the wide gulf that exists between sections of the judiciary and much of public opinion' (*Independent*, 13.4.95). Thus, despite the export of live animals currently being a legitimate economic trade, the protesters consider it immoral and are campaigning vehemently for a change in legislation to prohibit the trade. It is in this sense that a legal trade has indeed become a moral issue.

Case study: Brightlingsea

In January 1995 the first convoy of lorries containing live animals arrived at the seaports of Shoreham and Brightlingsea. This development acted like a catalyst—hundreds of people in the first town and thousands in the second took to the streets, blockaded the roads, and the lorries were initially turned back. They returned, however, the export trade continued, and the people resolutely continued to express their indignation. The campaign to ban live exports had entered a new phase. To explore this in more detail, Brightlingsea serves as a case study.

The protests at Brightlingsea attracted unprecedented local, national and international media attention, much of which was generally sympathetic. For example, it has been suggested by writers in the *New Left Review* that the media coverage 'remained far removed from the hegemonic hostility which has characterised media treatment of industrial action by workers, as well as other more obviously comparable forms of protest action, such as those of campaigners against the Criminal Justice Bill, hunt saboteurs and motorway protesters. It is also significant that no major public figure disputed the moral case advanced by the protesters, though there were numerous attempts to discursively reconstruct the issue.'[5] The protests also occurred at a time when the campaign to ban live exports had been very much in the news the previous year—thus a climate had been created which meant that the media and the general public were both sensitive to the issue. Finally, the fact that the people involved in these protests challenged the media stereotype which had come to be associated with animal rights/welfare campaigns, this perhaps enabled 'ordinary' law-abiding people to identify with the protesters. This was exemplified by the plausible and articulate presentation of the spokesperson for the local protest group Brightlingsea Against Live Exports (BALE).

The activity of protesting does not occur in a spatial vacuum. Geographical location and related infrastructure provide a context, which influences who participates, how one protests, and the experience of protesting. These factors provide valuable information pertaining to the resources, opportunities and constraints which people engaged in the activity of protesting have to negotiate in order to achieve their goal. Here we consider two aspects. Firstly, were the protests at Brightlingsea no more than a NIMBY (not in my back yard) response? Secondly, it is suggested that the infrastructure of Brightlingsea played a significant role in bringing into urban public view the live farm animal which is usually out of sight. This raises an interesting point about the relationship between the degree of proximity to the issue of concern and the level of response. The further away one is, the more objective, rational and detached one can be; the closer one is, the more informed, engaged and emotionally involved one may become.

'NIMBY'ism?

The residents of Brightlingsea did not have to initiate or manufacture an interest; the issue was brought directly to their doorstep every weekday until October 1995 — when the trade of live animals ceased going through their town. It was widely reported in the media that the protesters at Brightlingsea challenged the stereotype commonly associated with those active in the animal rights movement — they 'lack the youth, the dreadlocks, the crusty dresses and the vegetarian boots that have come to characterise our visual images of these campaigns' (*Guardian*, 3.6.95). A local reporter observed that the police seriously damaged their 'image and reputation . . . and the wounds are going to take years to heal . . . had the protests mainly been comprised of scruffy rent-a-mob traveller types intent on causing mayhem, the police might have found a bit more support . . . the majority of those protesting were the sort of people who would normally count the police as allies — law-abiding locals, Mr and Mrs Averages, pensioners, young mums and children' (Evening Gazette, 17.5.95). A survey conducted by the present author in summer 1995 supports these observations: 82% of the sample associated with BALE were female, 73% were aged between 41 and 70, 38% were retired, 71% resided in the Brightlingsea area, and 80% had never protested before. Since the export trade of live animals was thrust upon them — a town of approximately 8,000 residents — without prior consultation, it could be argued that what arose was a NIMBY response. However, a survey sponsored by the town council at the height of the protests indicated that 71% of respondents were opposed to the trade irrespective of where it took place; 6% declared that their opposition to it was primarily a result of it going through Brightlingsea, whilst only 8% said that they had no objection to the trade at all; 79% of respondents proposed that 'even if the trade is lawful, it should be banned if it upsets the local community'.[6] On the face of it, only 6% gave a NIMBY response, but many of the 71% may also have been influenced by the experience of the trade going through their town.

It is interesting to note that when exports through Brightlingsea ceased, the local protest group continued to meet weekly, with 40 to 60 people attending on a regular basis. A further survey by the present author in summer 1997 indicated that 76% of them were female, 81% were 50 years of age or over, and 55% retired. BALE continued to up-date its telephone information lines on a daily basis and circulated its newsletter to supporters. In addition, coaches of demonstrators offered ongoing support to protesters at Dover, where exports of live animals continued. They have also travelled to other animal rights/welfare events in Britain and Europe. Some of the protesters regularly participated in watches at markets and lairages (temporary resting and feeding points for animals destined for market or export abroad), recording and if necessary reporting to officials, (e.g. representatives of the veterinary profession, the Ministry of Agriculture or local authority Trading Standards services) any breaches in animal welfare legislation. As a result, some of the participants have become well informed about relevant legislation and are in effect, voluntarily policing the system. The charge of NIMBYism seems to provide a partial explanation for the protests: 'I was stirred out of apathy about something I knew of, by the fact it was going through my town'; 'At first I was furious that anyone had the nerve to bring heavy lorries through our town without consulting us first'. Nevertheless, it fails to account adequately for the local residents that have remained active well after the trade of live animals stopped going through their town.

The live farm animal comes into urban public view

Most people in urbanised Western societies have little direct contact with animals. This can foster a detached and often indifferent attitude towards them.[7] Pet owners can act as mediators in this situation. They assume the responsibility of meeting their animals' physical needs and this may help them understand the needs of livestock transported for export or sold at market. The author's 1997 survey also showed that 71% of respondents currently owned or looked after a pet and 90% had at sometime in their lives owned one. It has been suggested that people who become involved in the animal rights movement are in part activated by their personal experience with pets and are influenced by concern for pet-like animals.[8] This observation is particularly relevant here. Week-old calves, with their appealing faces peering out of the lorries, can engender high levels of urban public sympathy, not unlike the anti-seal-culling campaigns in Canada during the 1970s.

The intensification of farming methods has been a significant factor in concealing farm animals from public view. When exporters had to find alternative seaports and airports following the ferry ban in 1994, their trade was much more evident. Dover is a 24-hour port accessed by dual carriageway, with the infrastructure to process convoys of lorries quickly. At Brightlingsea, on the other hand, the only vehicular access to the wharf is a three-mile narrow, winding road, lined with residential houses and a few small businesses. The structure of the road became a resource for the protesters to generate media attention. In one incident masses of sand, deposited in the road, had to be cleared before the lorries could get through. As Barbara Goodwin observed in her book, *Using Political Ideas*, 'civil disobedience need not cause a public nuisance, but the greater the nuisance, the greater the publicity'.[9] Moreover, Brightlingsea is more like a marina than a port. The transportation ship could only sail at certain times of the day, depending on the level of the tide. This had a bearing on who was able to protest: the afternoon made it difficult for people who were employed (predominantly men) to participate. Early morning or early evening allowed them to protest before going to work, or on returning. Brightlingsea's infrastructure, combined with the mass protests, slowed down the procession of lorries carrying their cargo of live animals, making it difficult for witnesses to turn a blind eye. This is conveyed by those involved in the protests, e.g. 'There is no escape from the daily convoys with the sight, sound and smell of the animals. I cannot turn my back on such suffering. While it all offends the sensibilities of so many people across the country, it is legal. I can't understand why it remains so.'

However, not only did the farm animal come (back) into view, the export trade itself became subjected to public scrutiny. Exposure to the trade increased public awareness of intensive farming methods, food production, European legislation and the economics which underpinned the trade. It has been suggested that the division of labour within the industry prevents anyone from accepting responsibility for the animal.[10] In relation to the export trade, does it lie with the breeder, farmer, livestock markets, transporters, exporters, slaughterhouses, butchers, advertisers, retailers, or the consumer? As consumers (potential protesters) become more informed about the trade, they increasingly challenge the status quo. The export of calves to the veal crate system, predominantly in France or Holland, illustrates this further. It is important to note, however, that in 1996 the EU banned the export of calves from Britain in response to the BSE crisis. At the time of writing this ban remains in place.

Veal crate system and European legislation

The majority of male calves destined for the veal crate system are an unwanted by-product of the dairy industry. In order to produce milk, cows have to produce calves. Female calves are reared to maintain milk production, but males have no value for the dairy farmer and are generally ill-suited for beef production. At about one week old, the latter begin their journey to the veal crate system in continental Europe. The veal crate is a solid-sided wooden box, with a slatted floor. Each calf is enclosed in a crate for the rest of its life, approximately 26 weeks. It is unable to turn round. No straw is provided because if consumed it could alter the colour of the veal from the preferred white to a pale pink. The calf is fed a reconstituted liquid diet, with reduced iron content, also to ensure that the flesh remains pale.

In January 1995, CIWF launched an investigative video made by a freelance filmmaker and a former BBC environment correspondent. They had followed a consignment of calves from Coventry airport to Rennes airport, then shadowed trucks to a veal crate system somewhere in France. Video footage, depicting the calves 'struggling against their chains, frightened and desperate', was shown on national television and attracted widespread newspaper coverage. CIWF suggested that these scenes 'have touched the nation's heart and roused public indignation at the dreadful injustice of this cruel export trade'.[11] Such strategies by the animal rights/welfare movement play an important role in focusing attention on what is usually hidden. The ideal viewer's response is: 'If this scrap of documentary evidence has been brought to light, how much more remains unseen?' The imaginary unseen may then carry greater symbolic weight than the images revealed.[12] Consequently, the people involved in the protests at Brightlingsea had certainly become more informed about the conditions and farming practices which would meet the calves at their destination.

The high-profile public demonstrations at the local grass-roots level provided a tremendous opportunity for animal welfare organisations, such as CIWF, to lobby for legislative changes at a European level. Two examples will be discussed. Firstly, the export trade of calves from Britain, destined for the veal crate system in Europe, raised fundamental issues relating to the principle of free trade within the European Single Market, which came into effect at the beginning of 1993. CIWF argue that 'it is morally unacceptable for the UK, having recognised the cruelty of the veal crate by prohibiting its use (in 1990), to continue to send calves overseas for rearing in crates'.[13] Article 34 of the Treaty of Rome prevents such trade restrictions, however, and the Minister of Agriculture decided that he could not ban live exports. Nevertheless, in 1995 CIWF, along with the International Fund for Animal Welfare, challenged this on the basis of a clause in Article 36 of the Treaty which permits a member state to impose partial or complete trade restrictions if this can be justified on grounds of 'public morality, public policy, or public security; the protection of the health and life of humans, animals or plants'. The case has reached the European Court of Justice and, according to Peter Stevenson, is the first time that an animal welfare organisation has been able to take its case this far. The Opinion of the

Courts' Advocate-General in Autumn 1997 appeared to indicate that Britain might be able to invoke Article 36 if there is scientific evidence that the veal crate system does have substantial health problems for calves and that the British public has clearly expressed the view that the trade is morally unacceptable. It is the latter aspect, i.e. the public morality clause of Article 36 which is of particular significance. Meanwhile, the European Agriculture ministers have conceded that the veal crate system will in any case be banned from the year 2008.

The other high profile campaign relates to the status of animals in European legislation. Under Article 38 of the Treaty of Rome, live animals are classified as 'agricultural products' together with other agricultural commodities, thus subjecting animals to the rules of free trade. CIWF has campaigned since the late 1980s to reclassify animals as 'sentient beings'. In 1991, it presented a petition to the President of the European Parliament with over a million signatures from citizens in the twelve member states (and the backing of European animal welfare bodies). In 1994 the European Parliament supported the recommended change in status, but amendment of the Treaty of Rome requires the consent of all member states. An Inter-Governmental Conference was scheduled for 1996 whereby such an issue could be considered. CIWF's campaign to change the Treaty gained the support of a coalition of animal welfare groups, known as the European Committee for Improvements in the Transport of Farm Animals, formed in 1993. In the summer of 1996, at the Amsterdam Summit, it was unanimously decided by the fifteen member states to recognise animals as sentient beings. The protocol which will be annexed to the Treaty commits the EU to 'pay full regard to the welfare requirements of animals' when formulating and implementing the Community's policies on agriculture, transport, research and the internal market. CIWF regards this as an opportunity to ban live exports, restricting trade to meat.

It is important to note that the campaign to ban live exports has not been promoted as a 'veggie issue', hence the significance of the phrase 'on the hook but not the hoof'. It has been noted that people who are involved in the animal rights movement tend to be vegetarian or vegan.[14] However, according to the author's 1997 survey, of those who continued to attend BALE's weekly meeting 64% continued to eat meat, fish or chicken. In this particular animal rights/welfare campaign the rhetoric of animal rights was evident but the campaigning styles and moral tone 'stayed firmly within the utilitarian-welfarist tradition'.[14] This enabled the campaigners to mobilise a wider base of public support, as in a poster: You Don't Have To Stop Eating Meat To Care—Ban Live Exports. It seems that those who were more ideologically orientated (i.e. adopted a more animal rights perspective and were more likely to be vegetarian or vegan) tended to assume a more proactive role in the campaign. However, it could also be argued that as the issue was transported to the residents of Brightlingsea, it engaged people who would campaign because of an interest in animal-related issues since they were unable to turn a blind eye.

Finally, as an issue of concern, the campaign to ban live exports appeared to transcend political affiliations to the left or right, leading to the suggestion that 'the moral case for animal welfare is close to a national consensus', hence, in this respect it is 'non-political'. Arguably, this was fundamental to the campaign in attracting and maintaining the breadth of public support it received at a local, national and European level.[15]

Conclusion

The campaign to ban live animal exports peaked in the 1970s and the mid-1990s. In the intervening period, the political, socio-economic, legal and moral landscape of continental Europe and Britain has changed dramatically. The issue of animal welfare has arguably moved from the margins into the mainstream, which is reflected by the high level of public support which animal welfare organisations such as CIWF, and its locally based protest groups, have attracted and maintained during the 1990s. The live animal has increasingly, and at times unexpectedly come back into urban public view. The BSE crisis and high-profile food scares have ensured that the animal, whether dead or alive, remains in view. The recent protests generated by the campaign to ban live exports appears to illustrate that the activity of protesting has become increasingly acceptable socially — as a mechanism which enables 'ordinary' members of the public to communicate and register their concerns to governmental bodies.

1 P. Stevenson, *A Far Cry from Noah: The Live Export Trade in Calves, Sheep and Pigs* (Green Print, 1994), p. 2. This is the first book to document the export trade in live animals and has generally informed the historical, political and economic background to the trade.

2 P. Stevenson. op. cit., pp. 24–8.

3 Information relating to CIWF and its campaigns has been taken from its quarterly magazine *Agscene* (1990–97).

4 *Agscene*, Spring 1994.

5 T. Benton and S. Redfearn, 'The Politics of Animal Rights — Where is the Left?', *New Left Review*, Jan/Feb 1996, p. 44.

6 See E. Tannenbaum, *Animal Transport Through Brightlingsea: Report of an Opinion Survey* (University of Essex, 1995), pp. 6.

7 See J. Serpell, *In The Company of Animals: A Study of Human-Animal Relationships* (Blackwell, 1986).

8 See W. Jamison and W. Lunch, 'Rights of Animals, Perceptions of Science, and Political Activism: Profile of American Animal Rights Activists', *Science, Technology and Human Values*, Autumn 1992, p. 448.

9 B. Goodwin, *Using Political Ideas* (John Wiley and Sons, 1992), p. 319.

10 See J. Serpell, op. cit.

11 *Agscene*, No. 117, (Spring, 1995), p. 16.

12 See S. Baker, *Picturing the Beast: Animals, Identity and Representation* (Manchester University Press, 1993), p. 221.

13 P. Stevenson, op. cit., p. 60.

14 See H. Herzog, 'The Movement is My Life: The Psychology of Animal Rights Activism', *Journal of Social Issues*, 1993/1.

15 T. Benton and S. Redfearn, op. cit., p. 51.

Second Runway at Manchester

BY STEVEN GRIGGS, DAVID HOWARTH AND BRIAN JACOBS

ON 31 May 1997, just a month after New Labour's landslide election victory, more than 300 protesting residents from Knutsford, Mobberley and Wilmslow marched around the two and a quarter mile long security fence surrounding the site of Manchester Airport's proposed second runway. After an hour's silence to mark the loss of the countryside, Terry Waite, the former envoy of the Archbishop of Canterbury who grew up in the nearby village of Styal, addressed the assembled crowd. He congratulated the direct action campaigners, many of whom were still buried underground, for their defence of the picturesque Bollin Valley, admonished the airport bailiffs, the notorious balaclava-clad 'men in black', for their Gestapo tactics, accused the authorities of illegally cutting down trees, and urged the government to order an immediate review of the runway plan (*Observer*, 1.6.97). Two days earlier, Liz Snook, nicknamed 'the Worm', was eventually forced from an underground chamber where she had been encased for several days with a noose around her neck, thus bringing to 127 the number of direct action campaigners arrested by police and security forces that week. It was to take another three weeks for the protesters to be finally evicted. Though other legal avenues would still be pursued by eco-warriors and local residents, the campaign to stop Manchester Airport from building a second runway was effectively over.

Citizen protests and mobilisation over the proposed construction and extension of airports are hardly new. Internationally, past campaigns have ranged from traditional bargaining between airport authorities and residents over levels of compensation for falling property prices, the problems of noise and air pollution, or environmental damage, to violent antagonisms between anti-state movements and political systems.[1] Plans to build London's Third Airport in the 1960s and early 1970s provoked considerable protest by local residents and environmental groups.[2] However, the campaign against the expansion of Manchester Airport was the first airport protest in Britain in which the mobilisation of largely middle-class residents was accompanied by the presence of a committed group of direct action protesters. These environmental protesters, who rapidly acquired a folk-hero status, capturing the popular imagination with names such as 'Swampy', 'Animal' and 'the Worm', were prepared to use sophisticated techniques of bodily risk to obstruct the construction of the proposed runway. This peculiar alliance of traditional middle class protesters and self-named eco-warriors, 'Vegans and Volvos' as *The Times* leader article put it (19.5.97), with their marked differences of identity, style, social characteristics and political orientation, grabbed the attention of the local and national media, and altered popular perceptions about environmental issues.

Here we explore the changing dynamics of protest as the anti-runway campaign unfolded, focusing particularly on the contingent alliance of groups which contested the decision and its implementation. In addition to standard questions raised by what has been called the politics of suburban social movements, the intervention of the eco-warriors raises a new set of questions. How was their alliance with local residents forged? Did their radical methods and ideology make a difference to the more established forms of mobilisation and protest? Did this conjunction of forces have a material impact on the decision to extend the airport? Is this campaign, along with the roads campaigns, a harbinger of a new form of politics in the 1990s? What role did the media play in the representation of the events?

Local opposition

Manchester is the UK's third largest airport in terms of air traffic after Heathrow and Gatwick. Successive governments have actively supported the expansion of air travel, recognising since 1978 the strategic national role of Manchester. The Thatcher and Major Conservative governments confirmed that regional airports would expand to meet the ever-increasing demand for passenger and freight services. These policy commitments led to substantial capital investment in Manchester's terminal facilities and the identification of the airport with the regional and international aspirations of the City of Manchester. Manchester Airport stated at the public inquiry that the airport would continue to grow with a capital expenditure programme of £530 million between 1994 and 2004. As a major player in the North West regional economy, it would attract new commercial and industrial activities and expand its 12,000 workforce, as well as generating jobs further afield. Accountable to its local authority stakeholders, it presented a vision of success that would benefit the wider regional economy. Strengthened by the Labour Party's embrace of the market, the Labour-controlled City of Manchester and the airport formed a powerful lobby which represented an almost unstoppable driving force behind the second runway.

For those who did not share this modernising vision, Manchester's King Kong was about to disrupt Cheshire's rural calm, avariciously devouring the countryside. They saw the second runway as a threat to an area that is one of the wealthiest and environmentally most pleasant commuter belts outside the South East. The communities south of Manchester around Knutsford, Mobberley and Wilmslow have been among the highest per capita income areas in Britain; they have attracted both those associated with 'old money' and those who have acquired 'new money' in the wake of the impressive growth of the North Cheshire economy. This is a part of Cheshire where the rapid economic expansion of the 1980s and 1990s resulted in sparkling service sector office developments, new high-tech research and development facilities, executive housing, state-of-the-art shopping centres and up-market leisure clubs.

The pace of change and the demands of developers for more land strengthened local conservationist groups. As early as the 1970s, village amenity groups in the area south of the airport, especially in Knutsford, Mobberley and Styal, had long been aware of the implications of economic growth and the expansionist zeal of the City of Manchester and its airport. The Styal Action group was formed in 1973 when it successfully fought the original plans for a second runway. There was therefore a strong and active conservationist tradition in the villages that formed the basis of the broad anti-growth coalition against the Airport's revived plans for development in the 1990s. The Mobberley Village Society was another well established civic society from which emerged the working group of residents in Mobberley to oppose the second runway. They were instrumental in the formation of the Knutsford and Mobberley Joint Action Group after the 1991 announcement of the planned expansion project. Together, they took the subsequent lead in founding the Manchester Airport Joint Action Group, the umbrella organisation representing all the village groups at the public inquiry. This was fully established by the end of 1992 during the Manchester Airport's public consultation phase.

The Joint Action Group assumed the task of coordinating a disparate set of village and suburban community organisations. Each constituent group retained its own identity, leaving the umbrella group to ensure a collective voice at the public inquiry. At its peak prior to the public inquiry, the supporters of the Joint Action Committee and its affiliated groups numbered an estimated ten thousand. It had the support of professional people who committed substantial expertise and resources to the campaign. It also had politicians from the various local authorities around the airport. All this allowed it to supplement the evidence of its expert witnesses at the public inquiry, thus lowering the cost of the campaign, as well as enabling it to answer the technical questions posed by the media and interested parties.

The Joint Action Group quickly organised high profile events that attracted the support of local villagers. £300,000 was raised during the run up to the public inquiry. The bulk of fund-raising occurred at events such as the summer ball in the grounds of Hill House, one of the listed buildings threatened with demolition. There were campaign stalls in the villages and posters (local newspapers reported that these were displayed in the windows of most affected residences). Tee shirts and sweat shirts were printed. Although the campaign centred on affluent Knutsford, activists were drawn from outlying towns such as Northwich and

Macclesfield to broaden the appeal of the campaign and attract media attention.

The Joint Action Group's committee members concentrated their resources on hiring expert witnesses and preparing their submission for the public inquiry. A working group identified issues that they intended to pursue and after considerable debate appointed a London firm of solicitors. While they were aware of the importance of publicity, they felt that they were battling against seemingly overwhelming odds when it came to getting their message across. This strategy provoked an important split when a spokesperson of one of the groups fell out with its committee, arguing that greater resources should be devoted to a national media campaign and lobbying activities at Westminster. He went on to form the Manchester Airport Environmental Network in April 1994 which later made a separate submission to the public inquiry.

In addition to the residents' groups, Macclesfield Borough Council also opposed the development, stressing the protection of the Green Belt and the enforcement of planning guidelines. The National Trust, English Nature and the Campaign for the Protection of Rural England opposed the runway on environmental grounds. In contrast, the Joint Action Group concentrated upon projected passenger growth, air traffic flows and other technical matters, as well as related issues such as health and safety. Before the inquiry, Cheshire County Council opposed the runway extension, but decided to switch sides shortly before the inquiry. The County Council, the Airport and the Manchester City Council agreed to an environmental mitigation package to offset the damage which would be caused by the construction of the runway; an unexpected agreement that left the Joint Action Group and its supporters weakened on the eve of the public inquiry.

The public inquiry

The Joint Action Committee and the Environmental Network regarded the inquiry as an opportunity to appear well informed on complex technical issues and were keen to attend (though believing that the process was weighted in favour of Manchester Airport by the exclusion of Liverpool from its consideration). Moreover, Manchester Airport had the resources to run a well-funded publicity campaign before and during the inquiry. The City Council and a line-up of influential political leaders in the North West backed the runway and echoed the Conservative government's call for improved economic competitiveness and inward regional investment. The inquiry thus became a battleground of competing expertise and technical competence.

The City was strongly committed to the second runway while admitting that there would be some negative environmental impacts. Listed buildings would be demolished, natural habitats would be disrupted and there would be recreational loss in the Bollin Valley.

Nevertheless, it argued that the expansion of the airport was an appropriate use of land within the Green Belt which had strong public support. Indeed, the project would contribute to 'the economic and social health of the city'. Moreover, a significant limitation of the environmental impact would be achieved by the Cheshire County Council's Environmental Mitigation Package, structured jointly with the Airport. The County Council admitted that ancient woodland, hedgerows, trees, grasslands and riverside habitats would be lost, but reassured the inspector that it would protect the natural environment and was committed to a 'no net loss' policy of biodiversity.

Presenting itself as the legitimate voice of the community, the Joint Action Group accepted that Manchester Airport was important for the region, but argued that it had overstated the potential economic benefits of the second runway. The group expressed doubts about the commercial viability of the project and disputed the official claim that the runway would lead to the creation of 50,000 jobs. It argued that Liverpool Airport could be expanded to handle more of the tourist charter traffic while Manchester could focus on the business traveller.

The Environmental Network lacked both the resources to muster the same extensive professional support and the widespread community support of the larger umbrella group. Its case relied upon its capacity to play the airport officials at their own game. Its evidence focused directly on technical arguments and comparison of Manchester with other airports internationally and therefore appeared less concerned with convincing the inspector that the group had a resonance locally. This meant that some of the strongest environmental arguments for the protection of badgers, wildfowl and natural habitats were left to groups such as the Cheshire Wildlife Trust and Manchester Wildlife. While English Nature was not an outright objector, concern was expressed about the welfare of the badgers, bats and great crested newts. The National Trust objected because of the landscape impacts of the proposed runway on its woodland and other property, arguing that the environmental threats affected nationally important sites and would destroy listed buildings and intrude upon recreational areas such as Tatton Park and the Styal and Dunham Massey estates. In contrast, the Greater Manchester Transport Action Group, which had in the past objected with Trafford Friends of the Earth to various motorway projects, concentrated entirely on trunk road traffic flows around the airport. Taken with the evidence of many individual protesters, such presentations left the inspector with a substantial amount of carefully argued material to assess.

Despite the turf battles between the inspector and the objectors over technical matters, the Joint Action Group and the Environmental Network maintained that the opposition won the argument in spite of the disappointing outcome of the inquiry. They remained suspicious about the role of John Gummer, Secretary of State at the Department of the Environment, who appeared to the group to be strongly favouring the runway. There seemed to be a long time lag between the end of the inquiry in March 1995 and the public notification of the ministers' planning permission for the runway, which suggested that the decision was difficult to justify. However, the inter-departmental process of consultation was complex, and the January 1997 letter explaining the decision of the Secretaries of State for the Environment and Transport to grant planning permission for the runway extension was notable for its frankness, giving credence to the opposition's claim that they had made a credible case. It indicated that the development plans for the runway site related to a designated area that was entirely in the Green Belt. Moreover, it stated that the second runway in the Green Belt could only be justified if there were very special circumstances. It conceded that there would be negative effects, but these were outweighed by the economic case for the runway and the fact that sufficient measures would be taken to protect wildlife habitats and compensate for other environmental damage.

Direct action

The January 1997 announcement in favour of Manchester Airport signalled the failure of the residents' campaign and the beginning of the campaign of direct action. The scene was now to shift decisively away from the committee meetings of the protest groups to the construction site and the muddy camps of the eco-warriors. Environmental activists across Britain had been alerted to the decision to build the runway at Manchester and they knew that construction teams were preparing to lay swaths of concrete over yet another precious piece of rural England. The runway extension was thus to become their next high profile environmental battle to be played out in the media spotlight. It was the ideal follow-up to the actions at Twyford Down, Newbury and Fairmile. Indeed, the week before the Manchester announcement there had been violent clashes and protests at Newbury as environmentalists marked the first anniversary of the start of work on the construction of the Newbury bypass.[3] In contrast to the Joint Action Group's respectable public inquiry strategy, green activists in South Manchester had experience generally of past failures of such inquiries and they scorned the public inquiry process as a result. The decision to grant planning permission ignited their own campaign. Militant activists, alerted by the communication networks which structure the environmental direct action movement, flowed into the Bollin Valley site as a new loose coalition called the Campaign Against Runway Two took shape. With organisational support from Manchester Friends of the Earth, it brought together the different cultures and strategies of the radical activists of Earth First, the Green Party, Manchester Wildlife and the local protesters of the Environmental Network.

On 25 January, green activists established Flywood Camp on the airport construction site in the Bollin valley. Over the following weeks, further camps, each with their own character (for instance, Zion Tree, Jimi Hendrix, Sir Cliff Richard, Wild Garlic and River Rats) were established as protesters began to dig in to delay the construction of the runway. They injected new tactics into the campaign, as well as knowledge gained through past protests, such as tree-houses, lock-ons and, in particular, the tunnelling skills first used at the A30 dual-carriageway road protest at Fairmile in Devon. Many of the environmentalists who had held media-attention at the A30 protest arrived at Manchester, including 'Swampy', 'Animal', 'Muppet Dave' and 'Ian'; four of the five 'moles' from the Fairmile Big Momma tunnel. For these direct action veterans, Manchester satisfied the need for new protests to provide continuity with past campaigns.

The new phase of direct action produced a campaign focused on the exploitation of the media, with campaign organisers seeking to highlight the tactics and the style of the protesters. Numerous articles appeared in the national press detailing not only the issues surrounding the construction of the runway, but also the background of the green activists and the experiences of journalists who stayed in the camps. Significantly, the arrival of 'Swampy' elevated him as the mouthpiece for a campaign of direct action. On 1 April, *The Times* reported that 'Swampy', with a Dig for Victory campaign banner and a ten-point manifesto, intended to stand as a candidate at the general election for the Never Mind the Ballots Party in the Blackley constituency of Airport Chairman and former leader of Manchester City Council, Graham Stringer. He also wrote a *Mirror* newspaper column for £550 per week. For the media, the activist campaign transformed Manchester into an issue of national significance.

These were remarkable developments for the Joint Action Group that had long striven to increase its media coverage in local papers. It had to adapt quickly to the new situation as the international media converged on Knutsford and the surrounding villages. Although it did have informal contacts with the Campaign Against Runway Two and the green activists, a major concern of many of its members was that they should not be seen to be endorsing illegal action. However, the intensity of the opposition to the runway meant, as a parish councillor insisted, that 'there were ordinary people in the village who were so disappointed with the outcome of the inquiry that they forged links with the eco-warriors'. The Mobberley Women, for example, established a support group, providing deliveries of free bread and cakes from the local baker and organising a rota for recharging mobile phones and car batteries. According to *The Times* (19.5.97), they were 'women in Barbour coats and Hunter Wellingtons who joke about having become surrogate mums to the dreadlocked and nose pierced protesters', but they formed strong personal ties with the eco-warriors that lasted after the main protest. One Joint Action Group committee member insisted that this was not just moral support for people who wanted a bath. We are talking about hundreds of people living in ancient woodland there, fenced in by razor wire fencing and 800 security guards. The one thing around here is that people know their rights, they are educated and they know what they have to do. If there was a security guard there, or the police were there and said you can't enter here, you have no legal rights to do XYZ, and that sort of prevailed, then there would be huge support, in terms of moral support, financial support, legal support — you name it'. Even Neil Hamilton, the Conservative MP for Tatton until his defeat in the 1997 said that he would meet 'Swampy'.

On 10 February, the Airport awarded contracts for the construction of the second runway to the AMEC-Tarmac Joint Venture. The developers made no immediate attempt to remove the protest camps from the Bollin Valley. Indeed, there followed throughout February and March, a 'phoney war' punctuated by a number of skirmishes between the Airport and the protesters. The camps held the first of a series of Runway Funday Sundays on 21 February whilst developers erected razor wire fencing around the camps. 'Swampy' was arrested for criminal damage on 16 March and 'Animal' was later charged with secondary picketing according to the Trades Union and Labour Relations Act 1992. In fact, the Campaign Against Runway Two and the runway consortium engaged in a media battle aimed at capturing public opinion. For instance, as the Airport repeatedly raised concerns over the safety of activists and the dangers posed to emergency services if called upon to rescue tunnellers, the Campaign Against Runway Two protesters let it be known that on 26 March police and private security guards had cut off the nearest water supplies to the camps.

On 27 March, activists obtained a two-week reprieve from the High Court in which to organise their case against eviction, but lost at the full hearing on 10 April. This signalled the start of the eviction of the camps. Protesters steeled themselves for the arrival of the bailiffs. Operation Fulcrum, led by the Under-Sheriff of Cheshire, began on 20 May with the storming of Zion Tree and Jimi Hendrix camps by 60 bailiffs and 100 police officers. Expert tree climbers, nicknamed 'cherry pickers' tackled tree-dwellers as black boiler-suited evictors drove across the camps on quad-bikes (*Manchester Evening News*, 21.5.97). This start of the eviction intensified the media campaign as both sides engaged in a battle over the issues of violence and questions of tactics. The newly-elected Labour MP for the nearby Wythenshawe and Sale East constituency, Paul Goggins, used his maiden speech to urge the green activists to go home. The Under-Sheriff declared his concerns over the safety of the tunnel at Zion Camp, particularly after rain fall, though this was dismissed by protesters as a ruse.

On the fifth day of evictions, there were an estimated 80 protesters still in the Bollin Valley, although Wild Garlic camp fell two days after Zion Tree and Jimi Hendrix. This all provided very newsworthy material nationally and locally. The *Manchester Evening News* (26.5.97) portrayed green activists who made an SAS-style river invasion up the Bollin to join the protesters still on site. However, as at Fairmile, as the ground camps were removed, media attention came to focus on the green activists holed up in the tunnels dotted throughout the construction site. As the Sheriff's eviction team, nicknamed the 'Men in Black', prepared to enter the tunnels, rumours circulated in the press of the booby traps waiting for the bailiffs. Meanwhile, activists threatened to sue the Under-Sheriff for assault. However, at the end of May, Liz Snook, the 'Worm', voluntarily emerged from her tunnel suffering as a result of the cold.

Fresh from his election victory over Hamilton, Martin Bell turned up at the site early on into the evictions. However, the most significant and high-profile support came from Terry Waite who having written against the runway to John Prescott, the newly-appointed Deputy Prime Minister, led a procession of 25 protesters to the site on 23 May. He told the Under Sheriff's representatives that he was denying democratic rights. He emphasised the moral authority of the environmental activists and claimed that the legal process was loaded from the beginning in favour of the developers. In fact, it was behind this media-profile of Waite that the campaigns of the residents and the green activists merged. Waite possessed the legitimacy necessary to mobilise the residents of Mobberley behind the demonstrations of the tunnellers. His end of May march around the security fence, accompanied by 300 residents was both the clear manifestation of the 'Vegan and Volvo' alliance and, the last desperate attempt of residents to stop the King Kong of Manchester invading the Cheshire Green Belt.

Attempts to prolong the campaign did take place. Green activists burst into woods near the construction site, establishing three further camps, 'we are over here, and over here, and also here', then announced plans to occupy derelict buildings, protest at suppliers to the contractors and to target the site of the planned airport eastern link road due to extend into Cheshire. Terry Waite also held out the prospect of a prolonged campaign. Launched by Waite, Green Skies, a pressure group endorsed by Friends of the Earth, the Ramblers Association, the Open Spaces Society, the World Wildlife Fund UK, the Council for the Preservation of Rural England, Airport Watch and others, pledged to reduce pollution caused by air transport. It demonstrated that the second runway was an issue stretching well beyond the confines of Mobberley and Knutsford. However, the last of the tunnellers, Matt Benson, eventually emerged after 18 days down the Cakehole tunnel. At the end of the eviction, 211 arrests had been made and the costs of security were alleged to have risen to six million pounds. The campaign of direct action did not stop the construction of the second runway, but as a supporter of the Environmental Network pointed out, local residents and eco-warriors were proud to have been part of an action which had disrupted the developers and had received international media coverage.

Vegans and Volvos

What conclusions can be drawn from the Manchester Runway case? It can be contextualised by reference to comparative studies of airport protests. Some question the popular impression that these really centre on environmental concerns, arguing that environmental interests were often evoked by property owners who employed the discourse of the environmental movement because they understood the greater public appeal of such demands to the wider community.[4] Others analysing the explosive near revolutionary episodes surrounding the building of Sanrizuko Airport in Japan for example, emphasise the role of ideological principle.[5] There, movement from interest to ideology marked a new stage in the campaign against the airport where the protest appeared to become a defining issue for all forms of citizen protest. The first perspective is firmly located within the interest group paradigm, with its attendant concerns of group formation and mobilisation, the overcoming of collective action difficulties, and the logics of instrumental bargaining between defined parties within formal institutions. The second perspective is closer to recent work on social movements, where emphasis is placed on the role of identities and values in unifying relatively disparate and loosely organised groups operating outside the formal institutions of the state on the terrain of civil society.

These two perspectives capture the difference between the residents' groups and the direct action protesters. Thus, in classical pressure group terms, the Manchester Airport Joint Action Group sought principally to influence the public inquiry, while also trying to turn public opinion in its favour. It mobilised local residents by campaign meetings, protest marches, petitions of councillors and local MPs, and it drew upon the technical expertise of its supporters to contest the Airport's case. While at times it presented its message in environmentalist terms, the predominant motivations were to protect its members' quality of life and material interests. Conversely, the eco-warriors sought to operate completely outside the formal channels of representation and interest mediation, preferring to obstruct and delay the plans to extend the airport by direct action. They regarded the public inquiry as a window-dressing exercise; they did not organise around self-interests, but on an ideological commitment to protect the environment. Moreover, their campaign was sustained by their own particular lifestyle and the impending confrontation with the authorities. For the green activists, Manchester was a mere episode in a long-term struggle against environmental degradation; for the Joint Action Group, it was the struggle.

However, this neat division should not disguise the complex interplay between the different phases and styles of the campaign. As the direct action campaign developed, Joint Action Group sympathisers and other residents, originally hostile to direct action campaigners, their lifestyles, but also their methods, came to identify with the environmental cause that the green activists championed. This was evident in their changing attitudes to the eco-warriors. Typically, local residents raised concerns that the campaign against the runway should remain within the bounds of the law. One parish councillor, urging residents not to join the direct action campaigners, argued that 'the law should be upheld, even if certain aspects of the law are an ass' (*Knutsford Guardian*, 22.1.97). Though reasonably representative of local opinion, such views contrasted with those of local residents as the campaign unravelled. One Joint Action Group committee member was 'quite astounded when I sat down and started talking to some of these people and found the knowledge they had'. As we have seen, groups like the 'Mobberley Mums' gave moral and material sustenance to the eco-warriors, providing food, shelter and psychological support. Similarly, high profile campaigners such as Terry Waite who commanded moral authority amongst the residents' groups, overtly sympathised with the direct action campaign. In short, the residents' campaign in 1997 took on a support role, backing up and providing solidarity to the outside protesters.

A number of factors help explain this contingent alliance of forces opposed to the second runway. First, connections were forced by the pro-Manchester Airport campaign. Tarring middle-class residents, their legitimate interests and forms of protest, with the same brush as the eco-warriors resulted in the creation of solidarity and a degree of identity between widely divergent forms of campaigning. This ideological branding of enemies was reinforced by the residents' own perceptions of the tactics employed by the Airport. The presence of black-shirted and balaclava wearing evictors, the alleged heavy-handed methods of the private security guards, rumours of phone tappings and personal insults increased the sense of outrage. Claims that opposition to the second runway would endanger the creation of 50,000 jobs in the region also angered the residents' groups whose members resented the accusations that they were rich Cheshire NIMBYS ('not in my backyard') opposed to economic growth. The emergence of an opposition between a dynamic Manchester seeking to expand its regional influence and an anti-growth movement that alluded to the Cheshire idyll thus structured the terms of the debate.[6] It served to make manifest the distinction between the forces favouring regional growth and those which managed, at least for a while, to establish some common purpose to upset the developers' project, in spite of the campaigners underlying differences and aims.

Second, the media's association of the residents and eco-warriors served to crystallise the antagonistic constructions around which the Campaign Against Runway Two and the pro-Airport lobby organised themselves. Images of eco-warriors and local residents side by side in their confrontation with the Airport authorities served to fix this unlikely linkage in the minds of the residents. Whatever the wider political consequences, one result was to legitimise the eco-warriors and their case. Just as New Labour assiduously courted the popular press, so did the direct action protesters. 'Swampy' may have been turned into an unlikely and at times unwilling media celebrity, but the attention certainly gained the protesters an audience previously denied them. In sum, there was a good deal of personalisation and even trivialisation of the protesters and their lifestyles, but its overall impact was to alter public perceptions of new environmental movements.

Third, there were important figures in the campaign who were able to function as policy-brokers between residents and eco-warriors. Jeff Gazzard, for instance, a local resident associated with the Joint Action Group and organiser of the Environmental Network and a key member of the Campaign Against Runway Two, was able to act as a link between the differently orientated groups in the campaign. The involvement of such people strengthened the residents' groups, and helped coordinate the opposition.

However, the most decisive factor in the overall campaign against the second runway was the decision of the public inquiry to recommend permission for the construction of a second runway. The Joint Action Group's supporters invested great faith in their case and in the inquiry to deliver a fair judgment. In theory, a public inquiry is the legitimate way for interested parties to make representations, but here (as in other inquiries) it undermined confidence in the value of such procedures. This coupled with a growing recognition by middle-class protesters of the unreliability of established democratic channels at local and national levels, resulted in a rapid disillusionment. It went some way in explaining the identification of many residents with the new forms of protest action.

1   E.J. Freedman and J. Milch, *Technocracy versus Democracy: The Comparative Politics of International Airports* (Auburn House, 1982); D.E. Apter and N. Sawa, *Against the State* (Harvard University Press, 1984).

2   C. Buchanan, *No Way to the Airport* (Longman, 1981); D. McKie, *A Sadly Mismanaged Affair: A Political History of the Third London Airport* (Croom Helm, 1973); D. Perman, *Cublington: A Blueprint for Resistance* (Bodley Head, 1973).

3   *Guardian*, 9.1.97; 13.1.97; *Sunday Times*, 12.1.97; *Sunday Telegraph*, 12.1.97.

4   E.J. Freedman and J. Milch, op. cit., p. 155.

5   D.E. Apter and N. Sawa, op. cit., 1984; D. Nelkin and M. Pollak, 'The Politics of Participation and the Nuclear Debate in Sweden, The Netherlands, and Austria', *Public Policy*, Summer 1977.

6   I. Taylor, 'Fear of Crime, Urban Fortunes and Suburban Social Movements: Some Reflections from Manchester', *Sociology*, May 1996; I. Taylor, K. Evans and P. Fraser, *A Tale of Two Cities: Global Change, Local Feeling and Everyday Life in the North of England. A Study of Manchester and Sheffield* (Routledge, 1996).

Opposition to Road-Building

BY BRIAN DOHERTY

PROTEST against road-building is not new in itself. In the 1970s John Tyme achieved notoriety as the leader of campaigns against the building of new motorways, and some of the local groups opposing new roads in the 1990s can date their campaigns back to this period. However, the protests in the 1990s were different in kind and much more widespread than earlier campaigns. They were also assisted by changes in the politics of transport due primarily to new evidence about the impact of road transport on the environment. Whereas Tyme had concentrated on disrupting the public inquiry process and much of the activity of anti-roads groups in the 1980s continued to focus on inquiries, in the 1990s new strategies emerged which shifted the focus. Groups opposing new roads concentrated their efforts on marshalling political opposition to a new schemes at local level outside the formal consultation process. This was based on the view that the remit of public inquiries was so restricted that in effect the choice was over the route of a new road, rather than the wider question of whether a new road should be built at all. Public inquires were viewed as an expensive trap in which the technical expertise of lawyers and planners tended to exclude effective public participation.

The most striking difference from the 1970s, however, was the growth of a counter-cultural protest movement of young ecological radicals. This group opposed the destruction of landscape and urban communities, but also voiced a deeper opposition to what it saw as the failings of modern progress culture: excessive consumerism, loss of contact with nature, and pollution. These eco-protesters mainly concentrated on disrupting the construction work on roads already being built. Thus after the end of the legal decision-making process, the direct action protesters undertook the last stand against the bulldozers by occupying the site for a new road or other development projects in order to delay and disrupt the work, and to draw attention to the destruction involved.

A further factor which provoked stronger opposition compared to the 1970s was the scale of the government's road-building programme. When in 1989 road traffic forecasts predicted that overall traffic growth on British roads would increase at rates between 83% and 142% by the year 2025, the Conservative government sought to deal with this problem by announcing what it, perhaps foolishly, called, 'the biggest road-building programme since the Romans'. An initiative by the EU to improve transport links within the member states (Trans-European

Networks) launched in 1992 also gave priority to new roads. The scale of the road-building projects led to the formation of large numbers of new local groups which were initially motivated by opposition to a specific local scheme. These groups were linked through a small London-based group called Alarm UK which had grown out of the successful coordinated opposition of 150 anti-roads groups to a comprehensive plan for new roads in London first released in 1988. The principal lesson that Alarm learned from the London campaign was that local groups needed to work together to avoid being played off against each other and to place local schemes in a national and European context. Thus briefings sent to the 300 groups nationwide affiliated to Alarm UK stressed the importance of seeing a local schemes not simply as a bypass to relieve traffic congestion but as part of a national or European route which taken as a whole was likely to generate more traffic and more in-fill development such as out of town shopping centres. In the years from 1989 to 1993 there were a number of quiet successes for these local campaigns such as the cancellation of new roads in Preston, Crosby, Hereford, Norwich and Calder Valley

The first evidence of the new counter-cultural direct action movement was the formation of Earth First! groups in 1991. Initially, these groups concentrated their actions on issues other than the building of new roads. It was only in 1992, as Earth First! and other eco-radicals began to protest against the first stages of construction of the M3 through Twyford Down near Winchester, that local opposition to roads and the new eco-protest groups became linked. There had been long-standing local opposition to the plan to extend the M3 through Twyford Down, led mainly by pillars of the local Conservative establishment in Winchester. Once the dreadlocked and body-pierced eco-protesters began to camp on the Down, the local anti-roads group was divided over how to receive them. Some continued to place hopes in the support provided by the Environment Commissioner of the EU who had ruled against the British government for its failure to carry out an environmental impact assessment on the schemes. However, agreement between the EU and the government was reached as part of the preliminary negotiations prior to ratification of the Maastricht Treaty, leaving no legal avenue to prevent construction. Friends of the Earth had made a significant effort to assist the Friends of Twyford Down in symbolic actions against the first stages of construction work, but it withdrew from protest activity when advised that it could face sequestration of its assets if it continued. To some in the local campaigns this meant the end of their struggle, but the eco-radicals saw no reason to give in. They had no assets and so were not vulnerable to the same threats. They continued to disrupt the work and were supported by some of the local opponents of the road who formed a new group the Twyford Down Association to continue the fight. To the eco-radicals it was a cause of some bitterness that they received no help from Friends of the Earth. This was in part because of an over-cautious view of the legal situation, and partly because Andrew Lees, then Campaigns Director of Friends of the Earth had a contemptuous view of the eco-protesters whom he believed were likely to undermine the attempts of Friends of the Earth to make the environmental movement more respectable and to broaden its political appeal.

The violent eviction of the Dongas camp on 2 December 1992 brought national attention to the small scale campaign of disruption that had been waged since spring of that year. It encouraged others sympathetic to the eco-radicals to lend their support and it also succeeded in showing local groups that the eco-radicals were prepared to endure danger and violence while remaining non-violent themselves. To local groups facing the end of an institutional battle, the determination of eco-radicals to confront the developers had a strong emotional appeal, and this was a powerful factor in making the alliances between local groups and eco-radicals work.

Protests continued at Twyford throughout 1993 but the focus gradually shifted to other sites, the most important of which was the extension of the M11 through Wanstead and Leyton in East London. As at Twyford, local groups had opposed the schemes for over a decade. Public inquiries had been disrupted in the late 1980s and there was no ambivalence about working with the direct action protesters. This made the boundary between eco-radicals and locals less clear cut. Some experienced eco-activists travelled to London, but many local opponents became eco-activists through their participation in the campaign. Because of its location in London, the M11 campaign was also able to draw on its networks of radical activists, celebrities and artists, who lent their support to what became a high-profile protest. Nevertheless, the No M11 campaign remained in essence a local form of resistance. This was deliberately evoked by those campaigners who squatted successive sites on the route naming each a Free State in evocation of the spirit of local resistance to planners of the Ealing comedy Passport to Pimlico, of an earlier Free State declared by London housing activists in the late 1970s and of counter-cultural Free States such as the Orange Free State in Amsterdam which, like that at Claremont Road, was intended to provide a pace of artistic expression and an experiment in showing how an alternative community could work.

By 1993 resistance to new roads had spread across the country. Direct action protesters were working with local groups at Jesmond Dene in Newcastle, Wymondham in Norfolk and Salisbury Hill in Bath. Friends of the Earth helped to organise a pledge signed by over 5,000 people to promise to oppose the construction of a Thames river-crossing through Oxleas Wood in South London. Anxious to avoid unnecessary confrontations, the government cancelled this scheme. By 1994 the pattern of local groups which had come to the end of the legal road but were working with direct action groups prepared to put their bodies in the way of the bulldozers was being repeated at most major new roads projects. In that year road protesters were evicted after spectacular and skilful confrontations in the trees at Preston, Bath and Glasgow. This gave the impression that any road scheme would provoke a confrontation.

Although opposition to new roads became the principal target of the eco-radicals, the breadth of their ideology meant that they also drew strength from other protests in what they saw as related issues. The protest against the live export of animals in 1994 seemed to show, like the alliances between eco-radicals and local anti-roads groups, that political barriers were being broken down and protest could spread beyond the core networks of the counter-culture. The opposition to the curbs on civil liberties in the 1994 Criminal Justice Act also reinforced the impression that there was a growing extra-parliamentary opposition movement embracing young counter-cultural radicals and 'middle England'. The failure of the Labour Party or the Liberal Democrats to oppose the Act helped to convince the eco-radicals that they represented the only real opposition left in British politics. It also created links between previously diverse groups such as anti-roads protesters, ravers, hunt saboteurs and New Age travellers. Motivated by what was seen as an attack on alternative lifestyles, groups such as the Freedom Network and the Brighton based group Justice? established to oppose the CJA, were added to the network of the direct action groups.

The highpoint of anti-roads campaigning was the eviction of the 28 camps at Newbury between January and April 1996. The drama of the treetop battles to evict protesters at Newbury was replayed nightly on TV screens and helped to sustain the sense of a crisis over road building. Divisions had begun to emerge in the government and among its supporters about the wisdom of road building. At Winchester, Bath and Newbury aristocrats and well-heeled Conservatives had been picked out by the media as prominent among the local opponents of the roads. Others, such as the editor of the Conservative-supporting *Sunday Telegraph* and, following his resignation as Minister for Roads, Steven Norris spoke out against the Newbury bypass,. The strongest evidence for the new acceptability of eco-protest came after eviction of the protest camps against a new part of the A30 at Fairmile near Exeter in January 1997. The seven days endured by one protester ('Swampy') in a tunnel, dug to prevent bulldozers approaching trees, made him a national celebrity. Fêted by the Conservative-supporting tabloid press and given his own weekly column in the Labour-supporting *Sunday Mirror* as well as coverage in a host of other publications, the lionisation of Swampy showed that the protest movement had become an accepted part of the political scene.

After Fairmile the focus of direct action protesters switched to other issues. The cuts in the roads programme which the government had begun in 1994 and continued in 1995 and 1996 meant that there were no significant new roads to oppose by 1997. These cuts had partly been a response to Treasury pressure to curtail public spending, but the fact that roads were cut also signalled a new phase on the politics of transport in which the need to cater for continued car growth was being questioned. In 1992 roads had been protected from the cuts made in public expenditure although cuts were made in spending on railways. In 1994, however, as protests against new roads was spreading, the determined resistance of the Department of Transport was undermined by the publication of two official reports which questioned the principles on which road building was justified. The report of the Standing Advisory Committee on Trunk Road Assessment supported the claims made by anti-roads groups that new roads often generate more traffic, while the Royal Commission on Environmental Pollution said that pollution from road vehicles was so serious that it required measures to reduce traffic growth. Combined with a new confidence from the Department of the Environment in targeting traffic growth as a major environmental problem, there was considerable evidence of opposition to road building from within government. The Treasury in particular was anxious to see cuts in public spending. Thus it is difficult to weight the effect of anti-roads groups on the cuts in the roads programme. As well as the cuts, however, there has been a much wider debate in the media and by the Conservative and Labour governments about the need to rethink transport policy. This debate was not evident before 1992 when transport was viewed as a dull issue only of interest to specialists. There is also evidence from surveys of public opinion that road-building is seen as a much more significant environmental problem than it was before 1990.[1] Although it is impossible to be precise about the how much of this can be ascribed to the roads protesters it seems unlikely that the debates would have moved as far or as fast without their actions.

Friends of the Earth and Greenpeace under attack

Roads protests began outside the existing environmental pressure groups and until 1996 they remained so. This was partly because much of the impetus of ecological protest has come from those who were dissatisfied with the passive character of membership of the existing environmental groups. Among the eco-protesters there was a perception that the leaders of the environmental pressure groups were middle-aged, male and white and out of touch with younger greens, and had become too close to the establishment. Paradoxically, the group with the strongest network of active local groups, Friends of the Earth, has been the most heavily criticised by road protesters. As one Earth First! activist put it: 'Friends of the Earth is now a middle-class social club, patronising the working class' (*Guardian*, 28.2.92). Environmental pressure groups certainly played a role in opposition to road-building. There were meetings of the major groups, including Friends of the Earth, the

National Trust and the World Wide Fund for Nature in 1993 to consider how they would oppose the roads programme. Friends of the Earth claimed that it had a significant role in anti-roads campaigns, even if this was not always obvious to others, for instance by privately lobbying Conservative MPs opposed to the widening of the M25. And in 1997 Friends of the Earth helped to draft the Road Traffic Reduction Bill, submitted to parliament as a private member's bill to parliament by Cynog Dafis, the Plaid Cymru MP. However, despite this conventional political action, environmental pressure groups failed to recognise the potential for protest action in the early 1990s.

A summit meeting of environmental activists was called by George Monbiot (an academic and green activist) and others in Oxford in December 1994 at which many criticisms of the pressure groups were aired. Leading figures from most of the major environmental pressure groups attended, and to the surprise of many there was endorsement of legal protest actions from conservation groups such as the National Trust and the World Wide Fund for Nature. Yet these groups were in reality too closely associated with lobbying from within the system to have any real effect in encouraging their memberships to become involved in protests. Friends of the Earth and Greenpeace were in a more difficult position. In the 1990s Greenpeace UK had shifted its emphasis from attempts to influence government policy to pressure on private business, which meant that it had not concentrated on transport policy. Greenpeace had also been subject to the criticism that it was too hierarchical and that, as the largest of the campaigning environmental groups, its reluctance to support ordinary members taking protest action in its own name had hindered the growth of environmental protest. It had achieved a certain tacit acceptance from some road protesters by donating money and other resources to anti-roads groups. It did also make efforts to respond to the new situation. A former Greenpeace volunteer who had been involved with the M11 campaign was recruited to develop a wider involvement of Greenpeace's supporters in direct action. Among the results of this shift were the mass site invasions at the nuclear plant at Sellafield and the nuclear weapons research establishment at Aldermaston in spring 1995.

Friends of the Earth was held particularly responsible for the failure to mobilise its local groups to join protests. At the Oxford meeting, Charles Secrett, its Director, accepted that it had made a major mistake at Twyford and committed the organisation to more direct support for road protests. Some of its local groups had taken part in protests, notably those in the vicinity of the M11 Link, but for road protesters the absence of any push at the national level suggested that it was still too concerned about losing respectability in the eyes of political elites if it supported direct action. The strategy of Friends of the Earth had also been criticised by local groups and by some working in the national office and in the years after 1992, with changes in the campaigns staff, there was a shift towards providing more resources for local groups. Only with the Newbury campaign in 1996 did Friends of the Earth associate itself more directly with the protests and provide some more significant resources to the local campaign. But by then the roads movement had a life of its own and it was reacting to it rather than leading it. One of the most important consequences of the anti-roads protests is that they have introduced a new, more radical, protest network into British environmentalism which is autonomous from the existing pressure groups.

Movement organisations

The first challenge to the status of Greenpeace and Friends of the Earth as representatives of supposedly the most radical kind of environmentalism possible in Britain was the formation of groups modelled initially on the US green direct action network, Earth First! The initiators of the movement were two 18 year-old members of Friends of the Earth and Greenpeace. The first British groups announced themselves in 1991. Like their American equivalents they had no national structure or formal posts: their organisation was restricted to a network of local contacts and a newsletter. By 1997 there were around 60 active groups and the 1997 annual 'gathering' was attended by around 400 activists. The nature of Earth First! makes it difficult to be sure about its size, since it has no formal membership and because it is impossible to establish a clear distinction between Earth First! and the wider eco-protest movement. There is also no clear evidence about the numbers involved in the broader eco-radical movement, but most activists stress how small the core of activists is. In interviews, participants estimated the numbers who had taken part in direct action at between two and four thousand.

When Earth First! made its appearance in Britain existing environmental pressure groups reacted with hostility. In the USA, Earth First! had been associated with covert sabotage actions against those seen as destroyers of the environment, such as the logging industry, and with misanthropic and racist sentiments expressed in its journal; despite a reaction against this from within US Earth First!, it was regarded by British environmental pressure groups as having the potential to discredit the whole green movement. A split emerged at the first national gathering of Earth First! in Brighton in April 1992 between those who wanted to concentrate on ecological sabotage in the tradition of US Earth First! and those who wanted a more open movement. Although, the role of violence remains a point of debate within the movement, the emphasis has been more on openness and protest directed towards the public than on covert action. A second reason for the negative reaction by Friends of the Earth and others was the fact that Earth First! in the USA had been formed in opposition to what was perceived as the incorporation of US environmental groups such as the Sierra Club by the political system, and the British Earth First! groups shared their anarchistic critique of established environmental pressure groups. The direct action movement as a whole reflects this loose anarchistic ethos. There is little interest in political doctrine and no real attempt to define a collective strategy. There are few opportunities for collective discussions between groups outside the annual national gathering. A clear doctrine is resisted because of the commitment to individual autonomy and the belief that actions speak louder than words. The principal role of Earth First! groups is to mobilise supporters to take part in protest action. By 1995 Earth First! had become sufficiently influential for the Director of Friends of the Earth to attend its national gathering in order to discuss ways in which the two might work together.

Despite the anti-organisational ethos of the direct action groups there have been sub-groups within the movement which have provided some forms of coordination. Within Earth First! the groups responsible for the network's Action Update have been able to influence debates through their choice of which issues to emphasise and by virtue of their ability to draw on resources, such as access to the facilities of students unions, not available to other groups.[2] At the height of the roads protests, permanent offices were created to provide more effective communication between protesters. However, the two main groups that functioned as the 'national offices' for the two wings of the anti-roads campaign were barely organisations at all. The first was formed by participants in the Twyford Down protests, but then renamed Road Alert. It provided regular e-mail bulletins, fuller newsletters, and a manual covering strategic, legal, personal, and logistical aspects of protest. However, it never sought to outline a strategy for the movement as a whole, remaining an information and coordination centre with four or five volunteers at a time and had only one substantial donation of a few thousand pounds from Greenpeace. After moving to Newbury in 1995, the office closed as the Newbury protests began, mainly because the efforts of sustaining a full-time office had taken too much of a toll on the main volunteers.

The second group, Alarm UK, also relied on volunteers, with one full-time and three others part-time. Its main work was helping the 250–300 local anti-roads groups, some of which had been in existence for decades, but which had not hitherto had any national coordination. Most of their work concentrated on preventing a road proposal being approved officially. Alarm UK compared their experiences, brought them together in national conferences to develop strategy and provided briefings to support local campaigns. Although it received help from Transport 2000, a group part-funded by the rail unions and mainly concerned with lobbying decision-makers and presenting technical alternatives to road dominated transport policy, it had few resources of its own: a small income from member groups; a small donation from Greenpeace and two larger ones from environmental benefactors.

Overall, however, the anti-roads movement seems to have worked effectively as a protest movement without any formal national organisation beyond these two groups. For the eco-protesters, email and the use of the world wide web provided efficient ways of distributing information cheaply and quickly, particularly to student activists. Moreover, their lack of structure conforms with the observation that decentralised organisations can be more effective because they do not have a head which can be lopped off by the authorities.[3] Both Alarm UK and Road Alert saw their role as temporary and in neither case was there any long-term prospect of institutionalisation. This biodegradable form of organisation reflected the strategy of the movement.

Identities and strategy

The anti-roads movement is an awkward combination of a radical new social movement and a more specific reformist environmentalism. The eco-protesters represent the radical wing, whilst local protest groups, Alarm UK and its local groups and Friends of the Earth remain primarily concerned with incremental change. For the latter groups, the main goals are achieving changes in policy. Most of the local groups dissolved after their road has been built or cancelled. In 1997, as the roads programme appeared to be winding down, Alarm UK considered joining Transport 2000 as a network of local groups campaigning for better public transport. In this sense, the local groups were conventional interest groups concerned primarily with local grievances and focusing on the single issue of road building. However, there were also differences between them with some (e.g. Glasgow for People) viewing themselves as part of a grassroots opposition to the local and national establishment, or raising broader issues, such as the priority given to affluent suburbs over deprived inner city districts. And even those groups with a more limited focus were not necessarily motivated only by NIMBY 'not in my backyard' concerns. Local groups along the route of trunk roads formed alliances to publicise the role of local schemes in national policy, such as (e.g. South Coast Against Roads (SCAR)) and accounts by activists from such groups speak repeatedly of disillusionment with the decision-making process and what was perceived as manipulation by the Department of Transport. There is some support in this evidence for the suggestion that groups that begin as NIMBY often become radicalised by the experience of political conflict and develop broader political concerns.

There is no real ambiguity, however, about the opposition character of the direct action eco-protesters. Their ideology is anarchistic, but they reject as irrelevant the doctrinal debates which have characterised many anarchist groups. They are hostile to politicians and believe that non-hierarchical ways of working empower individuals to take political responsibility themselves. This means that there is no prospect of any formal organisation being established to centralise resources or policy.

Drawing on romantic traditions of opposition to modern industrialism and materialism, some eco-protesters view themselves in tribal terms. This provides a link with the resistance of tribal peoples in industrialising societies. It also provides the basis for a strong collective identity which can be expressed in clothing and other styles which identify its members as different from the mainstream. The strongest expression of this is found in the Dongas tribe who grew out of the opposition to the M3 at Twyford Down. After the end of the Twyford protest some of the Dongas became travellers, living in tents and carrying their possessions by donkey cart. The development of a distinctive sense of national identity is connected to this tribalism. Protesters sometimes speak of themselves as the indigenous peoples of these islands or as Celts opposing the Romans. However, they use symbols which are intended to contrast with what they regard as the predominant jingoistic nationalism (the Union Jill, a version of the Union Jack in the colours of the suffragettes is a common sight at protests and Blake's Jerusalem is preferred to Land of Hope and Glory). Emphasising the importance of a rootedness in the land, some eco-protesters assert that they have a more authentic knowledge of its significance than is possible for those trapped in mainstream consumer culture.

Romantic traditions and the defence of ancient sites are associated with protest against development in rural areas, but different themes have been developed in urban areas, suggesting some differences of culture between rural and urban campaigns. The occupation of Claremont Road in Leytonstone, in the path of the M11, developed into an artistic site and open community space in a deliberate attempt to create a symbolic form of resistance. This meant that there was more emphasis on political engagement and less on autonomy and withdrawal. As one 'No M11' activist put it: 'Unlike Twyford, Bath or Preston, we are not just defending natural habitats, but an area of London. We have raised social issues as well as ecological ones'. The campaigns against the M11 in London, the M77 in Glasgow and the M66 in Manchester were all based in urban areas and gave priority to the theme that communities were powerless against planners. In contrast, at Twyford, the Dongas developed a deep ecological discourse that reappeared at Bath, Preston and at Newbury. In this, the 'rape of Mother Earth' and respect for landscape and trees were central. Neither approach was exclusive of the other, and each reflected their immediate environment, but each represented options for how the roads protests would develop.

By 1995 there were suggestions in parts of the movement that a more positive agenda than simple opposition to road building was needed. In that year seven activists from the M11 campaign reformed a group called Reclaim the Streets which had a brief existence in the early 1990s before being absorbed into the M11 campaign. Their demonstrations against the dominance of traffic in urban areas were attempts to free space from traffic, if only temporarily, but also occasions for alternative uses of streets. Beginning in London, they staged a car crash which blocked a busy shopping street in Camden followed by a street party which passers-by could join. This was repeated in other cities. They also blocked rush hour traffic in Greenwich for two hours to highlight the effects of air pollution on the health of local residents. Perched on precarious tripods which could only be dismantled at risk to their occupier, they could not be removed quickly. As at other protests, by combining a certain technical ingenuity and a willingness to expose themselves to danger, protesters were able to gain attention. Their greatest success came in July 1996 when they managed to block a motorway in West London, and 'reclaim' it with a party for 8,000 participants, the largest number to join an illegal roads protest in Britain.

A contrasting attempt to develop a positive agenda for the movement was made by a group called The Land is Ours in which the best known public figure was George Monbiot, an Oxford anthropologist. Arguing that the capitalist enclosure of common lands had led most Britons to lose touch with authentic traditions of land use allowed him to establish a link between the struggle of tribal peoples to retain control of their land and the struggle against destructive development being led by the British eco-tribes. The first major action of the group sought to evoke indigenous traditions of radicalism by occupying a site close to the commune established by the 'Diggers' in 1649. Land ownership and access to land has been a central theme for the British green counter culture for many years, a concern reinforced by the 1994 Criminal Justice Act. However, a campaign based upon land rights is unlikely to appeal so clearly to those primarily concerned about urban social and environmental issues. Perhaps in an attempt to offset rural bias, The Land is Ours occupied a derelict site beside the Thames in Wandsworth, South London in summer 1996. The 'Pure Genius' occupation (using the advertising slogan of the owners, Guinness) was intended to show how collective voluntary work could transform a site which had been left to deteriorate by its owners, but it became preoccupied with the problems posed by casualties of urban life, such as those with mental illnesses, who used the site as a refuge. Similar problems arose at other protest sites, exposing the difficulty of combining protest with experiments in an alternative way of life.

These eco-protest groups fit closely the ideal type characteristics of new social movements developed to define innovative features in the women's, peace and environmental movements. They are distinct to the extent that they seek to challenge cultural norms through provocative forms of action or alternative lifestyles rather than aiming to capture the state in order to build a new society. Their degree of novelty remains a subject of contention, and there is also much diversity within these movements. The groups that appear to fit best here are the most radical ones, usually relatively small, such as the British eco-protesters. It could be argued nevertheless that their cultural impact has been significant Protesters tend to argue that simply by continuing their challenge, even when they cannot hope to prevent a road being built they are achieving change. As one activist from the M11 commented: 'Our secret truth: however hard we fought, we knew that everything would end up as part of the rubble . . . Knowing that the future is rubble gave us the strength to approach the eviction as a game. An elaborate game, one which we had carefully prepared, a game to unveil power and make visible real issues.' Thus a central purpose of this kind of protest is to pose a cultural challenge to mainstream society which makes people question the existing way of life.

Cultural continuity and non-violent direct action

While the approach of the new social movement theorists is useful other insights from a political process approach to social movements may offer more in explaining how the forms of action favoured by the eco-protesters have been developed.[4] This shows how protesters always work with forms of action partly inherited from previous protest campaigns. In thinking about how to act they draw on shared memories of earlier protests. Also important is the influence of networks of activists who overlap between different movements in passing on skills and cultural assumptions about forms of action.

The British roads protests are relatively unusual for counter-cultural protests in their commitment to non-violence and, unlike in the peace movement, this is not accompanied by significant philosophical debate about the relationship between means and ends. One may ask why there has been so little violence at eco-protests. The answer may partly lie in the national traditions of legitimate protest. The levels of violence have been low compared with countries such as France and Germany, despite the fact that centralised political systems such as Britain's are usually seen as more likely to provoke violence because protesters have such limited opportunities to influence policy.[5] Yet, Britain's student movement was relatively quiescent and the principal protests of the 1970s by feminists and 1980s by the peace movement were non-violent. On the other hand, there is a significant tradition of non-violent direct action. In the 1980s the most radical wing of the peace movement engaged in a sustained campaign of civil disobedience, breaking into bases, obstructing missile convoys. A significant parallel with the eco-protests was the establishment of peace camps, of which the Women's camp at Greenham Common in Newbury was the most famous.

The founders of Earth First! had all had some previous experience as members of green or peace movement groups.[6] The repertoire of Earth First! (UK) was in part inherited from existing and earlier social movement campaigns. The guidance in the main road protesters' manual reproduces much of the advice thirteen years earlier in a peace movement guide to preparing for non-violent direct action. It was this repertoire which activists felt was most appropriate in a British context. In later years there was a swing towards greater militancy as construction companies and the police adapted to protesters' tactics. Many protesters justified their action as a direct attack on the road-building industry as much as an appeal to public opinion, but there was little challenge to the commitment to non-violence.

In order to prolong their occupations and blockades without using violence campaigners, have had to rely on their own ingenuity, developing a series of techniques to make eviction more difficult, such as embedding tubes in concrete which can be used to lock the protester to almost anything; digging tunnels to make it dangerous to move heavy machinery, or walkways and tree-houses above ground level which required specialist teams of climbers to make eviction possible. Developed during the campaigns, they became part of a repertoire available at subsequent protests. The most constant feature was that their effectiveness depended upon the willingness of protesters to expose themselves to danger. In this sense, for all the discussion of the repressive character of the state, they were playing a game of bluff with the construction companies and the authorities. Protesters exploited the limits on aggressive action by the police and security guards in order to frustrate and delay road building.

The commitment to non-violence and the exploitation of vulnerability have been central to the ability of the eco-protesters to achieve a high level of positive media coverage. This also explains the relatively limited use of force by the authorities during evictions. Any move towards violence on the part of protesters would probably end any public sympathy, would break the links with local groups important to the legitimacy of direct action and to the ability to endure the long campaigns and would justify the use of more repressive tactics by the authorities.

The political impact of the roads protests

The principal political impact of the roads protests has been to alter the previously unchallenged hegemony of roads in transport policy. In 1989 there was relatively little public criticism of the government's road policy. The policy community was secure, indeed the position of the roads lobby had been strengthened by the cuts in spending on public transport during the 1980s. By the mid-1990s the debate about road-use had become the central focus of environmental politics in Britain. Transport issues had been politicised in a way never seen before and the arguments against roads and cars were now widely disseminated and by 1997 the Labour government accepted the need to reduce road traffic. Local anti-roads groups had been successful in preventing new roads in a number of areas, but, precisely because these were quiet successes, it is unlikely that they would have provoked the same level of public debate about car use if there had not been such sustained high-profile activity from the eco-protesters. Each wing brought qualities to the criticism of new roads that were lacking in the other.

The most successful campaigns by local groups have avoided focusing on the limited opportunities for public consultation and debate offered by the official planning process. The narrow remits of public inquiries and the misleading information provided by the Department of Transport has induced a scepticism that local groups share with eco-protesters about the democratic character of decision-making on new roads. Thus, even when there were tensions at Twyford Down and Bath between a local campaign and the eco-protesters, there was enough common ground to sustain a joint campaign. The non-violence of the eco-protesters was essential to their gaining some level of acceptance and helped to make protest events inclusive enough for moderate locals to join in on occasion. So, rather than a defeat, the end of legal battles saw the beginning of the dramaturgy of direct action which, whilst almost bound to fail, increased the emotional intensity of the campaign. Moreover, the complementary character of the two wings of the movement fits well with the general pattern for social movements that are successful in gaining access to the media.[7] The direct action groups helped to create a story, whilst the more moderate groups were able to fill the new political scenario with political meanings, arguing the case against roads on technical grounds. In turn, this also allowed for some surprisingly positive media coverage of the counter-cultural idealism of the direct action groups.

Conclusion

Despite the obvious failure of direct action to halt a road scheme once construction has begun, in certain respects the anti-roads movement can claim qualified successes. The road programme has been substantially cut to a third of the size envisaged when it was launched in 1989. The cuts may be partly attributed to the Treasury's desire for reduced public expenditure, but they also became more politically acceptable, forcing the government to reconsider its overall transport strategy in the face of widespread public debate about the environmental consequences of motor vehicles. The direct action groups are only one part of the broader anti-roads coalition, but it is probable that without their protests the issue would not have remained at the centre of national political debate.

1 See B. Taylor, 'Green in Word . . .', in R. Jowell et al. (eds), *British Social Attitudes: the 14th Report* (Ashgate, 1997).
2 See D. Wall, *The Politics of Earth First! UK* (Routledge, 1999).
3 See L. Gerlach and V. Hine, *People, Power, Change* (Bobbs-Merrill, 1970).
4 See S. Tarrow, *Power in Movement* (Cambridge University Press, 1994).
5 See H.P. Kriesi et al., *New Social Movements in Western Europe* (UCL Press, 1995).
6 See D. Wall, op. cit.
7 W.A. Gamson, and G. Wolfsfeld, 'Movements and Media as Interacting Systems', *Annals of the American Academy of Political and Social Science*, July 1993.

Nuclear Power at Druridge Bay

BY ROB BAGGOTT

ONE can identify a number of cases in recent decades where local protest campaigns have met with success, often against all odds. Examples include the Cublington campaign against the third London airport in the early 1970s, the protests during the mid-1980s against proposals to create low-level nuclear waste sites in Lincolnshire, Humberside, Bedfordshire, and Essex and during the 1990s the campaign to prevent road building in Oxleas wood in south east London. Nonetheless, most local protests are regarded as relatively ineffective—a nuisance rather than a threat—particularly when opposing large-scale capital developments backed by central government and large corporations. This assertion is supported by the fact that even controversial schemes attracting national attention have gone ahead despite widespread local protests, as illustrated by the cases of Twyford Down and Sizewell B nuclear power station.

Why do some well-supported local protest campaigns fail and others succeed? Here we seek to shed some light on this question by examining what can be regarded by most standards as a highly successful local protest group, which faced not one but two powerful interests in a war of attrition lasting over two decades. The Druridge Bay Campaign, directed first against plans to build a nuclear power station and then against the commercial extraction of sand, provides an illustrative case and highlights some of the problems of analysing local protest.[1]

Opposing nuclear power

Druridge Bay is a six mile long stretch of Northumbrian coastline, 20 miles north of Newcastle. For most of the year it is a windswept wilderness. When the weather is less inclement it attracts people from all over the region because of its isolation and natural beauty. The bay contains four nature reserves, includes a Site of Special Scientific Interest and is just to the south of the designated Area of National Beauty running down the coast from Berwick to Amble. The vicinity of the bay is not untouched by industrialisation, mostly opencast coal mining, though by now most of the old mineworkings have been restored to farmland or turned into nature reserves.

In November 1996, Magnox Electric announced it was selling land at Druridge Bay—previously purchased as a possible site for nuclear power generation—for agricultural and residential use. For local people this announcement signalled the ultimate success of a campaign against the siting of a PWR (Pressurised Water Reactor) nuclear power station in their midst. The campaign began almost two decades earlier with the news, three days before Christmas 1978, that Druridge Bay was being considered by the Central Electricity Generating Board as a possible site. This led to the formation of a pressure group—the Druridge Bay Association—in March 1979, following a series of meetings at a local public house. The participants were mostly people living in the immediate vicinity of the proposed development with the central protagonists drawn from the 'educated middle class'—including a teacher, a manager, an engineer, a scientist and a librarian. A few were also members of environmental and civic groups, but the motivation for collective action was based largely on the perceived threat to the individuals and their immediate locality (i.e. a NIMBY response) rather than any ideological commitment to green issues or opposition to nuclear power in principle.

The Association had some success in mobilising public protest, despite having limited resources. It attracted support from of one of the local district councils (Castle Morpeth) but not from the Northumberland County Council which adopted a 'wait and see' approach at this stage. The Association realised that its campaign would be strengthened enormously by County Council support, and its primary aim was to secure this. It published a pamphlet setting out the case against nuclear power and circulated this locally. It also launched a petition opposing the development, which eventually attracted around 30,000 signatures (one in ten of the adult population of Northumberland) and organised large public gatherings—including a rally of 3,000 people at the bay in July 1979. The Association also participated in public consultation meetings on the issue, attracting local media attention in the process— as on one particular occasion when its members led a walk-out at a consultation meeting. Finally, it sought to win support from MPs, trade unions, environmental and anti-nuclear pressure groups, conservation groups and civic societies.

In 1980, this pressure paid off as Northumberland County Council came out against the proposed development, but this did not prevent the Central Electricity Generating Board embarking on a series of drilling tests at the site and in December that year the site was declared viable for a PWR nuclear power station. Meanwhile the UK's first proposed PWR, at Sizewell in Suffolk, was to be the subject of a public inquiry and this, coupled with a further public inquiry regarding the planned PWR at Hinkley in Somerset, presented additional opportunities for opponents of the Druridge scheme to participate in the nuclear power debate. For example, two of the local authorities involved, Wansbeck District Council and Northumberland County Council, made representations at the Sizewell public inquiry.

The delay could also have given the Druridge Bay Association valuable time to generate even greater public opposition, but seemed to have the opposite effect. It became difficult to sustain the campaign in the lull between official announcements and actual events, such as test drilling: there was a real danger that local people, particularly those living outside the immediate area earmarked for development, would become complacent and lose interest in the issue. Also, time constraints on members of the Association made it difficult to sustain the campaign: more than one activist upset their employer because of the amount of time they spent campaigning.

A further problem was lack of coordination. Although there was a great deal of local opposition to the development, a number of competing perspectives arose. Despite their common interests, civic groups, anti-nuclear protestors, conservation and environmental groups, local authorities and trade unions were unable or unwilling to work together on the issue. Tentative moves to overcome these differences came to nothing and the Association began to run out of steam. Between 1981 and 1983, the campaign became almost moribund, even though the nuclear power 'threat' remained ever-present. In 1982 , news that Druridge Bay was on a short list of six sites focused minds on the need to reinvigorate the campaign and improve coordination between local groups. A key factor was the creation of a local Friends of the Earth group in 1983, which led to a more effective link between local green activists and local councils. Another was the networking of anti-nuclear activists on Tyneside within local trade unions, which brought these organisations firmly behind the campaign. Eventually in 1984 the strands of opposition were brought together in a new group: the Druridge Bay Campaign, a federation of 38 organisations with an individual membership of 500 people. It was funded by contributions from the constituent groups (which included trade unions and local authorities) and later individual subscriptions as well , and was led by a committee representing the major players.

The formation of the new organisation was timely. In May 1994, the Central Electricity Generating Board began to undertake detailed test drilling of the site. Then in December 1984, four years after the site initially had been declared suitable, it bought out properties near the proposed development. The creation of the Druridge Bay Campaign, which attracted considerable publicity from local press and television, had already by this time begun to mobilise opinion more effectively. After the purchase of the land and buildings the campaign moved up another gear. Local opposition was demonstrated in public rallies throughout 1985 as well as special events at the bay (e.g. such as a September Fair and a Christmas party, which along with a beach run became annual events) which attracted further publicity.

One of the key turning points occurred in 1986 when the Chernobyl disaster produced widespread fear about the safety of nuclear power particularly in areas earmarked for nuclear sites. Campaign members independently monitored the Chernobyl effect with a gamma monitor and were deluged with requests from the public and the media throughout the North-East who were desperate for data on possible contamination. During 1986 the organisation was strengthened with the recruitment of a part-time publicity officer and a part-time education officer, while sufficient income was raised, mainly from local authorities, to provide separate office facilities. These new arrangements were essential for the next phase of the campaign. With the approval of Sizewell B in 1987, and the opening of the Hinkley inquiry in 1988, the Druridge Bay Campaign began to focus greater attention on national lobbying. By now almost all the local authorities in the region had declared their support for the Campaign, and the local media and public opinion were strongly behind it. The Campaign also won explicit support from almost all the MPs in the region, with Alan Beith (Liberal, Berwick) and Jack Thompson (Labour, Wansbeck) being particularly active on its behalf.

Opportunities to lobby at a national level were increased by the Thatcher government's decision to privatise the electricity industry. The passage of the legislation enabled all the local and national groups opposed to nuclear power to attract a wider audience. It also gave them an opportunity to persuade MPs to introduce amendments to the legislation in an effort to undermine the expansion of nuclear power. Given the government's large Parliamentary majority, these amendments were unlikely to succeed, but they at least ensured that the case for nuclear power would be critically debated in public. In November 1988 Friends of the Earth organised a national lobby of Parliament bringing together the various local protest groups, which attracted considerable publicity. Throughout the passage of the bill, local MPs and peers were lobbied in an effort to put pressure on the government. One notable victory was a House of Lords' amendment requiring the privatised electricity companies to promote energy efficiency: although diluted by the Commons, it attracted further publicity for those who argued that an expansion of nuclear power was unnecessary given the potential for energy conservation.

The situation then changed dramatically. The nuclear power stations were suddenly withdrawn from the electricity privatisation programme after the government's own financial advisers found that nuclear waste disposal and decommissioning costs were higher than previously estimated. Moreover, the government placed a moratarium on the building of new nuclear power stations pending a review of the industry. The review, completed in 1994, confirmed that no more nuclear power stations would be built with public sector support. Subsequently in 1996 the nuclear power industry was part-privatised, with the older Magnox reactors remaining in the public sector. In the meantime the Druridge Bay Campaign maintained pressure on government. Campaigners believed that it was vital that the land still owned by the nuclear industry did not end up in the hands of the privatised company—British Energy. Although it was unlikely that the private sector would take on the commercial risks of building a new nuclear power station, the government did not rule this out. On the other hand, since the government had already committed itself to a moratorium on new nuclear power stations in the public sector, it was possible that if the site was allocated to Magnox Electric (the public sector body responsible for the older rump of the industry) it might be sold back to the community. In the event, Magnox Electric was given the land and, following persistent lobbying from the Druridge Bay Campaign, agreed to sell the site for agricultural or residential use.

Sand extraction

A second front for the Druridge Bay Campaign opened up in 1990. This time the adversary was Ready Mixed Concrete whose subsidiary, Northern Aggregates, was engaged in sand extraction at the bay. This had been going on for many years: the original planning permission was granted back in the 1960s, and even before this time sand had been extracted for industrial uses though on a much smaller scale. Sand extraction nevertheless became an important issue for the Campaign and its affiliated organisations. They believed that excessive quantities of sand were being taken from the site, causing disruption to those wishing to use the bay as an amenity, to wildlife, and to people living on the main access routes. They also attributed problems associated with coastal erosion to the cumulative effects of extraction.

Campaigners had a number of options. They could seek to revoke planning permission, but this would be expensive as the company could sue the local authority for compensation. Another option was to persuade central government to use default powers under the planning legislation to revoke permission, but this could still have resulted in the local authority paying compensation. A third option was to seek protected status for the bay in the form of a coastal protection order, but this had the additional disadvantage of being a convoluted process, whereas the problems of the bay required a speedy response. The final option was to persuade Ready Mixed Concrete and its subsidiary to wind down its operations voluntarily. This became the main strategy, although the Campaign continued to lobby for the second and third options with the proviso that any compensation claims be met by central government.

As with the anti-nuclear power campaign, the local authorities were useful allies and they continued to provide financial resources. A public campaign was launched including a petition (which eventually attracted some 20,000 signatures) and events aimed at attracting publicity (e.g. a beach party) in addition to annual community events launched by the anti-nuclear campaign during the mid-1980s (see above).

The campaign adopted King Canute as a symbolic character, with members dressing up to attract publicity in various locations (e.g.

outside the Department of the Environment, and outside the offices of Ready Mixed Concrete). All this added a bit of fun to what was of course a serious issue. This new approach also refreshed the media's presentation of the Campaign thereby maintaining interest locally. The Campaign also bought a share in Ready Mixed Concrete, enabling it to raise concerns at the Annual General Meeting. It tried to persuade local builders and DIY stores not to use sand taken from the bay: given the difficulties of identifying the source of supply, this was seen by most users as impractical, but it did attract further publicity for the campaign.

Meanwhile on the parliamentary front local MPs began to lobby the Department of the Environment on the issue. Parliamentary Questions were asked and an adjournment debate was raised. Following this, with encouragement from the government, Ready Mixed Concrete opened a dialogue with the Campaign and the local authorities. In 1993 it stated that it would agree to a phased withdrawal from the bay, but only if alternative sites could be found in the region. The failure to identify suitable alternatives meant that extraction at Druridge Bay continued. Then, in 1996, Ready Mixed Concrete announced the cessation of its activities at the bay abandoning this relatively small but profitable extraction site 56 years earlier than legally obliged to do so. At the same time it withdrew an application to quarry sand at another sensitive site near the Northumberland National Park. These decisions were announced a week after the decision by Magnox Electric to sell the site earmarked for the nuclear power station.

Once its main aims had been achieved the Druridge Bay Campaign closed down its office. However, it still exists as a voluntary group and maintains a membership list. It has also generated other organisations which are still actively involved in environmental, conservation and energy issues, including a group known as PIANA (Proper Insurance Against Nuclear Accidents) and Northern Energy Associates, a renewable energy consultancy.

Analysing the campaigns

The Druridge Bay case raises a number of broader questions about local protest groups. How should the success of such groups be judged? How are their achievements related to key variables such as political circumstances, organisation, public support, and the choice of strategies and tactics? What does the campaign tell us about contemporary political culture and in particular the rise of 'new social movements' and new forms of politics?

Relating to the first question, an evaluation of any campaign is highly dependent on the timing of one's judgement. As late as 1993 the achievements of the Druridge Bay Campaign were limited. Only in 1996, with the proposed sell-off of the site previously earmarked for nuclear power generation and the ending of sand extraction, could one reasonably judge its efforts as successful. At the present time and for the foreseeable future, both threats are substantially diminished. Most observers would regard this as a considerable achievement. After all, other communities have fought either against nuclear power or the encroachment of commercial interests keen to exploit natural resources—and have lost. However, as the campaigners themselves are well aware, future threats to the bay cannot be ruled out.

Even before the 1996 announcements regarding the future of the bay, the campaign could claim some success in stimulating local opposition and, perhaps as important, in contributing to national debates about nuclear power and energy conservation. Druridge Bay may have been a part of a much bigger picture, but like other local battles, many of which achieved far greater prominence nationally, it formed part of a groundswell of concern which forced environmental and nuclear power issues on to the political agenda in the 1980s and early 1990s.

It is too simple, however, to see local campaigns like Druridge as merely drawing strength from a national shift in public opinion: they contributed a great deal it themselves, over and above the efforts of Greenpeace, Friends of the Earth and other environmental, conservation and anti-nuclear groups at national level. As the Druridge Bay case illustrates, it was at the local level where the interaction of developers and conservationists took place. Local groups also rallied behind national groups when presenting their case through the media and in lobbying Parliament and government. In the nuclear debate for example, they helped to highlight key issues such as under-insurance, waste disposal and decommissioning costs—which ultimately produced a major shift in government policy.

In short, the Druridge case illustrates that local campaigns can benefit from favourable political circumstances, but that these circumstances are often partly of their own making. It also illustrates that the political climate can assist some local groups more than others. Some schemes cannot be halted by protest, no matter how favourable this climate. Too much political and financial capital has been invested in them, making abandonment virtually impossible. But others, nearer the drawing board stage, can more easily gain a reprieve. Druridge Bay was on the short list for nuclear power, but was fortunate in that others ranked above it. The Hinkley and Sizewell campaigners in contrast were fighting a much tougher battle—against the clock as well as the nuclear industry and the government.

Other circumstances certainly assisted the anti-nuclear campaign at Druridge. Accidents in America at Three Mile Island in 1979 and in Russia at Chernobyl in 1986 had a major impact on public attitudes towards nuclear power. In the UK, public support for building more nuclear power stations fell from 23% to 11% between 1985 and 1986 and by the end of the decade stood at only 14%.[2] Another crucial factor was the Thatcher government's decision to privatise nuclear power. This gave protestors a fresh opportunity to mobilise public and parliamentary opinion. Furthermore, the privatisation plan exposed the industry's finances to the scrutiny of financial advisers, who declared it an unattractive investment for the private sector, largely because of the hidden costs associated with waste disposal and decommissioning. This forced a review of the industry and a moratorium on public sector investment in new nuclear power stations. As a *Guardian* journalist observed at the time, the woolly-pullovered environmentalists staunchest ally turned out to be the sharp suited city accountant. However, as already noted, campaigners played a major role in highlighting the costs of decommissioning, waste disposal and under-insurance of nuclear power plants. It is possible that this publicity influenced the financial advisers' rising estimates of the industry's costs: certainly the absence of such activity would have made privatisation appear a more viable option.

Circumstances also played an important part in the sand extraction campaign. Ready Mixed Concrete and Northern Aggregates were seeking to develop other sites in the region and it is possible that Druridge was a useful card to play in negotiations with the local planning authority. For it was by no means certain that the Druridge site would have remained an economic proposition in the future and was therefore possible that extraction could have ceased anyway before planning permission expired. One thing is clear. The disruption and adverse publicity caused by the Druridge Bay Campaign significantly altered the balance of cost and benefits to the companies: a small but profitable operation became a liability in terms of public relations.

Another point regarding circumstances is that the sand extraction campaign undoubtedly benefited from the previous campaign against nuclear power. Although the sand issue attracted public concern in its own right, it is doubtful that on its own it would have had the same resonance. The second campaign rode on the back of the first, drawing on the level of public support already built up and benefiting from its effective organisation and political networks.

Good organisation was crucial to both of the Druridge campaigns. The initial group—the Druridge Bay Association—mobilised local opinion on the nuclear issue and was successful in generating media interest and promoting local authority opposition to the plans, but it failed to draw together other interests opposed to nuclear power in such a way that resources could be maximised. Residents, trade unions, local authorities, civic societies, conservation and environmental groups all had their own perspective on the issue. The unions were mainly concerned about the impact on the coal industry, the conservationists were concerned about harm to the local environment. Some campaigners were mutually suspicious of each other, particularly the anti-nuclear groups and the unions on the left against the middle-class conservation and civic groups located the centre-right of the political spectrum. Nevertheless as the threat to bay loomed larger, a federation emerged in the form of the Druridge Bay Campaign. Care was taken to ensure that all perspectives were represented on its executive committee with seats for unions, parties, local authorities, and environmental and civic groups. This strengthened the campaign, though it remained crucial that strategies and tactics adopted should not alienate any of the affiliated organisations. Some groups, particularly those with conservative inclinations, were keen to avoid outright opposition to nuclear power in principle, but gradually, even these underwent a learning process and eventually endorsed policies that they would not previously have countenanced.

Two factors stimulated the formation of the Druridge Bay Campaign: the prospect of detailed test drilling at the site, which meant that the development was more than a vague possibility, and the formation in 1983 of a Friends of the Earth group in mid-Northumberland, providing a link with national campaigns and facilitating relationships with other opposition groups locally. Once established, the Druridge Bay Campaign began to coordinate opposition far more effectively than the Association had been able to. It also brought additional resources as affiliated groups and individual members contributed funds. Further resources were made available in 1986, by the local authorities, enabling the organisation to improve staffing and office facilities. As we saw earlier, this was crucial to the next phase of the campaign, which involved a great deal of communication with MPs, the media and other anti-nuclear groups at national level, activities that could not have been undertaken successfully by people working in their spare time from their own homes. However, the energies of individual activists were still needed. The key difference was that the Association—as a voluntary group sustained only by the energies of individuals—found it difficult to replace activists as they became jaded through their efforts or left the area, while the Campaign was a federation of groups and its key activists—members of the steering committee—could be replenished over the years.

The Campaign also had a more professional campaigning style than its predecessor, enhanced by the creation of the two part-time posts. Initially however, the majority of campaigners were neither experienced nor politically active. They developed political skills through experience. As a result some later embarked on new careers, one activist becoming a public relations officer for an MP, another setting up a renewable energy company; while some became involved in campaigning on other local environmental issues. The leadership of the Campaign was collective in the form of the steering committee, but with key roles for office holders (such as chairperson, treasurer, membership secretary). The people who undertook these tasks subsequently played a key role in the leadership of the organisation, though the Publicity and Information Officer, Bridget Gubbins, was perhaps not surprisingly regarded as the public face of the organisation.

Another factor in the success of the campaigns was the level of public support. The Druridge Bay Campaign built on the foundations laid by the Association, but was far more innovative, focusing not only on attracting media attention but on special events, as mentioned earlier. It also sponsored music festivals and the publication of an anthology of poetry celebrating the bay. This had a publicity value, but also helped to foster a much stronger community feeling among people in the North-East against the threats to the bay. The media played an extremely important role in mobilising public support behind both campaigns. Most of the newspapers in the area gave them sympathetic coverage. Local radio and television maintained a keen interest in the issue, but had to be careful about accusations of bias, where powerful commercial and public sector corporations were involved. Nevertheless, their coverage certainly benefited the protestors, allowing them to air views and generate public support.

The seeking of media coverage was part of a deliberate publicity strategy. Campaigners sensed that they were pushing at an open door as far as local journalists were concerned, who found the 'David and Goliath' type story highly attractive. The Druridge Bay Campaign became adept at using the media, issuing regular press releases, thinking ahead about the timing of events, devising events that would attract interest. Plenty of thought went into using the media to define campaigns in the public's mind. For example, the anti-nuclear campaign was launched by building a cairn at Druridge Bay, a landmark to symbolise the determination of the protestors; the sand extraction campaign used the more light-hearted symbol of King Canute, but the effect was much the same.

The media strategy was effective in persuading local authorities and politicians at Westminster to support both campaigns. Local authority support was absolutely crucial: local authorities in turn pressured central government and Parliament, and provided funds for both campaigns. They also took on the developers directly at various stages of the planning process. On the anti-nuclear issue it was by no means certain that local councils would unite to oppose the proposals. Gradually, they lined up behind the Druridge Bay Campaign following media and public pressure. One case, that of Alnwick District Council, illustrates how this pressure was exerted. Councillors were initially opposed to the anti-nuclear campaign, but reversed their decision after the Druridge Bay Campaign began to promote its cause among their constituents. The other major tactic of the campaigners was to target Parliament. In some cases they were again pushing at an open door. Two MPs in particular, Alan Beith and Jack Thompson actively supported the Druridge Bay Campaign on both the nuclear and sand extraction issues. All but one Labour MP in the North-East wholeheartedly supported the anti-nuclear campaign (the exception was sponsored by the then pro-nuclear Amalgamated Union of Engineering Workers).

During the 1980s, the three Conservative MPs from the region did not endorse the anti-nuclear campaign, hardly surprising since the expansion of nuclear power was a central plank of government energy policy in this period. However, the Campaign did not concede defeat, knowing that it was important to secure cross-party support, and eventually one of the three Conservatives (Neville Trotter, Tynemouth) expressed his opposition to the proposed development at Druridge Bay, while remaining committed to nuclear power in principle.

On both issues, the Campaign's supporters in Parliament raised Questions, adjournment debates and contributed to other relevant debates in both Houses, they also advised it on how best to put its case. Finally, they acted as go-betweens, arranged meetings with other parliamentarians, ministers and civil servants. Gradually, through its supporters in Parliament, the Druridge Bay Campaign built up a dialogue with government: it communicated with the relevant government departments on both the nuclear and sand extraction issues during the 1990s. Although not achieving insider status in the sense that it was consulted regularly, the Campaign nevertheless earned the respect of government as it explored how the outstanding issues could be resolved.

Neither the Association not the Campaign explicitly endorsed direct intervention. This contrasted with some anti-nuclear groups in other parts of the country. There was some sabotage at Druridge Bay in 1980, during initial test drilling of the site, but campaigners disassociated themselves from this act, arguing that such activities damaged their cause. During the sand extraction campaign, two members of the Campaign did attempt to prevent the lorries from removing material but this was not officially sanctioned by the organisation and did not provoke a serious outbreak of disorder. The Campaign did urge a consumer boycott of sand taken from the bay—a form of non-violent direct action, but as explained earlier the main impact of this was in terms of publicity value.

In summary, the Druridge Bay Campaign clearly operated within the bounds of the conventional political system. It mobilised public opinion and built political support slowly but surely. It did not resort to legal or illegal direct action to achieve its objectives. But then it did not have to, as the conventional political system responded to its efforts and ultimately delivered the outcome it desired.

Analysing protest

What do these campaigns reveal about contemporary political culture? Certainly they indicate that far from being apathetic, people can be persuaded to take an interest when their life-style or immediate environment is threatened. Public interest was high, and was sustained over a number of years. However, the case suggests that even on issues of great concern to the community, campaigns are often organised by a core group of activists. At its peak the Druridge Bay Campaign had no more than 500 individual members; the number of 'key players' was much smaller, at around 20–30 people. This does not mean that it was poorly supported; it merely confirms that political activism is not necessarily a mass activity, even when public support is strong and localised: there is evidence of 'anticipatory democracy', with activists seeking to shape and respond to the public mood rather than create systems of mass participation.

The Druridge Bay Campaign also illustrates the conventionality of participation. It eschewed direct action, preferring to build support amongst the public, the media, local authorities and in Parliament. Campaigners were also prepared to open a dialogue with government and with opposing interests such as the Central Electricity Generating Board and Ready Mixed Concrete. Demonstrations took place, but this was done a peaceful and well-ordered manner, attracting rather than alienating public support. Of course, it could be that Druridge Bay is an unusual case, but at the very least it provides some evidence to challenge those who assert that contemporary protests represent a completely new form of politics.

Further, the Druridge Bay Campaign illustrates the problems of analysing protest politics. The 'new social movement' label has been criticised as overused, underdefined and open to a wide variety of interpretations.[3] However, it is generally equated with emerging forms of political participation that emphasise protest, informal organisation and collective action outside the conventional political system. In particular, new social movements have been identified around issues relating to social exclusion, political identity and environmental degradation.

Even in the terms of this rather loose definition, the Druridge Bay Campaign cannot itself be regarded as a new social movement because of its highly specific and localised nature. However, its activities may be viewed as forming a small but significant part of the broader environmental and anti-nuclear movement, both in terms of its contribution to the national campaign against nuclear power and as a local battleground where environmental and conservation issues have been fought out. Another aspect of the campaign which strikes a chord with social movement concept is its strong cultural element and in particular the relevance of 'identity politics'. The North-East is traditionally regarded has having strong sense of community and regional identity and these features were reflected to some extent in the Druridge campaigns. Indeed both campaigns had an important cultural element — aiming not only to rally local people but to demonstrate a much broader appreciation of the bay's significance to the local community and, more widely, to the North-East region. On the other hand, some of the features normally associated with new social movements were not found in the Druridge campaigns. Far from being informally or loosely organised, the Druridge Bay Campaign was extremely well-organised. Its strategies and tactics were not unconventional, direct action playing a very small and insignificant part. Furthermore, its success depended to a great extent on these organisational and tactical factors, not to mention political and financial support from elements of 'old' rather than new social movements—such as local authorities, trade unions, and traditional conservation groups.

This study has therefore highlighted some of the inadequacies of the new social movement concept as an analytical tool. It is of little value in explaining the activities of local protest campaigns, particularly where use is made of the conventional political system and where alliances are forged with traditional interest and cause groups.

Finally, the case also highlights the shortcomings of conventional approaches to understanding local protest. It is true that the kinds of factors identified here as possible explanations for the success of the Druridge Bay Campaign can be found in most studies of pressure-group politics: for example, good organisation, use of the media, building public and parliamentary support, dialogue with decision-makers. Nonetheless, there has been little academic interest in local protest groups and consequently their role has not been fully analysed. Such studies as there have been tend to regard these groups as weak and peripheral—largely ineffective sporadic interventionists.[4] This assertion is belied by the Druridge case, which shows that in particular circumstances such groups can be highly effective. Conventional wisdom also doubts the durability of protest groups and thereby the possibility that they may live on to fight new campaigns as happened with the Druridge Bay Campaign. Furthermore, it is often assumed that such groups, because of their local nature, are isolated and focus wholly on the periphery. As this study has shown, this is not necessarily the case: they may interact with other local and national groups in a synergetic way. Moreover, they may influence policy outcomes by participating directly in national as well as local policy arenas, thereby shaping the way issues are perceived by the public and decision-makers.

I am grateful to Bridget Gubbins of the Druridge Bay Campaign for her assistance.

1 B. Gubbins, *Generating Pressure The Campaign Against Nuclear Power at Druridge Bay* (Earthright Publications, 1991); B. Gubbins, *Power at Bay* (Earthright Publications, 1997).

2 K. Young, 'Shades of Green' in R. Jowell, L. Brook and B. Taylor, *British Social Attitudes*, 6th Report (Social and Community Planning Research, 1991).

3 P. Byrne, *Social Movements in Britain* (Routledge, 1997); A.G. Jordan and W. Maloney, *The Protest Business* (Manchester University Press, 1995).

4 A. Brier and R. Hill 'Participation in Local Politics: Three Cautionary Case Studies' in L. Robins (ed.), *Topics in British Politics* (The Politics Association); R. Dowse and J. Hughes, 'Sporadic Interventionists', *Political Studies*, March 1977.

Brent Spar, Atlantic Oil and Greenpeace

BY LYNN G. BENNIE

IN February 1995, the British Government approved a proposal by Shell UK for deep sea disposal of the 14,500 tonne, 463ft Brent Spar oil storage and loading buoy in the north Atlantic. There followed a sustained, highly publicised campaign by Greenpeace, backed by European governments and public, which included occupation of the oil platform by Greenpeace activists. After pressure from its sister companies in Europe, Shell UK abandoned the proposal. There followed a two-year-long reappraisal and study of other disposal options by Shell, while the Spar had a temporary home in Erfjord, Norway. In January 1998, Shell announced the oil structure would be recycled into a series of rings which would be sunk onto the seabed to form an industrial quayside at the port of Mekjarvik, near Stavanger in Norway. Deep sea disposal has now become politically unacceptable, with Labour announcing the government's apparent reversal of support for sea dumping shortly after it came to power, and in July 1998 European governments meet to debate a European wide ban on sea disposal.

The Brent Spar episode is now commonly regarded as a symbol of the power that political protest can exert over the powerful interests of big business and big government. While interpretations of events vary, the political significance of the Greenpeace campaign and of Shell's actions is universally recognised as a defining period or benchmark in the relationship between business, the government, the public and the environment. Detailed accounts of the events leading up to and surrounding Greenpeace's occupation of the Brent Spar on 30 April 1995 have been extensively documented elsewhere.[1] Here the focus is on events which occurred after Shell's policy reversal and, more importantly, the consequences of these events for the relationship between Greenpeace, the public and the oil companies.

Brent Spar

The myth of public protest? The central issue surrounding the Brent Spar debate was not new—toxic waste dumping has been taking place for a long time. Nor were the tactics of Greenpeace new—its creation of dramatic pseudo-events was a tried and tested formula. However, its skilful public relations campaign appeared to have special resonance and seemed to project the issue on to the public agenda in a uniquely dramatic fashion. The campaign against deep sea disposal of the Brent Spar involved a moral stand against the double-headed monster of business and government and it appealed to the emotions of the general public. Greenpeace's central and lasting message was that if the Brent Spar had been dumped, it would have sent the wrong signal to industry — that this was an acceptable form of waste disposal. It argued that dumping in the sea was wrong and that industry could not use the ocean as a dustbin. The constant use of the term 'dumping' (a term originally used by the oil industry) was an effective tactic. It had a stigmatising effect, similar to labelling the Community Charge the Poll Tax. The seizing of the moral high ground, and the use of symbolic, emotionally charged moral messages has been a common theme throughout Greenpeace's campaigning history. The battle was David and Goliath: sympathy for the little guy overcoming the interests of big business and big government.

Shell's Brent Spar climb-down has been almost universally regarded as a victory for Greenpeace and the public. Newspaper articles at the time pronounced that the Shell turn-around was an example of people power. The *Daily Mirror* declared that the policy change was, 'a victory for Greenpeace, a victory for the *Mirror* and other newspapers which campaigned against scuppering the platform. But most of all it is a victory for the people. The people whose boycott of Shell forced it to back down'. The *Guardian* argued that Shell's decision 'to bow to public protests' meant that 'people still count' and 'boycotts can still work'. The *Independent* said that 'the deciding factor' had been 'the ability and willingness of ordinary people to boycott Shell products'. These accounts of the Brent Spar campaign assume that the public were in some way involved in the Greenpeace protests against Shell. Is this an accurate reflection of the relationship between Greenpeace and the public, or has a myth of public protest grown up around the whole affair? While Greenpeace was successful in appealing to public sympathy in Britain, the Brent Spar campaign did not result in dramatically high levels of public protest.

There is little doubt that Greenpeace won the battle for public opinion. A MORI survey a month after the Brent Spar policy reversal found that 63% believed that Greenpeace 'won the argument' rather than Shell or the Government, and 71% that Shell should not have sunk the Brent Spar. A poll by Opinion Leader Research in February 1996 found that of those who had heard of the controversy surrounding the Brent Spar, 74% believed Greenpeace should continue with its campaign against the dumping of oil platforms. In summer 1996, a MORI survey showed 76% agreeing that 'British companies do not pay enough attention to their treatment of the environment', a seven point increase in one year.

However, to what extent does public sympathy for Greenpeace translate into behaviour or activity in Britain? The 1996 MORI data indicated that between 1993 and 1996 a steady two-thirds of the public disagreed with the statement that, 'There isn't much that ordinary people can do to help protect the environment' and 24% said they avoided using the services or products of a company that they considered had a poor environmental record (up nine points on 1989, the year when concern for the environment peaked in Britain). Worcester argues that green consumerism (when purchase decisions are based on environmental friendliness) is now well established and that industrialists and politicians were wrong to underestimate the level of environmental concern in Europe, pointing to a 1994 finding that 16% of people in 21 countries would 'boycott a product or country targeted by Greenpeace'.[2] Nevertheless, the polls suggest that the British public, while as concerned about the environment, may be less likely to be environmental campaigners than other Europeans.[3] Indeed, the extent of public protest against Shell in Britain over the Brent Spar is often over-estimated. One of the most interesting aspects of the Brent Spar case was the internationalism of the campaign. One can argue that it was the reaction of other European publics and governments which forced Shell to reconsider. In Germany, for example, sales fell by 30%. In Britain, while public sympathy for the campaign was evident, this did not manifest itself in the form of mass public protest or a widespread consumer boycott.

Playing to the media gallery. The relationship between Greenpeace and the media is central to understanding why the Brent Spar campaign was so successful. Greenpeace successfully used the media to mobilise public support. Prior to Brent Spar, a number of observers had noted the positive media image enjoyed by Greenpeace across Europe, and the importance of this. Indeed it has been argued that gaining the support of the media was its primary objective: all other functions were subordinate.[4] It has also been said that Brent Spar was an example of 'the role of modern systems of communication in the transformation of meanings concerning the natural environment' and that Greenpeace was the gatekeeper of information in the early stages because it was supported by the news media.[5] In other words, uncritical media coverage of the Brent Spar affair meant that Greenpeace was the most important player in the 'definitional' period.

After Brent Spar the media seem to have felt they had been led by the nose throughout the events and as a result they are now more cautious about supporting Greenpeace claims. Following Greenpeace's summer protests against oil exploration in the Atlantic in 1997, the *Financial Times* (12.8.97) wrote: 'The warriors of Greenpeace have a cause, which merely makes them look silly. They want to stop oil production in the deep waters west of the Shetland Isles. This hardly has the emotional resonance of earlier campaigns, such as saving the whale. And intellectually it is risible.' While such robust criticism is not typical of all recent media coverage, it provides a flavour of the cooling of relations between the news media and Greenpeace. The media seem to have been less enthusiastic campaigning partners. As Grant Jordan notes, Greenpeace 'may have inoculated the media against a repeat infection'. The problem is that by scoring a victory against powerful energy interests, the environmentalists no longer appear as underdogs. The media are now more likely to question the power of Greenpeace, an unelected pressure group. The risk for Greenpeace is that direct action protests are viewed as stunts to attract media attention. Greenpeace's response is that such action is still a genuine attempt to prevent environmental destruction. Chris Rose, deputy executive director of Greenpeace UK, acknowledges the need to adopt new campaign methods: 'We are even changing the way we communicate. We are children of the media, but now we must communicate directly with those who create problems. The media will always play a central role. But why use a comment piece in the Independent, for instance, to send a message to business? Meeting business people face to face — either in private in the spirit of cooperation, or with a megaphone outside the director's home — often does the trick more effectively' (*Independent*, 22.11.94).

Before Brent Spar the media respect enjoyed by Greenpeace was partly explained by the organisation's use of scientific expertise to substantiate its more emotive arguments. Following errors in its Brent Spar campaign, there has been a marked decline in respect for the Greenpeace expert, although poll evidence reveals that confidence in all scientific experts fell between 1995 and 1996. However, the media are partly responsible for declining confidence in experts because they inevitably simplify complex scientific and technical information, to suit short and snappy news bulletins. Greenpeace respond with suitable pre-packaged material.

Of course, 'scientific facts' are often disputable. Greenpeace scientists present a very different view of possible climate change from energy industry experts. One of the interesting features of environmental politics since Brent Spar is that the media are increasingly entering the scientific debate, but they have problems interpreting competing claims, and a high level of faith in scientists. Media reports of Greenpeace and its battles with multi-national companies, for example, tend to be written by environment rather than science correspondents which may lead to a distortion of its message and may be harmful to Greenpeace. This may explain the suggestion that it should find ways of communicating 'more directly'. It was acutely embarrassed by inaccuracies in its Brent Spar claims because in recent years it has developed a more professional approach to scientific research, now regarded as an important organisational weapon and campaigning tool.[6] It now has an active scientific director, reports are distributed to scientists before publication, and press releases refer to scientific journals. It has undergone a 'conversion towards science and the more conventional rigours of research'.[7] Although Brent Spar was a set-back for the group's attempts to build a reputation for scientific excellence, surveys show that journalists are still more likely to trust information coming from environmental groups than from government or industry. In 1995 journalists claimed that domestic NGOs were the single most useful source for information about conservation and environmental issues; 70% claimed they were 'very useful', 33% said the same of government agencies/departments in their own country, and only three per cent found companies or corporations in their own country very useful sources of information.[8]

The Atlantic Frontier campaign

Direct action. In 1997 Greenpeace mounted a campaign against the expansion of oil exploration in the North Atlantic. Its scale was much more ambitious than for Brent Spar—it involved an attempt to stop the development of new oil fields around the world. It argues that oil extraction has reached a point of unnecessary overproduction, and that burning excessive amounts of oil for energy is likely to create serious rises in temperature and sea levels and unpredictable ecosystem damage. It accuses the oil industry of being unwilling to accept these threats of climate change and emphasises the need to develop alternative forms of energy production to the burning of carbon/fossil fuel.

The Atlantic Frontier—the edge of the continental shelf—lies 100 miles west of Shetland and has only recently been licensed by the UK for oil exploration. Exploration is centred on Rockall and Shetland, expected to be exceptionally oil rich. 30 oil companies, led by BP and Shell, have developed leading edge technology to cope with the deep waters that are more difficult to drill than the North Sea. In 1997, Greenpeace led a summer-long campaign to disrupt oil exploration in this area. Activists employed various stunts in the campaign against the oil companies: they occupied the tiny island of Rockall for 48 days (living in a high-tech yellow pod—a solar survival capsule); dressed in suits and carrying copies of the *Financial Times*, they manacled themselves to furniture in the London offices of Conoco; they tied oil drums to Conoco's equipment; they disrupted seismic data gathering; and they delivered a petition signed by over 250,000 people to the Prime Minister.

The most publicised confrontation was the week long Stena Dee rig protest in August, when campaigners tied the yellow pod containing activists to the leg of a British Petroleum (BP) chartered exploration rig. This was an attempt to stop, or at least slow down, the progress of the oil drilling platform to BP's Foinaven oilfield west of Shetland. BP obtained a court order freezing the assets of Greenpeace and demanded compensation of £1.4 million. An order was served on the Co-operative Bank in Glasgow—preventing 65 Greenpeace employees being paid—and would also have enabled court officials to seize Greenpeace assets, including ships, in UK jurisdiction. The activists gave up their occupation when BP began this suit which threatened to bankrupt it. Greenpeace claimed that this was an attempt to cripple it and stifle the democratic protests of a legitimate public interest group. The oil industry, for its part, appeared better prepared than at the time of Brent Spar. BP's spokesman said that Greenpeace was not above the law and argued that its revenue was £90 million in 1996, according to its own accounts, more than enough to pay for losses suffered as a result of its action. Greenpeace challenged this, saying that its bank accounts only held £180,000 and that there was no secret bank account or assets (*Guardian*, 19.08.97).

Legal action. The Atlantic Frontier campaign also illustrates the use made by environmental groups of the law. In a reversal of the action taken against them by BP, Greenpeace was involved in High Court action against the Department of Trade and Industry (DTI) and 30 oil companies, one of them BP. It argued that the award of licences in the seventeenth-round contravened a number of European Commission directives by failing to protect sensitive cold-water coral reefs, grounds for judicial review. However, leave was refused due to delay in bringing the application. Legal action is increasingly being used by environmental groups to win over public and business.[9] Judicial review applications are used to challenge the granting of permits or licences to energy companies, for example. Greenpeace is recognised as having 'sufficient interest' (the relevant test for standing to bring a judicial review application).

Internet. Another Greenpeace campaigning tool is the Internet. Greenpeace highlight the fact that its world-wide web sites are award-winning, including one on French Nuclear Testing in 1995. It launched a general UK website in March 1997 at www.greenpeace.org.uk, and in November 1997 Greenpeace International launched its 'Stop Ocean Dumping' Internet site. The new look site gives the Greenpeace account of the battle over Brent Spar ('Greenpeace is proud that it could stop the Brent Spar becoming a serious precedent for industrial behaviour') and includes ten key demands for the UN-designated International Year of the Ocean, one being that European governments should 'ban the dumping of oil platforms and other offshore installations at sea'. It also focuses attention on the action which governments in Europe should take at a conference in July 1998 in Lisbon to prevent marine pollution from toxic and radioactive wastes, as well as from the offshore oil and gas industry. The Web can communicate campaign developments in the quickest way possible to an international audience, while Internet users can tip off Greenpeace on any suspected or proposed dumping plans in their country.

Cooperating with business. Since Brent Spar Greenpeace has shown remarkable willingness to cooperate with the business community. It is now in regular and often friendly contact with the oil industry; the tone

of Greenpeace public comment is often conciliatory, rather than confrontational. In October 1997, it organised a Greenpeace business
conference, aimed at 'pursuing solutions through strategic business
alliances', with the group chief executive officer of BP invited to give
the leading address. Is this the start of a new era of cooperation?
Perhaps most significantly, there are signs that the government is being
left out of consultation exercises. Lord Melchett states, 'People at the
top of a company like BP are thinking faster and more intelligently than
anyone I have come across in government . . . Business has more power
than the politicians now. With deregulation and free trade, politicians
have ceded some of the ground they occupied to business, and they are
starting to look at things in the way that governments should' (*Sunday
Telegraph*, 30.11.97). As a balance to such 'cosying up' Greenpeace has
tried to combine cooperation with the more traditional high profile
activism, as its Atlantic Frontier campaign showed. Melchett describes
this as a 'double-fisted' approach: talks are seen as thoroughly compati-
ble with direct action tactics.

The Greenpeace effect on industry

Shell and BP. The Greenpeace Brent Spar campaign had a dramatic
impact on business attitudes towards the environment. Commentators
have observed how Shell, a company that was bureaucratic, slow to
respond and unwilling to engage in open consultation, has been
transformed. Keen to seek public endorsement for its plans, Shell
concluded that it needed to find a way of working with Greenpeace
rather than publicly opposing it. Greenpeace was one of the representative bodies involved in the review of (over 200) options available for
disposing of the Brent Spar, aimed at identifying the Best Practicable
Environmental Option, participating fully in 'Seminars for Brent Spar
Dialogue'. Heinz Rotherman, managing director of Shell Expro, said
that the dialogue exercise was not a decision-making forum but a
genuine attempt to sound out views and incorporate these into
decisions. Shell's move towards transparency is a very significant change
from past decision-making practices.

Shell has acknowledged the need for action to prevent changes to the
world's climate, following in the footsteps of British Petroleum. Many
of its public comments involve an apparent acceptance of the Greenpeace position. During the Best Practicable Environmental Option
consultation exercise Chris Fay, chairman and chief executive of Shell
UK, remarked, 'We should remember the debt we owe to environmentalists for awakening society to the environmental challenges we
face. They remain a vital strand of opinion in our environmental
considerations.' It has also taken practical steps: Royal Dutch/Shell lead
the way in research into renewable energy sources. The company has
reorganised itself around a new five-business structure, establishing a
new fifth core business—Shell International Renewables—to concen-

trate on development of renewable energy sources, in addition to its traditional business sectors exploration and production, oil products, chemicals, and gas and coal. In 1997, the company announced its intention to invest $500 million in renewable energy over the next five years, including solar and wind power, and in 1998 the company set up a Social Accountability Unit responsible for policy issues like the environment and dealing with oppressive regimes.

BP's response to the Greenpeace Atlantic Frontier campaign indicated that it had learned a number of lessons from the Brent Spar case. It handled the direct action protest of Greenpeace very carefully. Shell had been damaged by dramatic images of water jets directed at Greenpeace activists; BP allowed the protesters to board its rig undeterred. It appeared better prepared to counteract the actions of Greenpeace than Shell had been, suggesting that Greenpeace itself was a profitable organisation and could easily afford to cover losses suffered as a result of the protest. It challenged the legitimacy of Greenpeace's activities and attempted to portray it as the Goliath of environmental groups — wealthy, internally undemocratic and unaccountable. This improved ability to deal with Greenpeace has been combined with a reappraisal of its approach towards the environment. For example, BP has been instrumental in setting up mechanisms through which local communities and other interested parties can express concerns about environmental aspects of industry operations in the Atlantic Frontier area. Shell and BP have concluded that the public interprets industry silence as reluctant acceptance of the Greenpeace argument.

Winning public hearts and minds. A glance through oil industry journals indicates that 1997 was regarded as a watershed for the industry. The public comments of oil industry representatives suggest that ethical and environmental considerations are now an integral part of good business decisions. Responsibility for this lies mainly with market forces and the success of recent Greenpeace campaigns. Companies face the ever-present imperative of operating more efficiently in the global market-place. The rational choice economist's analysis is that individual firms will not take action 'if society does not hold them accountable', in other words, if they are not compelled to do so. This is the classic problem of collective action. However, the meaning of good business is changing in the oil industry. There is evidence of movement from conventional economic calculations of short-term outputs and inputs to a considera-tion of potential public reaction — even if public reaction/disapproval is unlikely, Brent Spar has taught them that the possibility must be recognised. Two writers refer to a 'philosophy of industrial greening' which is seen as 'a matter of good business, good public relations, and good corporate citizenship'.[10]

Following Brent Spar, the oil industry was faced with what it saw as a crisis in public confidence. A MORI poll, commissioned by the industry, revealed a decline in public approval over the last twenty years, from over 70% approval to only 32%. James May—director-general of the oil industry lobby group the UK Offshore Operators Association—has conceded that companies are viewed as 'arrogant, profit-oriented multinationals, secretive, too cosy with government and not to be trusted', arguing that an image change is essential for the industry. Some of those active in the oil industry may still feel that deep sea disposal of oil equipment is a viable option, based on good science. However, the industry has been forced to admit that there is rarely a black and white scientific answer and that industry and environmentalists are not on a level playing field. The public are more likely to find 'neutral' views of the environmentalists persuasive than 'biased' industry sources. The industry now recognises that public scepticism about the motivations of oil companies is a problem and that handling of environment related issues is important; it recognises that image and emotion play a vital role and it is seeking to use all the communication tools available to get its message across.

The industry argues that oil structures differ—they do not have the same range of options—therefore, a case by case approach is fully justified. Accordingly public relations campaigns have involved attempts to persuade the public that deep-sea disposal is not environmentally dangerous and wasteful. The Offshore Operators Association uses the term 'extending public confidence' to describe a process which involves education of the public. While resisting regulatory initiatives, it is keen to publicise its environmental successes, from the publication of annual reports documenting progress to advertisements in newspapers and magazines. This might also involve an outside public relations firm to deal with difficult cases or events; the Association hired a PR firm following the events of the Brent Spar. The public's reaction to environmental matters is unpredictable. Concern for the environment competes with other issue priorities in the minds of the public. However, it is clear that potential public reaction is now seen as sufficient to merit action by oil companies. Bosso comments, 'Absent major disasters or crises, public concern for environmental protection does not translate automatically into support for specific policies. It transforms only into opportunities to transform attitudes into action'.[11] Greenpeace attempts to capitalise on these opportunities, while oil companies such as Shell and BP attempt to guard against this by anticipating Greenpeace campaigns and the public's response. Conscious of a long-term decline in public trust and confidence in business organisations, the industry has accepted that there is potential for consumer militancy—green or ethical consumerism. The accepted position now is that oil industry engineers and scientists must challenge Greenpeace by being proactive and ready to communicate ideas in the international public arena through the media. If they fail in this task, 'Public approval will not be fully measurable but disapproval will have immediate and major financial impact'.[12]

Are the recent activities of oil companies cosmetic attempts to pacify environmentalists' demands, designed to ultimately destroy Greenpeace, or have they been convinced by the environmentalist argument? It would be naive to argue the latter, but the language and actions of companies like BP and Shell suggest more of a philosophical commitment to a moderate form of corporate environmentalism, whether this is due to the fear of consumer backlash or a more fundamental commitment. For sure, the oil industry is engaged in a process of 'greenwashing' which is an attempt to change public image that may be genuinely motivated or not and involves emphasising the positive environmental aspects of an industry's activities. Such a strategy has attached risks. The first problem it leaves itself open to is the charge of hypocrisy, the second is that the industry faces division over the issue of climate change. Greenpeace is now able to charge oil industrialists with hypocrisy as its new rhetoric is not matched by continuing efforts to search for more oil. Furthermore, as some companies move from denial of the climate change problem to reluctant acceptance, gaps are appearing in their arguments and in their ranks. For example, while Shell is beginning to recognise the dilemmas behind oil production, Esso denies climate change is happening.

There can be little doubt that the oil industry in Britain has been influenced by recent Greenpeace campaigns. It has accepted that Greenpeace can be a serious threat to opportunities because it plays on the public's negative perceptions of industry. It has given up fighting the particular battle of the Brent Spar, although it remains genuinely convinced of the advantages of deep sea disposal. While it doesn't accept that the policy was wrong, it does accept that its communication approach was wrong and needs to be improved. To this end, the industry has developed a more sophisticated approach to communication and public relations. It has recognised that it needs the trust and confidence of stakeholders, employees, partners, customers and communities, and that it must offer solutions as perceived by society. Industrialists are now attempting to explain themselves through open dialogue with NGOs, concerned interest groups and the public at large. In the process, they have gone a long way towards accepting that neither side is totally wrong or right. George Watkins—UK chairman of Conoco—provided an example of how far the industry has moved towards the Greenpeace position in a speech in London in September 1997: 'I have a great deal of respect for Greenpeace and what they stand for . . . they are not always right and they are not always wrong . . . reducing carbon dioxide emissions and developing alternatives is the right long-term goal that we should all be working towards.'

Problems faced by Greenpeace

The Brent Spar episode led to the suggestion that Greenpeace had perfected the protest formula. It appeared that pushing the right media buttons allowed it to secure publicity and support for its cause. However, as Grant Jordan notes, the Brent Spar was probably more about a chance pattern of (international) events—a set of one-off circumstances—than strategy perfection. This has raised a number of problems for Greenpeace in the period following the Brent Spar.

Since then, Greenpeace has been in regular consultation with the oil industry and European governments, while continuing to manipulate protest through direct action activities. Consultation brings with it the pressure to play by the rules, which, in turn, can threaten to 'deradical-ise' group demands. Radical, grassroots-oriented environmentalists would argue that this will inevitably compromise the Greenpeace position. It may also appear that the environment has been successfully placed at the heart of the policy agenda—that Greenpeace has achieved its objectives. In that case, one might have expected Greenpeace supporters to have drifted away, satisfied that it had won the battle. However, membership in Britain stayed relatively steady through the 1990s at around 300,000.

Conversely, Greenpeace has been criticised for its high-profile cam-paigns. A view has been developed that these are more about institu-tional maintenance of Greenpeace, and that they may even be detrimental to liberal democracy.[13] Following the Brent Spar, Hugo Young commented, 'One vast oil company and several democratic leaders, accustomed to agreeing and deciding, have been intimidated into reversing themselves by a single pressure group' (*Guardian*, 22.6.95). The *Daily Telegraph* and *Sunday Telegraph* pressed the theme that the input of Greenpeace was suspect in a democracy because it was not only interested in the public good but its own good: 'Pressure groups are an important part of the Western democratic system. But with their power to raise public awareness comes responsibility. The suspicion remains that Greenpeace chose not to campaign about indus-trial fishing because it might have challenged the prejudices of its angst-ridden supporters in Holland, Germany and Denmark. And that could have lead to a reduction in donations. One should always remember that the primary objective of a modern pressure group is its own perpetuation' (*Daily Telegraph*, 12.6.95).

According to this view, Greenpeace income depends on the public thinking that it is getting something for its money. The problem with quiet influence lies in persuading financial supporters that they are making an impact. Even an unsuccessful stunt has more impact than successful insider negotiation. From this perspective, the Atlantic Fron-tier campaign differs from the Brent Spar campaign in a number of important respects. Its scale is much more ambitious than the issue-specific, and company-specific, Brent Spar case. The effects of global warming are much less visible than the effects of deep-sea disposal of an oil structure. Greenpeace was able to project an image of the Brent Spar to the public in a way that is much more difficult to achieve with climate change. It needs a direct link between actions and their outcomes, including policy changes. For organisational maintenance, its supporters need to be persuaded that Greenpeace can make a difference.

However, the success of campaigns is sometimes impossible to measure. When Greenpeace focuses on global issues, such as climate change, the result of campaigns are difficult to identify. This may be interpreted as the 'coming of age' of an environmental pressure group, when it can focus on things that really matter, but such things are difficult to communicate through the short-term mass media. Issue particularity and demonstrating the link between cause and effect is important: 'The quality of particularity is important because it assists public and political identification of the nature of an issue, the situation out of which it arises, the causes and the effects, the identity of the activities and the groups in the community which are involved with the issue'.[14] Since Brent Spar, Greenpeace has chosen to focus on complex global issues which are difficult to explain and, more importantly, it is difficult to apportion blame for them; nor do they tug at the heart strings of the public.

A related problem is that recent campaigns do not involve clear suggestions to the public about what they can do to support Greenpeace. In the case of the Brent Spar, its recommendation was a boycott of Shell. However, recent campaigns against oil exploration and extraction have assumed a different relationship between the group and the public. Greenpeace says that to reduce the emissions that cause climate change, society needs to give up reliance on fossil fuels. If this is to occur, one must first stop the expansion of fossil fuels. More emphasis is placed on the producer than the consumer. Greenpeace protest is often viewed as a form of public protest, but is this now the case? Greenpeace seems to protest on behalf of the public, rather than asking the public to become directly involved (beyond providing necessary financial support). The Brent Spar was an exception to this rule. The most sceptical interpretation of the relationship between Greenpeace and the public is that it manipulates public opinion. According to this perspective, the public might be viewed as the tools of a single-issue pressure group, rather than democratic participants.

The public as jury

Traditional approaches to agenda setting and issue definition have defined political action as the actions of government. However, what this case study reveals is that it is not always the actions/reactions of government that are most important. What is perhaps most interesting about developments since Brent Spar is that government's role can be seen to have been restricted. Greenpeace developed the status of 'principle definer' of the decommissioning issue, and in the period following the Brent Spar the response of the oil industry was crucial, rather than that of the government. This has been a story of the relationships between groups representing different interests and competition between these groups for public sympathy.

The style and venue of conflict resolution between the participants in this study is relevant. Both Greenpeace and the oil companies have adopted a conciliatory approach, and the primary focus/venue of their activities has been the international public arena, rather than the British government, Parliament or civil service. Greenpeace was able to transfer decision-making about decommissioning from the British policy community to the more open international issue network. However, the case in question clearly indicates that the globalisation of politics — the importance of global consumerism and the fact that territorial boundaries of states are becoming less clearly defined — means that policy process models are becoming more difficult to apply and that we increasingly need to add categories of exception to these models.

The debate is now centred on the responsibility of special interests. The emphasis placed on the international public arena as a negotiating venue raises the possibility of a different democratic model. Consumer behaviour may be regarded as one form of democratic expression, so is this an example of global consumer democracy? The scientific 'facts' of the debate between Greenpeace and the oil industry have become less and less important; the public perception has become paramount. The oil industry has acknowledged the importance of democratic legitimacy — of gaining the public's trust: unfortunately for the industry people still trust environmental groups more than politicians or industry.

Nevertheless, we should not over-estimate the level of public protest. In 1995 Greenpeace successfully mobilised sections of the public in Europe against the behaviour of a multi-national oil company, but its activities since have been conducted on behalf of the public, not with their direct involvement. Some oil companies meanwhile have modified their language and behaviour on the basis of potential public reaction. The sleeping giant of the oil industry has woken up to the possibility that consumers can from time to time pass ethical judgements on the behaviour of multi-nationals, and Greenpeace can provide a channel through which the public are mobilised — it can be an agent of change.

As the events of the last few years indicate, the search for agreement is exceptionally difficult when the parties involved have fundamentally different demands, priorities and values. The competition between the oil companies and environmental groups involves a battle over fundamental values which takes place in a cultural arena and involves the public, media and science. Moreover, it has been shown that conflict cannot be resolved solely on the basis of either facts or expertise. It is too early to argue, and very unlikely, that there has been an integration of environmental values into national and/or international policy making, but without doubt there has been a change in the behaviour of the actors involved.

1   L. Dickson, and A. McCulloch, 'Shell, the Brent Spar and Greenpeace: A Doomed Tryst', *Environmental Politics*, 1996/1; G. Jordan and L. Bennie, 'Political Aspects of Decommissioning' in D.G. Gorman and J. Neilson (eds), *Decommissioning Offshore Structures* (Springer, 1997).

2   R. Worcester, 'Business and the Environment: The Predictable Shock of Brent Spar', MORI Research Paper, 1995, p. 24.

3   D. Upsall and R. Worcester, 'You Can't Sink a Rainbow', MORI Research Paper, 1995, pp. 16–17.

4   D. Rucht, 'Greenpeace and Earth First! in Comparative Perspective' in W. Rudig, *Green Politics Three* (Edinburgh University Press, 1995), p. 71.

5   A. Anderson, *Media, Culture and the Environment* (UCL Press, 1997), p. 8.

6   R. Eyerman and A. Jamison, 'Environmental Knowledge as an Organisational Weapon: The Case of Greenpeace', *Social Science Information*, 1989.

7   F. Pearce, *Green Warriors: The People and the Politics Behind the Environmental Revolution* (Bodley Head, 1991).

8   R. Worcester, 'Not so Green as Cabbage Looking: Comparing Environmental Activism of the Public and of Journalists', MORI Research Paper, 19 May 1996, p. 25.

9   J. Blain, 'Green Action in the Courts', *Energy Day*, December 1997.

10 D. Press and D.A. Mazmanian, 'The Greening of Industry: Achievement and Potential' in N.J. Vig and M.E. Kraft (eds), *Environmental Policy in the 1990s* (Congressional Quarterly Press, 1997).

11 C.J. Bosso, 'Seizing Back the Day: The Challenge to Environmental Activism in the 1990s' in N.J. Vig and M.E. Kraft (eds), *Environmental Policy in the 1990s* (Congressional Quarterly Press, 1997), p. 54.

12 P.A. Meenan, 'Technical Aspects of Decommissioning Offshore Oil Structures' in D.G. Gorman and J. Neilson (eds), *Decommissioning Offshore Structures* (Springer, 1997), p. 50.

13 See G. Jordan and W. Maloney, *The Protest Business?* (Manchester University Press, 1997).

14 W. Solesbury, 'The Environmental Agenda: An illustration of how situations may become political issues and issues may demand responses from government: or how they may not', *Public Administration*, 1976, pp. 384–5.

Pesticides, Sheep Dips and Science

BY ALAN GREER

THE regulation of pesticides has been politically controversial and provided fertile ground for single-issue protest campaigns and pressure group activity throughout the industrialised world. Pesticides and veterinary medicines include a wide variety of biologically active and dangerous substances which are designed to control diseases in crops and animals. Concern about the hazards of pesticides in the UK goes back at least to the early postwar years, for although their use arguably has many benefits for society, including improved agricultural productivity and food quality, it also poses a potential threat to humans, animals and the environment generally.[1] The 1979 report by the Royal Commission on Environmental Pollution, for example, identified the widespread use of toxic chemicals as one of the most worrying developments of modern farming. In the 1960s, Rachel Carson's book *Silent Spring* provided a focus for public unease and much of the impetus for subsequent protests against pesticides containing DDT. More recently, although safer pesticides have been developed, protest campaigns have been waged against the use of products such as organophosphates.[2] The modern use of organophosphorous (OP) compounds in agriculture developed from the work of scientists in Germany in the 1930s and 1940s, work which more disturbingly contributed to the development of chemical weapons and nerve gases. Concern was already evident fifty years ago about the impact on wildlife but there has been increasing worry about the potential adverse effects on humans of low-level, long-term exposure. More recently, there has also been much speculation about a connection to 'gulf war syndrome' and to the suicide in 1997 of Gordon McMaster, the Labour MP, who himself linked his tiredness, depression and severe mood swings to overexposure to OP pesticides during his work as a gardener.

In its concern with dangerous chemical products such as OPs, the role of the state is essentially regulatory. A wide range of interests are involved in a complex administrative system — industrial manufacturers, workers, farmers, environmentalists, and domestic users. The Ministry of Agriculture is the lead department for the approval and supply of agricultural pesticides and veterinary medicines, working through its executive agencies. The Health and Safety Executive, on the other hand, an agency of the Department of Education and Employment, oversees the reporting of incidents, and the use of hazardous substances in the workplace; compliance with regulations rests primarily with its agricultural inspectors. Other features of the British administrative style are also found here—a preference for voluntary arrangements (although a statutory scheme for pesticides was introduced in the mid-1980s), reluctance for state agencies to be pro-active in extending controls, and the incremental development of legislation.

There are two parallel administrative structures for pesticides and veterinary medicines. OP compounds are used in a wide range of agricultural products, but sheep dips are regulated as veterinary medicines rather than pesticides because the matter is classed as one of animal health. This has some important implications: while the pesticides approval process is relatively open, that for veterinary medicines is subject to the stricter confidentiality provisions of the Medicines Act. Overall policy on OP sheep dips lies with the Ministry of Agriculture in conjunction with the Health departments, acting on the advice of an independent Veterinary Products Committee of scientific experts such as vets, pharmacists and toxicologists. The main administrative institution is the Veterinary Medicines Directorate, now an executive agency. It has a general duty to ensure the safety, quality and efficacy of veterinary medicines in the UK, safeguarding the health and safety of farmers, workers, consumers and the environment generally as well as that of animals. It is responsible for the licensing of products, administering the suspected adverse reactions surveillance scheme (both important in the sheep dip debate), the regulation of manufacturing premises and monitoring residues in meat. It provides policy advice to Agriculture ministers after consultation with other agencies, departments, the veterinary profession, the pharmaceutical and livestock industries, and consumer and other organisations. EU institutions are also now relevant.

Although OP compounds are found in everyday products such as wood preservatives and flea collars, they are predominantly used in agriculture where high levels of productivity and the economic prosperity of farmers has become increasingly dependent on extensive chemical and fertiliser use. Their use to counteract problems such as sheep scab has become increasingly controversial and given rise to a persistent protest campaign for tighter regulation. For example, a 1995 enquiry by the House of Commons Agriculture Committee, ostensibly focused on the organisation of government agencies for pesticides and veterinary medicines, prompted numerous submissions on the issue. The first OP sheep dip had been authorised in 1972 and sales peaked in 1984: OP products accounted for some 95% of the entire sheep dip market before 1993/4, falling to 60% then and continuing to decrease. The first suspected adverse human reaction was reported in 1985, and ten years later the Veterinary Medicines Directorate had received some 570 such reports involving 656 individuals. The Ministry of Agriculture attributed a fall in the number of reports of adverse reactions between 1993 and 1995 to tighter controls on the use of OP products. However, the number of suspected cases had increased in the four years before 1993 and this could be consistent with long-term effects, with the subsequent reduction in reports due to less use of OPs following adverse publicity. On the other hand, the government has argued that because the use of OPs has been falling steadily, the sudden increase in reports of suspected adverse reactions in the early 1990s is explained by much greater awareness of the issue.

Despite a persistent and vigorous campaign against the use of OP sheep dips, supported to some extent by established bodies such as the House of Commons Agriculture Committee, the government has resisted all calls to limit the availability of OP products. Precautions on the use of OP sheep dips have become increasingly stringent however; for example, all those involved in sheep dipping with OPs are now required to hold a certificate of competence, introduced because many farmers were not using adequate protective equipment. A four-year research programme was also announced by the Ministry of Agriculture in 1995, after a report by the Institute of Occupational Health suggested that OPs could harm the human nervous system. Nonetheless, the constant official position, based on the advice of the Veterinary Products Committee, has been that there is insufficient scientific evidence to justify a ban on OPs which are perfectly safe to use provided that the recommended precautions are taken. As the Minister of Agriculture told the Agriculture Committee in 1995, if evidence was forthcoming, the department would ban OP dips as it had banned other products in the past. This position has since been repeated. Moreover, although the Labour Party was critical whilst in opposition, it has also acknowledged that there are difficulties in introducing a ban. The issue is thus generally regarded as one where the primary determinant of government action is technical and scientific evidence rather than ideology or public opinion.

OPs and public protest[3]

Essentially, the protest campaign has been directed at the use of a small number of sheep dip products containing OP chemicals. The first preference of many of those involved is for a total ban on the use of OP sheep dips, but fall-back positions include an immediate moratorium pending the outcome of a full public enquiry and, at the very least, much stricter regulation. The campaign has been persistent, regionalised and relatively low key, but has flared into general public consciousness on several occasions. Although the number of individuals who have reported health problems as a result of OP exposure is measured in hundreds rather than thousands, the issue arouses much wider concern amongst workers manufacturing the products, users such as farmers and gardeners, doctors and other health specialists, consumers worried about residues in meat, and those concerned more generally with the adverse environmental effects of chemical use.

At the core of the protest are those lobby and self-help groups organised to assist individuals who are convinced that their health has been directly affected by OPs. Most notable in this respect are the Organophosphates Information Network (a successor to the South West Environmental Protection Agency which was set up after the Camelford incident), the National Action Group and the Pesticides Exposure Group of Sufferers. The last, established in 1988 and based in Cambridge, has over 450 documented cases of health damage as a result of exposure to OP sheep dips, provides counselling for sufferers and publicises the issue. The National Action Group was set up in 1991 to press for recognition of the problem by a Devon farmer forced to quit the industry because of health problems associated with OP use. Also reflecting the geographic location of many of the reported cases, the Cornwall-based Organophosphates Information Network, an independent group, campaigns strongly, arranges meetings, counsels, acts as a focal point for over 600 sheep farmers who have suffered from chronic ill-health through OPs, and is an important information resource. It also acts as a political protest group, coordinating the input of a growing number of sympathetic scientists, lawyers, doctors and journalists. One recent development has been the formation of the OP Scientific Forum of independent scientists who work closely with the Network. There are also links with the various groups representing Gulf War veterans. The approach, therefore, combines voluntary action and protest with more conventional political tactics. Small demonstrations are occasionally mounted outside places to be visited by ministers but much emphasis is put on the collection of reliable case data and scientific evidence which can be presented to the relevant authorities.

For some commentators, this sort of approach, involving self-help, loosely organised local groups forming networks of interaction, and a concern with lifestyle, is linked to a new politics centred on protest campaigns and social movements rather than more traditional party and pressure politics.[4] In this interpretation, new forms of political mobilisation emerge alongside more conventional patterns. Moreover, social movements question several of the central tenets of advanced industrial society and established political processes. Some of this is clearly evident in the OP sheep dip issue where campaign groups such as Friends of the Earth use individual case histories in an attempt to ensure that OP sheep dips are banned but also to influence public consciousness and promote a cultural shift in attitudes. The protest is thus part of a wider challenge to what are regarded as the excesses of chemical-dependent modern industrial agriculture. Indeed, Friends of the Earth has a long history of campaigning against pesticides in this context. Organisations such as the Pesticides Trust, a science-based charity concerned with their health and environmental implications, also promote the development of safer alternatives and reduced use of chemical products. However, one important criticism voiced by groups such as the Soil Association, representing organic farmers who do not use OPs, is that the alternatives are generally much more expensive. Moreover, the costs imposed by the regulatory system prevents the development of more environmentally friendly products by small companies and result in a bias towards the large chemical companies committed to producing toxic pesticides with a large market potential.

Media exposure is vital and is perhaps the most important tactic of the anti-OP campaign. Much of the protest is directed at gaining official recognition that a problem exists, and coverage in the press and TV is central to achieving the cultural shift sought by many of the critics of OPs. Individual campaigners and 'dissident' scientists also play an important role, not least in drawing attention to the issue. People such as Mark Purdey (the Somerset farmer who describes himself as an environmental journalist and toxicologist and who was one of the first to draw attention to the issue in the mid-1980s) work assiduously through conventional and unconventional channels. The OP issue was initially contained within established political parameters, for example Purdey's submission to the Agriculture Committee's 1987 investigation into the effects of pesticides on human health and in the letters pages of *Farmers Weekly*, the journal of the National Farmers' Union. However, the issue has impinged more directly on wider public consciousness, demonstrated by significant media exposure in popular press, radio and television. Much press coverage of the effects of OPs followed the death of Gordon McMaster MP and has also surrounded the debate about Gulf-War syndrome. The issue has been raised in many factual TV and radio programmes; for example in 1997 a two-part *World in Action* documentary covered the wide range of OP use. Perhaps the clearest sign of the way in which the debate on the use of OPs in sheep dipping has seeped into the public realm has been its incorporation into episodes of fictional programmes such as *The Archers* and the TV series *Mortimer's Law*.

More conventional political channels have also been used. The issue has been aired frequently in Parliament, both in the investigations of the Agriculture Committee and in debates and questions. Sympathetic MPs such as Tom King and Jean Corston have voiced a concern which transcends party boundaries and which reflects its relevance to region and constituency. Anti-OP campaigners were also lucky in that the Countess of Mar, a sheep farmer who herself has suffered from OP exposure, was able to exploit her membership of the House of Lords to highlight the issue. As a vocal campaigner on Gulf War syndrome as well, her activities demonstrate the close connections between the two causes. There is evidence, however, that opponents of OP use are bypassing the established political processes and are putting increasing emphasis on action in the courts. Faced with government opposition (attributed by some to a desire to evade liability for damage to human health from compulsory sheep dipping), trade unions have taken up complaints from members about adverse health effects, pursuing cases of individual redress and at the same time participating in the wider campaign. As the Transport and General Workers Union (representing agricultural workers) has commented: 'We support a ban totally . . . We will be supporting full compensation claims for our members. This is a battle in the war against pesticides.' Whilst some regard judicial action as inappropriate because of the difficulty of identifying liability, negligence and causation, claims on behalf of members for compensation against employers are increasing. It is also likely that many cases have been settled out of court. In February 1998, for example, in what could herald a flood of similar compensation claims, a shepherd represented by Unison obtained an £80,000 out-of-court settlement from Lancashire County Council. This case also demonstrated a commonality of interest between the sheep dip critics and the groups representing Gulf War veterans which welcomed the settlement in the belief that it would strengthen their campaign for a full investigation into the use of chemicals and OPs during the conflict with Iraq.

The vested interests

For many critics of OP use the villains of the piece are those stuck on the treadmill of industrial agriculture—the Ministry of Agriculture, the chemical companies and the National Farmers' Union. Friends of the Earth argues, for example, that problems with products such as OP sheep dips have arisen 'largely because the power and influence of MAFF and the chemical companies has gone unchallenged for so long: it is only in the past few years . . . that grassroots and media pressure have forced a change.' Indeed, it is partly the difficulty of challenging such entrenched interests successfully which leads many of the campaigners against OP use to find alternative channels of expression. As the organisation representing many of those affected or at risk, it might be expected that the National Farmers' Union (NFU) would be at the forefront of the anti-OP campaign. In fact, it has experienced acute internal difficulties as grass-roots pressure and mounting other evidence have forced it to take the OP issue seriously. It sponsored a joint seminar with the British Medical Association in June 1995 at which its leadership was subjected to sustained criticism from the floor, and there was a groundswell of opinion in favour of a ban amongst those who attended. Much of the protest came from farmers in south western counties, where the NFU regional director was well known for his anti-OP views. A Somerset farmer said 'I am glad that the NFU have actually got off their backsides and got this meeting today but I wish they had listened before.' However, the dilemma for the NFU leadership is that many sheep farmers have suffered no ill-effects. An NFU representative described these critics as 'a silent majority who are not represented noisily in this room'.

So although many grass-roots members of the NFU have complained about OPs, the problem is that a majority have used such products without adverse effects and the leadership maintains support for a policy of industrial agriculture based on the continued use of chemicals. Its leadership declares confidence in the existing regulatory system. (Some critics attribute reluctance to act to its close links with the NFU Mutual insurance company and the payout costs if a definite link were established between OPs and ill-health.) Whilst the concerns about OP sheep dips are taken seriously, the NFU points out that the relevant compounds are licenced and very useful to farmers. If serious adverse effects are proved to result from their proper use, then they will be banned through the regulatory process, just as other dangerous substances have been withdrawn in the past. It therefore tries to reassure members, while providing regular advice on sheep dips to make farmers more aware of the symptoms of exposure and encouraging the use of protective clothing, and it promotes research into the effects of OP exposure as well as into safer alternatives. The result, according to Friends of the Earth, is that farmers have little confidence in their Union and 'have been forced to turn to voluntary bodies for the support and help they need to tackle their problems and find their way through the maze of laws and regulations'.

If the organisation representing most sheep farmers is somewhat ambivalent on the OP issue, no such uncertainties beset those who manufacture the products. For pesticides and veterinary medicines there are influential organisations representing manufacturing companies, the British Agrochemicals Association for the former and the National Office of Animal Health for the latter. They maintain that what is important is accurate information, a choice of products and the minimisation of risk rather than a total ban on OP sheep dips. Clearly any successful protest campaign against OPs would threaten the profits of the manufacturing companies concerned and they lobby strenuously against stricter controls, arguing that the costs of more regulation threatens the availability of a wide range of affordable animal medicines. In a mirror image of the Friends of the Earth critique, the manufacturers complain about the undue influence of the environmental lobby and of government departments or agencies such as those for the environment, health and safety at work. The National Office of Animal Health believes that the Ministry of Agriculture needs to defend its territory against encroachment from other departments trying enlarge their power and introducing costly legislation.

For some people, there is an unhealthily close relationship between the Ministry of Agriculture and the manufacturing companies, with the National Farmers' Union making up the unholy trinity. Fears of regulatory capture are heightened by the fact that much of the funding of the approvals and licensing work of the Veterinary Medicines Directorate comes from the pharmaceutical industry. There is unease, for example, about the location in the same agency of responsibility for the approval of veterinary medicines and the investigation of adverse health effects. Some argue that this makes the ministry reluctant to promote a reduction in chemical usage. Trade unions tend to argue that safety aspects of regulation should be given to the Health and Safety Executive to avoid potential conflicts of interest, together with more resources for enforcement. However, allegations of collusion with the ministry are disputed by the chemical companies, which describe the relationship between the industry and its regulators as 'tense rather than cosy'.

Public protest and professional opinion

Phrased in terms of the well-known pressure group typology, the anti-OP campaign is essentially 'outsider' in so far as the groups involved have found it difficult to get their voice heard in the corridors of power. For the OP Information Network it has been a long struggle to persuade ministers and civil servants of the seriousness of the issue, the official attitude being described as 'smiling indifference' and 'hitting a brick wall'. However, there is evidence of increasing access to government (including the Ministry of Agriculture) and of a greater willingness to listen to the concerns of the OP protesters, particularly since the election of the Labour government in 1997. Nonetheless, it is the 'insider' groups such as the organisations representing farmers and manufacturers which have had the ear of government and the established links with the Ministry of Agriculture. The result is that the protest campaign combines traditional lobbying techniques with alternative approaches such as the formation of self-help groups and attempts to use the media to change public attitudes. The OP Information Network provides journalists with reliable material on which to base stories.

Established political forms are also challenged by the anti-OP campaign in another important way. It is not simply a matter of using unconventional techniques but of calling into question the very procedures themselves through which official decisions are taken. Regulation of dangerous chemical products, such as those contained in pesticides and animal medicines, has always been fundamentally technocratic. Scientific research and expertise are of crucial importance in many areas of government policy. Dependence upon experts to interpret ambiguous, if not contradictory evidence, influences both the nature of the policy process and the manner in which problems are understood. 'Thus, scientific teams are inevitably drawn into the process of policy-making and the type of expertise that is called upon will be significant in giving lay policy-makers an understanding of the problem.'[5] As a result, the debate on OPs reflects a fundamental dispute about the role of government in complex technical areas, about the role of scientific research and advice, and about relative value of scientific knowledge and lay expertise. Government policy on OPs relies heavily on the experts: the advice of committees such as the Veterinary Products

Committee, is invariably accepted. In evidence to the Agriculture Committee in 1995, the Minister of Agriculture, William Waldegrave, stressed the need to make decisions on difficult technical issues like the effects of OPs on the best available scientific evidence and lamented the intrusion of populism into such matters. Moreover, where alternative research-based advice was offered, he said 'It is very unwise for a minister, in my view, to depart from the clear advice of his or her scientific advisers in these matters.'

This view seems to be supported by the NFU. Decisions about whether particular products should be banned or not are the responsibility of government, guided by advisory committees of independent experts: 'It is improper to ask an association of farmers whether they want a chemical banned or not. We do not have the expertise.' According to the National Office of Animal Health, ministers were being forced onto the defensive by pressure from an 'alliance of an unsympathetic media and radical pressure groups' and needed to recognise 'the real damage that is being done by their attempts to appease and even pre-empt criticism'. What is needed is 'a science based' licensing system, not the addition of 'ephemeral, politically correct criteria to the international standards of safety, quality and efficacy'.

Critics of the use of OPs, on the other hand, are much more questioning of the science-based approach. Whilst opponents of OP sheep dips have worked within the legitimate channels of politics to a certain extent, they also challenge the whole technocratic approach to the issue. This reflects the problematic nature of science in contested contemporary areas such as risk assessment and the nature of environmental hazards. They question first the 'burden of proof' argument. What is needed is a 'precautionary approach' which recognises the limits of scientific knowledge: users, workers, consumers and the environment, therefore, must be given the benefit of the doubt and dangerous products should only be approved when all reasonable concerns about their safety have been removed.

The second strand of the argument about scientific expertise, sometimes called the democratic critique, holds that 'the primary problem is the failure of the regulatory agencies to incorporate a full enough range of values into their decision making'.[6] This is allied to criticism of the cloak of secrecy which surrounds the British policy process and to the way in which the legalistic and technocratic nature of established procedures disadvantages public protest groups. The democratic response is more lay representation on scientific advisory committees and for a more open and accessible decision-making process. Studies in the USA show that a crucial feature of the 'new politics of pollution' is the break down of older specialist policy communities composed of a limited number of producer representatives, politicians and bureaucrats, and the incorporation of new groups and interests, including consumers and environmentalists.[7]

Resources are also crucial. Friends of the Earth has a reputation for technical competence, the professionalism of its staff and its ability to put forward viable alternatives. Its overall strategy and claims to legitimacy rest 'on the technical rationality of its arguments rather than on its ideals. Accurate information is seen as the most important prerequisite for effective action'.[8] Indeed, as its intellectual authority has increased, the organisation has put much less emphasis on unconventional tactics such as direct action, although a media-centred approach remains. In the OP campaign, the Friends of the Earth case was put comprehensively in the 1993 publication *Scab Wars*, which rehearsed the history of OP use, the effects on sufferers and the technical arguments, then called for the complete withdrawal of OP sheep dips. It has been argued that one of the reasons for increasing openness of policy communities on environmental issues is that organisations such as Friends of the Earth have been able to 'demonstrate technical competence, both in the way that they were able to challenge the premisses of policy and in the way that they were able to exploit the political opportunity structures that were open to them'.[9]

Although the voice of environmental and public health groups and of consumer interests has become increasingly heard in the UK, the policy community on relatively invisible issues such as veterinary medicines remains closed and specialist. Besides demonstrating expertise, therefore, it is vital for opponents of OPs to open out and democratise the debate, not least because the well-resourced manufacturing interests are able to control the research agenda within the narrow confines of established technocratic structures. This situation has been exacerbated by the decrease in state funding which means that research expenditure is increasingly met by the chemical industry itself. The dominance of the research agenda by manufacturers often means that it 'may well not pose the questions, let alone provide the answers to important community, consumer and user concerns about pesticide safety that the rest of us wish to have addressed'.[10] As the Farm and Food Society comments, for example, 'independence, and impartiality, hitherto the cornerstone of scientific debate, can no longer be taken for granted. What is and is not published, is to a large extent dictated or influenced by companies financing research'.

It is in this context that protest movements and campaigns challenge conventional political structures which confine the debate to a handful of powerful interests and scientific experts. Here the case of OP sheep dips links to wider debates about the risk society and the tensions between experts and lay knowledges.[11] There is a view that risk society is characterised by the politicisation of science and a situation in which experts 'are relativised or dethroned by counterexperts. Politicians encounter the resistance of citizens' initiatives, industrial management that of consumer organisations. Bureaucracies are criticised by self-help groups'.[12] For others, the problem is the failure of the mainstream scientific community to take account of lay specialisms, expertise and concerns: as a result the 'healthy scepticism and common sense of some members of the public and non-expert groups now appear to be closer to the truth on pesticides than the views of certain groups in the scientific and medical community'.[13] The public authorities tend to be dismissive of such lay or unofficial expertise. For example, Mark Purdey's memorandum to the Agriculture Committee's 1987 investigation was disparaged by the ministry as 'unsupported', 'flawed', 'questionable interpretation' and 'lacking both objectivity and accuracy'. Going further, established notions of scientific knowledge and certainty have been questioned, not just because of 'scientific' disagreements but because 'Vernacular, informal knowledge which lay people may well have about the validity of expert assumptions about real world conditions is usually systematically under-recognised.'[14]

For many critics, therefore, it is the conventional technocratic approach itself which has contributed to the emergence of serious problems such as the adverse health effects of exposure to OP products. Indeed, in a 1987 report the Commons Agriculture Committee drew unfavourable comparisons between the British regulatory system and those in the USA and Canada, characterised by greater openness and the incorporation of a wider range of interests. As early as 1981 the Health and Safety Commission drew attention to the need to involve representatives of users, workers and the community generally in the risk evaluation process alongside the scientific experts. The Transport and General Workers Union has campaigned for formal and effective representation for those with experience of problems in the field including worker and consumer representatives, environmentalists and developmental bodies. Even the National Office of Animal Health has argued for outside observer seats on expert committees in order to allay suspicions about regulatory capture and give reassurance about the operation of the system.

Conclusions

The recent debate over the use of organophosphates highlights a number of themes in the general area of protest campaigns. Such campaigns do not necessarily mobilise large numbers of individuals and can just as easily be small-scale and localised. Exposure to OPs has directly affected hundreds of individuals and there is a clear regional character to the incidence of suspected cases, with most concern in the south west of England. Another characteristic is the low party-political salience of the issue. Concern about the potential health problems arising from OP use links MPs of all parties. In this respect, the rural and regionalised nature of the OP campaign is more important than ideology or party allegiance. Partly this is a consequence of the regulatory nature of the issue but, more importantly, also of its high technocratic content. Media exposure is especially vital to those groups striving to highlight the nature of the problem, especially where the public authorities are reluctant to recognise its scale or even existence. Obtaining cover in the popular press and broadcast media is linked to the desire to effect a cultural change amongst the public generally, as well as the attempt to secure a specific political objective. The media also report court cases; indeed, increasing recourse to the judicial system may be seen as another way in which traditional political processes are increasingly by-passed. Bodies at the core of the campaign, such as the Organophosphates Information Network, the National Action Group and the Pesticides Exposure Group of Sufferers are also of a markedly different nature from the more institutionalised pressure groups. These are more like loosely organised voluntary action groups, with no real formal structure or leadership. In addition, although they are concerned to gain official recognition of the problem of OPs and stricter regulation, they also act as conduits for self-help, counselling and the dissemination of information. This core is supported by a number of more established groups, ranging from those concerned with the environment such as Friends of the Earth to trade unions primarily concerned with the health of their members. Importantly, many of these anti-OP protest groups share a belief that they are largely excluded from the established political channels which are dominated by their 'opponents', namely those with a vested interest in the maintenance of chemical-dependent agriculture such as the Ministry of Agriculture, the manufacturers and the National Farmers' Union. This perception of 'outsider' status is important in understanding the tactics adopted by the groups, particularly the focus on media attention. However the challenge to conventional political forms also occurs in the way organisations such as Friends of the Earth question the very nature of the regulatory system. Long-established practices and procedures involving the incorporation of scientific expertise are confronted from the perspective of democratic or representative politics. In a risk society it is no longer acceptable for issues such as the safety of OPs to be decided within a technocratic structure. A wider range of interests, covering users, manufacturers, consumers, environmentalists and citizens generally, need to be incorporated into the decision-making process, buttressed by greater openness and freedom of information. This is what is particularly important about protest campaigns such as those on OPs—they not only draw upon a variety of conventional and more unconventional tactics in order to change government policy on specific issues, but they also embody a fundamental challenge to some central elements of the established political and policy system in Britain.

1   See e.g., N.W. Moore, *The Bird of Time: The Science and Politics of Nature Conservation* (Cambridge University Press, 1987).

2   See R. Norton-Taylor, *Whose Land is it Anyway?* (Turnstone Press, 1982), p. 158; S. Jasanoff, *The*

Fifth Branch: Science Advisers as Policymakers (Harvard University Press, 1990); A. Irwin, *Citizen Science: A Study of People, Expertise and Sustainable Development* (Routledge, 1995).

3   This account draws largely on the views of pressure groups and individuals provided in the House of Commons Agriculture Committee report on the Pesticides Safety Directorate and Veterinary Medicines Directorate (1994–95, HC 391); the report of the NFU seminar on Organophosphate Sheep Dips and Human Health (2 June 1995); the British Medical Association, *Pesticides, Chemicals and Health* (Edward Arnold, 1992); Friends of the Earth, *Scab Wars: The Impacts of Organophosphate Sheep Dips on Farmers, Livestock and the Environment* (1993).

4   See e.g., P. Byrne, *Social Movements in Britain* (Routledge, 1997).

5   A. Weale, *The New Politics of Pollution* (Manchester University Press, 1992), pp. 7–8.

6   Jasanoff, op. cit., p. 16.

7   C. Bosso, 'Transforming Adversaries into Collaborators: Interest Groups and the Regulation of Chemical Pesticides', *Policy Sciences*, 1988; A. Nownes, 'Interest Groups and the Regulation of Pesticides: Congress, Coalitions and Closure', *Policy Sciences*, 1991.

8   P. Lowe and J. Goyder, *Environmental Groups in Politics* (George Allen & Unwin, 1983), p. 127; see also Byrne, op. cit.

9   Weale, op. cit., p. 29.

10 A. Watterson, 'Pesticide Health and Safety Policy in the UK: A Flawed and Limited Approach?', *Journal of Public Health Policy*, winter 1990, p. 495.

11 See Jasanoff, op. cit.; Irwin op. cit.; S. Lash, B. Szerszynski and B. Wynne (eds), *Risk, Environment and Modernity: Towards a New Ecology* (Sage, 1996).

12 U. Beck, 'Risk Society and the Provident State' in Lash, Szerszynski and Wynne (1996), pp. 32–5.

13 Watterson, op. cit., pp. 497–8.

14 B. Wynne, 'May the Sheep Safely Graze? A Reflexive View of the Expert-Lay Knowledge Divide' in Lash, Szerszynski and Wynne, op. cit., p. 59; see also J. Clark and P. Lowe, 'Cleaning Up Agriculture: Environment, Technology and Social Science', *Sociologia Ruralis*, 1992.

Nuclear Weapons and CND

BY PAUL BYRNE

TALKING recently with one of the full-time staff at the Campaign for Nuclear Disarmament, I ventured the view that CND was no longer relevant to a discussion of protest in contemporary Britain. After all, a campaign which arguably dominated media coverage of 'protest' in the 1980s has virtually disappeared from the public eye. There was a sharp intake of breath before the incredulous response — but how can you say that? CND is 'the mother of all protest groups'. This may be so; as we shall see, CND can legitimately claim to be the precursor of organised, long-term protest campaigns in postwar Britain. The nagging doubt remains, however, that it may have moved on from the status of dynamic matriarch to one of respectable dowager. The issue of nuclear weapons, high on the agenda of the 1983 general election and Labour Party politics throughout much of that decade, has reverted to being an item of cross-party consensus, hardly figuring at all as a salient issue in the eyes of voters in the last two elections. The Cold War has ended, and there has been a significant reduction in the world's nuclear arsenals. The apparent lack of interest in CND is such that it has not held a mass demonstration for over ten years now, when at its height in 1982 its demonstrations could attract some 400,000 people onto the streets. Its membership is ageing and more likely to write to an MP than live up a tree or in a bender outside a military base. Perhaps most strikingly, a Campaign which once saw its commitment to the aim of unilateral action as immutable and non-negotiable now campaigns for a multilateral approach to the process of ridding the world of weapons of mass destruction.

Forty years of protest

Before we dismiss CND as an interesting historical relic, we should bear in mind that it has been here before. Forty years old this year, CND is now in its fourth phase of existence. It enjoyed truly national prominence between 1958 and 1963; was then virtually moribund until 1980; forced its way onto the political agenda once again between 1980 and 1987; and has dropped back again since that. It begs the question — is there the scope for a fifth phase? In a 'new' world order, and with a 'new' Labour government, is there any likelihood that such an 'old' campaign can once again rise from the ashes? In what follows, we try to establish what lays behind the ups and downs of CND and speculate on its future as a 'protest' campaign. Before this analysis, and given its low profile in recent years, it would be as well to remind ourselves of some the major developments in CND's history to date.

CND was formed in 1958, leading intellectual figures on the left in British politics joining with local groups of activists[1] who had started to campaign against nuclear testing the previous year. Its core demand was that Britain should renounce unconditionally the use or production of nuclear weapons and refuse to allow their use by others in its defence (hence the call, from 1960 on, that Britain withdraw from NATO unless the Alliance also renounced nuclear weapons). It has only ever concerned itself with weapons of mass destruction (i.e. nuclear, chemical and biological). Despite the fact that it has always attracted support from people who classify themselves as outright pacifists, it has never been a pure peace movement, in the sense of campaigning against 'conventional' weaponry. It questions the morality of a strategy for the defence of the realm which rests upon the threatened use of weapons of mass destruction, but has never endorsed the idea of the UK disbanding its conventional forces and adopting a wholly pacifist stance.

As far as tactics are concerned, CND has always used both conventional and unconventional methods of expressing its viewpoint. Some of its original leadership never envisaged the Campaign becoming a mass movement, assuming they could use their contacts within government, officialdom and academia to act like an insider group persuading decision-makers by reasoned argument alone. They were as surprised as anyone when there was an immediate ground swell of popular support, as people wished to make public their stance on the issue. In that sense, non-violent direct action (originally taking the form of demonstrations, marches and sit-down protests) was initially forced upon the leadership from below. Although such protest has since become a defining feature of its activities, the Campaign has throughout its life also sought to lobby decision-makers in the same kind of ways as any mainstream pressure group.

During its first phase of prominence, CND's prime target was Britain's independent deterrent and the testing programme its development required. By 1962, however, Britain and America had resumed their nuclear cooperation, and a pattern was established which would last until the 1990s. Britain had its 'own' nuclear forces (UK-manufactured warheads and submarines but missile systems bought from the Americans), and allowed the USA to base some of its weapons in the UK. Although the Campaign certainly objected to US nuclear bases in the UK, it concentrated upon the British deterrent because it was thought that, as one of only three nuclear powers in the world at the time, unilateral action by the UK could achieve a real impact around the world. Marches and demonstrations attracted up to 100,000 participants, and Labour's Annual Conference in 1960 adopted a unilateralist policy—though Labour's leader, Hugh Gaitskell, rejected the Conference decision and managed to have it overturned the following year. A movement which had seemingly spontaneously erupted, however, dwindled just as quickly in the mid-1960s. By the time protest against the Vietnam war took off in the late 1960s, CND had shrunk to a hard core of some four thousand supporters. What was left of the Campaign was split by the Vietnam issue, some arguing for a straight-forward anti-American, pro-North Vietnam stance, others that CND should concentrate upon 'ban the bomb'—campaigning against per-ceived American imperialism being best left to other groups and campaigns.

The Campaign remained in the doldrums until the end of the 1970s, with a membership of a few thousand, protest marches and events attracting no more than a few hundred. It was effectively kept alive by the support of two groups—Quakers (who saw in CND the closest thing to a national organisation reflecting their pacifist principles) and the then Communist Party of Great Britain (attracted by the anti-American, anti-NATO aspects of the Campaign's ideology). Everything changed in 1979, with the NATO decision to base new short-range nuclear missiles (Cruise and Pershing) in Western Europe and the election of the first Thatcher government which quickly announced it would be replacing Polaris with the much more powerful (and expen-sive) new Trident missile system. Cruise and Trident became the Campaign's main targets throughout the 1980s, and support mushroomed.

The rise was dramatic, membership rising from just over 4,000 members in 1979 to 9,000 in 1980, 20,000 in 1981, 50,000 in 1983 and peaking at c. 100,000 in 1984. As before, CND utilised both protest and more conventional tactics. Turnout at the annual demon-strations in the early 1980s regularly topped a quarter of a million. Peace Camps, most notably at Greenham Common and Molesworth, were established (although CND's involvement at Greenham was tangential). A wide variety of non-violent direct action took place, usually at military bases and nuclear weapons manufacturing/storage sites. Whilst some was organised by CND at a national level, the norm was for local initiatives, with national CND coordinating rather than directing. On a more conventional level, it continued to lobby within the parties and trade unions, and persuaded some 170 local authorities to declare themselves 'nuclear-free zones'.

As before, CND managed to persuade Labour to adopt its line. The 1980 and 1981 Annual Conferences passed resolutions favouring unilateral nuclear disarmament, but it was not until the 1982 Confer-ence that unilateralism was approved by the two-thirds majority neces-sary for it to become part of the party's official policy. Labour fought the 1983 election with a commitment to cancel Trident, refuse Cruise and remove all nuclear bases from Britain within five years—but also to remain in NATO and only get rid of Polaris through multilateral negotiation. The ambiguity was heightened by senior Labour figures such as Jim Callaghan and Denis Healey openly questioning the wisdom of unilateral action; Labour's leader, Michael Foot, was a long-standing CND supporter but was unable to unite his party around the unilateralist cause. Such internal disagreements, combined with a Conservative Party fresh from its Falklands victory, resulted in an election campaign in which defence and nuclear disarmament played an unusually important role — and Labour went down to its worst defeat since 1945.

Despite this, the Campaign maintained its momentum through to the 1987 election (with both Labour and the Liberal-SDP Alliance including the cancellation of Trident in their manifestos), but the writing was on the wall after 1983. The Conservatives had been largely successful in persuading the electorate that unilateralism was dangerously tantamount to a policy of a 'defenceless' UK. Even though many activists within Labour and the Alliance (especially the Liberals) remained loyal to the unilateralist cause, their leaderships spent much of the mid-1980s trying to drag their parties back to a multilateralist, pro-NATO, Atlanticist defence policy — a reversion to the norm of the 1960s and 1970s achieved by the end of the decade. The Gulf crisis of 1990–91 saw a brief resurgence of interest and support; but, as with Vietnam some twenty years earlier, whilst some within CND were happy to align with far left groups in what was seen as a struggle against American imperialism, others felt that the Campaign should concentrate on the nuclear issue and, for wider political reasons, were unhappy that CND should be seen as closely allied with 'extremists' of the far left. By the 1992 election, all the major parties had returned to the multilateralist fold, the Cold War had ended and unilateral nuclear disarmament was once again effectively off the national political agenda.

Protest and persuasion

Whatever its vicissitudes, the Campaign has always endorsed protest. Even when unilateralism appeared to be achieving the most impact on mainstream politicians, prompting calls from some within the Campaign to tone down protest in order to facilitate relations with the major parties, its activists insisted upon pursuing non-violent direct action alongside more conventional techniques of persuasion. The motivation and justification for non-violent direct action has always been twofold. On the one hand there have been those who argued that conventional tactics (lobbying, petitioning, etc.) would be ineffective and thus advocated non-violent direct action on the pragmatic grounds that it would serve to push the issue onto the agenda of public debate. On the other hand, there has also always been an element within CND which is wedded to non-violent direct action on principled or moral grounds.

The argument takes two forms, one based upon democracy, and the other on morality. The democratic argument focuses upon the very closed nature of nuclear policy-making. It is true that British Cabinets, let alone Parliament, have more often than not been kept uninformed about key decisions to acquire or update nuclear weapons. Given this apparent lack of democratic input to decision-making, CND argues that opposition also has to be outside the normal democratic channels. More important, however, is the moral dimension. Here, the argument is that the immorality of mass destruction is such as to justify reference to a higher order morality—i.e. one is not only entitled, but indeed compelled to break the law if that law is itself fundamentally unfair or immoral. As one might expect, many of those within the Campaign who adhered to this line of reasoning were actively religious, but it was not restricted to them—a survey of the membership in 1985 found that whilst only a quarter of respondents were practising members of a church or religious denomination, almost two-thirds cited the immorality of nuclear weapons as the 'most important' argument for unilateral nuclear disarmament.[2]

The commitment to non-violent direct action protest (which the 1985 survey revealed to be strongest among the most active supporters) was exemplified in the Campaign's relationship with what became the single best-known instance of such 'bearing witness' in the 1980s, the Greenham Common Women's Peace Camp. This was never a CND initiative; it emerged spontaneously from a mixed (male/female) march to the Cruise missile base at Greenham which quickly became a women-only protest. There were those among the leadership of CND at the time who not only objected to the idea of excluding men, but also questioned whether the media image of the camp (which often emphasised the lesbian/New Age hippie dimension, rather than the women's analysis of nuclear weapons as the ultimate expression of inherent male violence) might deter support from the middle ground of the electorate. Such misgivings received short shrift from the membership, however, as Greenham women received rapturous receptions at the Campaign's annual conferences. Whilst the majority of CND's members were reluctant to indulge themselves in non-violent direct action other than large-scale demonstrations, there was clear and vociferous majority support for those who were perceived as being prepared to put themselves on the front-line of protest.

Having said that, there was also consistent support for more conventional campaigning. CND put considerable effort and resources into persuading both the general public and those closer to the seat of power. Numerous books and pamphlets were published, most notably the Campaign's monthly glossy magazine, Sanity, which had a circulation of some 40,000 in the 1980s. There was a research section at national headquarters, which analysed government policy (British government's obsession with official secrecy being such that much of the illuminating information came from researchers despatched to archives in the USA) and produced scientifically-based rebuttals of government thinking. CND encouraged supporters within different professions to form their own affiliated groups (e.g. Scientists against Nuclear Arms, the Medical Campaign against Nuclear Weapons) and utilised their expertise. On a party-political level, supporters within the main parties were similarly encouraged to form their own specialist sections, giving rise to Labour CND, Liberal CND, Trade Union CND and Green CND. From the mid-1980s on (and still a part of contemporary campaigning), CND also encouraged its supporters to mobilise within parliamentary constituencies, monitoring the stance of their MP on the nuclear issue and mounting coordinated lobbying during the run-up to elections.

CND compared

The mixture of conventional and unconventional tactics, persuasion and protest, is not uncommon. It may be hard to imagine Swampy earnestly lobbying his local MP, or animal rights activists breaking off from firebombing a research laboratory to spend months drafting highly technical submissions to parliamentary select committees. Among the longer-established, more formalised challenging groups, however — such as Friends of the Earth or Greenpeace — such a combination of approaches is also the norm. Similarly, the kind of people motivated to join or support CND fit the mould we have come to associate with movements involved in protest. Ideas originating in America in the 1950s and 1960s — that protest was a last resort, turned to only by those who did not have the economic, social, intellectual and interpersonal resources to participate in normal politics — have long since been disproved by empirical research. As is the case with the women's and environmental movements,[3] CND has always attracted a preponderance of middle-class, well-educated people, who are active in mainstream politics as well as protest. Despite the rise and fall of support over the years, all the surveys of its supporters from the 1960s and the 1980s reveal the same picture — approximately two-thirds coming from the educated middle-class and concentrated in public-sector occupations such as education and welfare.

If there are similarities between CND and other groups, there are also important differences — and it is in these differences that the reasons lie for not dismissing it as a movement which has had its day. I think these differences stem primarily from the nature of the issue which CND is addressing. For those who support the cause, nuclear disarmament is literally a matter of life or death. With the possible exception of the animal rights movements, other protest groups or movements stop short of engaging in arguments about when, if ever, it can be right to kill. This gives the campaign a unique moral resonance, arguably as valid today as it was forty years ago.

A complication, however, is that its aims are far-reaching and can only be achieved through action by the political authorities. Roads protesters can hope for victories on specific projects; environmentalists and feminists can look to promoting change in people's personal behaviour, as well as changes in public policy. For CND, given that it is not an outright pacifist organisation, there is no 'personal' dimension. Nuclear disarmament would have major implications for the whole of British defence and foreign policy, especially given the NATO dimension. Nor can it point to apparent policy failures, in the way that roads protesters, for example, can point to the failure of past transport policy to address congestion. If anything, reductions in nuclear arsenals owes more to NATO insistence upon maintaining an arms race which finally crippled the Warsaw Pact countries and ended the Cold War, than it does to critical argument and protest.

Finally, CND is much more open than most other protest groups to being influenced by external events, especially in the international arena, and technological developments. New missile systems, new types of warheads, the state of the superpower relationship—these have been clear stimuli in the past. Granted, other protests are often triggered by specific events, especially in the environmental field—but few, if any, are quite so dependent upon the state of world affairs. It was the testing of nuclear weapons by the USA and the Soviet Union, as well as by the UK, which inspired CND's creation. Arguably, subsequent developments (such as the resolution of the Cuban missile crisis in 1962, and the conclusion of a Partial Test Ban Treaty in 1963) did much to lessen the feeling of urgency that something had to be done about nuclear weapons if the world was not to self-destruct. Similarly, there can be little doubt that the main spur for revival in 1979–80 was the Thatcher/Reagan axis (with its rhetoric about the Soviet Union as an 'evil empire') and the NATO decision to site Cruise missiles in Europe. Likewise, it is clearly not coincidental that CND's second period of decline after 1987 coincides with the collapse of the Soviet Union, the end of the Cold War, the consequent removal of Cruise and other weapons (by the end of 1998 Trident will be the UK's only nuclear weapons system), and the Anglo-Russian agreement that neither country would target the other.

All of this places CND in a distinctive position in the panoply of British protest. If we adopt the resource mobilisation perspective, which seeks to explain the development of challenging groups in society in terms of their ability to mobilise 'conscience constituents' (people who do not stand to make any immediate personal gain from involvement), one can appreciate that CND has advantages which other protest movements do not. It can lay claim to the moral high ground—thou shalt not kill millions in one fell swoop arguably having greater clarity and urgency than even the environmentalists' plea to preserve the planet in the long term. It can legitimately claim that everyone is threatened by nuclear devastation. On the other hand, it also faces difficulties others do not. It cannot prove its case. It is possible to prove that greenhouse gases have a detrimental effect on the ozone layer, for example, but no one knows whether possession of nuclear weapons makes Britain secure or a certain target in the event of international conflict. If all CND wanted to do was enlist the support of hundreds of thousands of people, this would not be too problematic; the lack of hard causal evidence can be out-weighed by an appeal on moral grounds. However, popular support is necessary for CND, but not sufficient. If it is to achieve its aims, it must persuade government as well as the electorate.

CND *and the parties*

Given the configuration of British party politics, what this means in effect is that CND has an inextricable relationship with Labour. Whilst the Conservative Party postwar has never seriously contemplated a defence policy which did not rest on a nuclear deterrent and membership of NATO, Labour has always contained at least some prepared to question both tenets. Concern over nuclear weapons was expressed within the party before CND existed. Popular with the Labour left, unilateralism looked to be gaining some headway until Aneurin Bevan gave his famous conference speech in 1957 pleading with delegates not to send a future Labour Foreign Secretary 'naked into the international conference chamber'. It was the realisation that the party's leadership was not prepared to contemplate unilateralism that led directly to the formation of CND as an extra-parliamentary campaign.

Since then, CND has certainly worked to persuade the minor parties of its case. It always had some support among Liberal activists, although their influence has declined significantly with the influx of ex-SDP supporters (Labour's then shift to unilateralism being, together with Europe, one of the main reasons for the departure of the 'gang of four'). It has enjoyed considerable success with the nationalist parties of Scotland and Wales—to the point where, in 1998, every SNP and Plaid Cymru MP is claimed as a supporter. Until the advent of a much more proportional electoral system and/or fully-fledged independence for Scotland and Wales, however, Labour remains CND's only realistic hope of seeing its goals turned into reality.

On the face of it, although the present regime may not look too hopeful, CND can at least claim to have succeeded in converting Labour not once, but twice—even if the first conversion was short-lived and the second a significant factor in Labour's electoral disaster of 1983. The uncomfortable fact remains, however, that CND's influence within Labour is at its height when Labour is not only in opposition, but also in disarray. It has been said of CND in the fifties and sixties that it represented a symbol—a symbol not just of values which were at odds with those dominant in the political culture of the time, but also of fundamentalist left-wing credentials at a time when Labour was locked in internal combat over Clause Four.[4] The same could be argued of the early and mid-1980s. The right of the party was associated with the uninspiring record of the Wilson/Callaghan governments of 1974–79, and the left was convinced that the appropriate response to the rise of the New Right in the Conservative Party was to shift decisively to the left. As before, the cause of unilateralism was seized upon with enthusiasm by the left. This is not to argue it was entirely a cynical decision on the part of the left—many, after all, had been long-term supporters since the 1960s. It is to argue, however, that support for CND was a relatively low-cost option compared with other causes. Both environmentalism and feminism had their critics within Labour, not least from trade unionists concerned about the possible impact on the employment prospects of their members of equality in the workplace or a move to renewable energy sources. Nuclear disarmament had minimal consequences for employment (and, in any case, CND had a carefully worked-out strategy for converting jobs in nuclear weapons facilities to more peaceful purposes). It was an issue around which the left could unite with little difficulty.

CND today

What, then, are we to make of CND's present situation? CND has certainly changed during the 1990s. During 1991–92, it finally made the change that past leaders like Bruce Kent in the 1980s had been unable to achieve, the move from arguing for unilateralism, pure and simple, to advocating a multilateral approach. It now argues that Britain and all other nuclear weapons states should declare a policy of 'no first use', not develop any new weapons, and agree to base their existing weapons only on their own soil or in their own territorial waters. The policy on NATO has also changed, no longer calling for British withdrawal but against further expansion of membership. This should facilitate dialogue with New Labour, and, to some extent, this is happening. CND was invited to make a submission to Labour's current defence review and claims to have had a number of private meetings with senior Labour figures, though it seems unlikely that the government will endorse even the 'freeze' strategy CND now calls for.

It is easy to see how CND has made this shift. Its membership may have held at around the 40,000 mark, but it will freely admit that the bulk of this membership is largely passive. It also seems that very few are new members—CND estimates that approaching half its supporters are now aged over 60. The activists who insisted on retaining a commitment to both unilateralism and withdrawal from NATO in the 1980s have either changed their minds or moved on. CND would argue the former: with the end of the Cold War, there is simply more scope now for multilateral agreements, and that is why supporters are happy with the toning down of its demands. There is a counter-argument, however. After all, Britain still has nuclear weapons; convoys carrying them still regularly travel up and down the country; CND estimate that there are some 4,000 tons of military nuclear waste stored here. The threat of super-power conflict may have receded, but the potential for nuclear-related accidents remains. Yet the enthusiasm for decisive unilateral action has virtually disappeared; reasoned persuasion, rather than protest, is now CND's chosen modus operandi.

Latent protest?

It is my contention that protest could well return, but it is dependent upon two factors, one international and one domestic. The experience of the 1970s and 1980s suggests that the salience of nuclear disarmament relates to the climate of international affairs—in other words, there has to be a fear factor in operation. If the motivation for protest was simply British possession of nuclear weapons, protest would have continued. The evidence of the last two decades also suggests that suspicions that much of the protest was inspired more by anti-American (anti-imperialist) sentiments than pro-unilateralism are unfounded. Although Cruise aroused more interest than Trident in England, neither Vietnam nor the Gulf crises saw people flocking to CND as a mobilising force for critics of the US stance. If nationalism were the root cause of much anti-nuclear protest, one would also expect to see more interest being shown in Anglo-French nuclear co-operation (the 'Euro-bomb', as CND terms it) than there has been to date.

Having said that, one area where nationalism may well coincide with anti-nuclear sentiments is Scotland. The fact that the UK's only nuclear weapons are based in Scotland, that Trident has consistently been more unpopular with the Scottish electorate than anywhere else in the UK, and that all the present SNP MPs are claimed as supporters by CND, makes it likely that the issue will at least be raised in the Scottish parliament. The configuration of internal politics in Labour is also important. It has only been when the left is in open rebellion that unilateralism has been seized on by large numbers of Labour supporters. One might argue that the 'new world order' and New Labour mean that neither of these factors is present, or likely to be in the near future. My point, however, is that the potential for such a revival still exists. A nuclear accident in Britain would have much the same effect of making people nervous as the Cold War had. And while New Labour may be relatively disciplined at the moment, disillusion may set in as the government pursues its 'modernisation' of the welfare state and continues to curtail public expenditure. In such a situation the left may again cast around for an issue which symbolises their rejection of the prevailing consensus in British politics. Were that to happen, CND's claim to the moral high ground could once more spur and justify the kind of protest activity it has been so successful in mobilising over the last forty years.

---

1 The Emergency Committee for Direct Action against Nuclear War—usually referred to as the DAC; see F. Parkin, *Middle-Class Radicalism* (Manchester University Press, 1968); R. Taylor and C. Pritchard,

The Protest Makers (Pergamon, 1980); and P. Byrne, *The Campaign for Nuclear Disarmament* (Routledge, 1988) for accounts of CND's early years.

2   Survey of CND national membership, 1985 — see Byrne, op. cit., chapter 4.

3   P. Byrne, *Social Movements in Britain* (Routledge, 1997), ch. 5.

4   Parkin, op. cit.

Representing Women in Scotland

BY ALICE BROWN

'LABOUR'S plans to guarantee equal representation for women in the Scottish parliament and Welsh assembly have been thrown into doubt by a legal challenge from a leading councillor in Wales ... Plans for twinning constituencies, which would together pick a male and female candidate to contest both seats, were drawn up under pressure from women's lobbies in both Scotland and Wales' (*Observer*, 15.3.98). It could be argued that this quotation represents both good and bad news for women activists who have exerted political pressure to promote the policy of equal representation of women and men in the first elections for the new Parliament in Scotland and an Assembly for Wales. It is positive in the sense that it acknowledges the influence of women's agency in ensuring that representation is now a salient political issue, but negative because it reports potential legal challenges to the Labour Party's mechanism for achieving gender balance.

This study examines the way in which the tactics of gender have been employed to keep the issue of women's representation high on the political agenda in Scotland, both in the run-up to the 1997 general election and in the referendum campaign which followed. It charts the strategies used by political activists, the way in which they have operated both inside and outside the political parties, and assesses the success of their campaigns. Finally, it asks whether such mobilisation of women can be categorised as part of what has been described by some as a third wave of feminism.

At first sight, mobilisation around the issue of representation may not appear to fit into the category of protest politics, at least not in the same way as some of the other movements described in this volume. More-over, it may strike others as odd to relate this activity to a possible new wave of feminism, especially at a time when many commentators have questioned the relevance of that in the late 1990s or have asserted that the women's movement is in decline in Britain. It will be argued that the emphasis given to representation in political office and public arenas in Scotland is part of a wider, worldwide campaign by women to ensure that they have a greater say in the decisions that affect their everyday lives. Their 'protest' on this question may not take the form of other protest movements, but nevertheless it is possible to identify political strategies that give some support to the view that it would be premature indeed to write the epitaph of either feminism or the women's movement.

Background

Before looking specifically at the debate and campaign surrounding political representation in Scotland, it is necessary to situate this within the broader context of pressure for change at international, European and UK levels. Thus, whilst the constitutional question in Scotland has opened up real opportunities to advance the representation of women, it should be interpreted as part of a wider movement.

First, at international level the fourth United Nations World Conference on Women was held in Beijing in September 1995. Its aim was to review the advancement of women against the objectives agreed at the last world conference on women held in Nairobi ten years earlier. The UK government sent a written submission describing progress made in the UK in achieving equality since 1985, which included the views expressed by a number of non-governmental organisations including some Scottish agencies. Nevertheless, it was felt that this report did not capture the specific concerns of women in Scotland. As a result, the Scottish Women's Coordination Group organised a consultation with women throughout Scotland which formed the basis for a Scottish Report (the Group was formed after the 1992 election with representatives from different women' groups in Scotland as well as representatives from the Churches, the Scottish TUC, the Campaign for a Scottish Parliament, etc.). The key areas of concern highlighted there were summarised under three headings; poverty, violence, and participation in key decision-making arenas, including a Scottish Parliament. A separate report was submitted to the Beijing Conference by the Wales Assembly of Women.

The conference agreed a Global Platform for Action which set out strategies to be adopted by governments and other governmental and non-governmental agencies in twelve key areas — poverty, education, health, violence against women, armed conflict, women in the economy, women in decision-making, national machineries for the advancement of women, human rights, women and the media, women and the environment, and the girl child. Under women in decision-making, the declaration notes that improving women's social, economic and political status depends on the sharing of power between women and men at all levels, from household to government, and calls on governments to commit themselves to a goal of gender balance in governmental bodies, public administration and the judiciary. The fact that the UK government had been party to the agreement prompted the Women's National Commission and the Equal Opportunities Commission for Great Britain and Northern Ireland to draw up a National Agenda for Action with ten detailed policy papers, including their recommendations on women's participation in decision-making. The Women's National Commission and the Equal Opportunities Commission drew attention to their proposals during the general election campaign in 1997.[1]

Experience at the European level was also relevant. For example, campaigners often cited the low representation of women in the House of Commons compared to the high levels of participation evident in many other European countries, notably the Scandinavian countries. The European Fourth Action Programme on equality between women and men provided another forum for promoting the case for improving representation in decision-making bodies. Women's Forum Scotland used this opportunity to identify the views of the voluntary sector and submitted a report with key recommendations. Its 1995 Report called on the European Commission to establish a framework of rights and standards in relation to women and decision-making and to introduce a directive to ensure appropriate strategies throughout the EU, and on the UK government to establish a Scottish Parliament with statutory provision for gender equality.

Significant developments in the UK have also influenced the Scottish campaign. Representatives from the Women's Coalition in Northern Ireland have participated in events organised by the Scottish Women's Coordination Group to share their experiences of participating in the political process.[2] Some parallels can be drawn with the involvement of women in the constitutional debate in Wales.[3] The election of a record number of women MPs at the 1997 general election (102 Labour, 13 Conservatives, 3 Liberal Democrats and 2 SNP—a representation rate of 18%) also had an effect on developments in Scotland.

Joni Lovenduski discusses the factors contributing to the election of 120 women to the House of Commons, including the part played by the Labour Party's policy of all-women shortlists in half of the party's most winnable constituencies.[4] The policy was dropped in 1996 following a successful challenge to an Industrial Tribunal by two men, but not before it had influenced the number of women selected. The fact that the number of women elected to represent both the Liberal Democrats and the Conservative Party in 1997 did not show the same significant increase supports the view of some activists that positive action mechanisms are necessary in order to remove some of the structural and institutional barriers that militate against women in the selection processes of the political parties. Recognition that 'voluntarism' does not produce parity and that intervention is necessary helped fuel the campaign for change in Scotland.

What have women done?

In 1996, the present writer charted the role of women in Scottish politics, their campaign for gender equality in a Scottish Parliament, and their participation in the Scottish Constitutional Convention and the Scottish Civic Assembly.[5] New organisations, such as Engender, have been established; new networks and coalitions forged between women both inside and outside the political parties. Much of the campaign has been brought together by the Scottish Women's Coordination Group which has published information and campaign leaflets on women and politics, organised seminars and conferences; invited women from other countries to share their experiences and strategies for change; organised questionnaire surveys of political candidates for local, Westminster and European elections; lobbied politicians and others in decision-making positions; and held press conferences publicising the key objective to achieve 50:50 representation in Scotland's first Parliament since 1707. A major achievement of the Coordination Group was its success in brokering an agreement between representatives of the Scottish Labour Party and the Scottish Liberal Democrats in which they accepted the principle of gender balance and gave a commitment to field an equal number of male and female candidates in winnable seats at the first elections for the new Parliament. This Electoral Contract was subsequently endorsed by the Scottish Constitutional Convention and included in its final report *Scotland's Parliament, Scotland's Right* published in November 1995.

There have been significant political developments since the publication of the Convention's report in 1995, including the controversy that followed the Labour Party's announcement in 1996 that it would hold a referendum on constitutional change if it won the coming election.[7] In this climate, the debate on gender balance was somewhat overshadowed. However, the Scottish Women's Coordination Group and other women's organisations played their part in keeping the issue on the political agenda during the election campaign, in spite of the media's preoccupation with the views of male politicians. For example, they produced material setting out the case for a 50:50 Parliament and suggested questions to be asked of candidates. In contrast to previous elections, the 1997 campaign saw 'the active intervention of feminist advocacy organisations determined to raise the profile of women in the election'.[8] The advocacy of women in Scotland was further galvanised by the substantial increase in the number of women MPs elected to the House of Commons and by the fact that the new Labour government kept its pre-election promise to make constitutional change a key aspect of its programme, publishing a White Paper on devolution in July and announcing its intention to hold the two-question referendum in Scotland on 11 September 1997 (whether voters agreed that there should be a Scottish Parliament and it should have power to vary tax).

Immediately following the election, the Scottish Women's Coordination Group organised a conference inviting Henry McLeish, the new Minister for Women's Issues also Minister for Devolution and Home Affairs at the Scottish Office, to give the keynote address. He reaffirmed Labour's commitment to gender balance in the elections for the Scottish Parliament, his intention to promote the representation of women in public life and his desire to create a woman-friendly Parliament. Gender balance was endorsed by the representatives from the other political parties, the Scottish Liberal Democrats and the SNP, which were also represented at the conference.

The women activists in Scotland went on to play their part in the broad-based campaign for a Yes/Yes vote organised by Scotland Forward. Again, they used the opportunity for a cross-party event, holding a press conference at which Rosemary McKenna MP (Labour), Roseanna Cunningham MP (SNP) and Marilyn McLaren (Liberal Democrats) reaffirmed their parties' support for constitutional change and for equal representation in Scotland's parliament (the Conservatives, then still opposing a Parliament, were not represented).

The referendum produced a substantial endorsement of devolution, 74.3% voters agreeing that a Scottish Parliament should be established and 63.5% that it should have the power to vary taxation by 3p in the £. Following this, the government published a Scotland Bill in December 1997. As its more detailed proposals for a Scottish Parliament began to emerge, women political activists turned their attention to such matters as the standing orders and procedures of the new Parliament and other legislative provisions for equal opportunities.

How much success?

Having outlined the way in which women have 'protested' against their under-representation and used different strategies to stake their claim for equality, it is necessary to assess how successful they have been in their campaign. As is evident in the following discussion, there are both positive and negative outcomes to report.

First, the positive developments. The government's White Paper on devolution endorsed the Scottish Constitutional Convention's proposals for a Parliament with 129 MSPs elected on a version of the Additional Member System. Asking who will be eligible for selection and election, it was 'keen to see people with standing in their communities and who represent the widest possible range of interests in Scotland putting themselves forward for election. In particular the government attach great importance to equal opportunities for all — including women, members of ethnic minorities and disabled people'. It urged 'all political parties offering candidates for election to the Scottish Parliament to have this in mind in their internal candidate selection processes' (*Scotland's Parliament*).

The new Minister for Women's Issues has appointed a small Women's Advisory Group to brief him on the issues of key concern and proposals for change (one commentator dubbed it New Advisory Group (NAG)). One outcome of this development is the setting up of a new consultative process with women and women's organisations in Scotland. The Scottish Office published the consultative document, *Reaching Women in Scotland*, in October 1997 in which it invited views on proposals for taking forward measures to ensure that the Parliament is woman friendly and to establish a Scottish Women's Consultative Forum to provide a direct channel to government. To provide further support for this process, it was to appoint a woman's issues research consultant.

The second positive development is the continued resolve by three of the main political parties in Scotland to devise mechanisms to maximise the participation of women in the new Parliament. Joni Lovenduski and Pippa Norris have noted that the policies adopted by political parties to redress gender imbalance normally vary across ideological lines, with more left-orientated parties favouring positive action.[9] Alice Brown and Yvonne Galligan have classified the response of political parties to pressure from women activists into three broad categories: adherence to the 'status quo' with no specific policies targeted at women; 'promotional strategies' to encourage more women to participate through training and other measures; or 'active intervention' such as the use of quotas or the legal system to effect change.[10] The Conservative Party adheres to the status quo, all of the others have adopted strategies for active intervention, taking account of the Additional Members electoral system. As it will gain most of its seats on the constituency side of the elections, Labour intends to twin constituencies so that both men and women can compete for selection as candidates for a pair of parliamentary seats: the man with the highest votes will be selected for one constituency, the woman with the highest number for the other; any gender imbalance in the constituency election results will be redressed through the top-up list. The Liberal Democrats propose to put forward two men and two women in the constituency selection process and will also use the additional seats to achieve gender balance. The SNP has encouraged women to put themselves forward for selection for constituency seats and also intend to use the top-up list.

It is also necessary, however, to record that not all the aspirations of the women activists have been met. Against the hopes of the women campaigners, the government decided that equality legislation should continue to be a reserved power at Westminster and that the Equal Opportunities Commission should not be included as a cross-border political body with responsibility for both reserved and devolved matters (although the Scottish Parliament will have responsibility for ensuring the operation of equal opportunities in all its areas of competence, including education, economic development, environment, health, housing, local government, social work and transport).

The second area of disappointment surrounded the government's decision not to include a clause in the Scotland Bill exempting the selection processes of the political parties for the first elections for the Scottish Parliament from the provisions of the Sex Discrimination Act. This was sought by women activists in order that the political parties should not be inhibited from introducing selection procedures to maximise women's representation. The issue became politically contentious with the leaked Cabinet committee minute in which the Lord Chancellor, Lord Irvine, was reported as saying that such an exemption would not protect the parties from a challenge under domestic law and that even with it a challenge could be made under the European Equal

Treatment Directive. In setting out the issue and the proposal from Donald Dewar, Secretary of State for Scotland, that the Sex Discrimination Act should be amended for the first elections to the Scottish Parliament, he stated: 'Donald described the recent history of the issue in Scotland and the particular pressure which had led him to make his proposal.' He added that 'It was particularly awkward that Donald's proposal was limited to the first elections to the Scottish Parliament, because this would allow it to be presented as an artificial and expedient response to a particular political problem' (*Guardian*, 3.3.98). There was some argument that Dewar's original attempt to achieve parity would have been supported by EU jurisprudence and the Treaty of Amsterdam but, given the weight attached to the advice of legal officers, it is unlikely that the desired amendment to the Scotland Bill will be accepted. This will not necessarily stop parties pursuing the mechanisms they have agreed to improve the representation of women: whether legal challenges will be made remains to be seen.

Assessment

Although political activists in Scotland have not achieved everything they wanted in the plans for the Scottish Parliament, it is widely acknowledged that without the constant pressure from a cross-section of women at every stage in the long campaign for constitutional reform, the advances made would not have been so extensive. Women were successful in gendering much of the debate, using the language of democracy, participation and representation to stake a claim on behalf of women. Commenting on the debates within the Scottish Constitutional Convention, Yvonne Strachan, a leading member of the Scottish Women's Coordination Group, said, 'The men's agenda was different, and we had to keep raising the issue. Although some men on the Electoral Reform Group were supportive and sympathetic to our demands, we doubt whether they would have pursued the issue. We were the ones who had to argue the case again and again.'

The tactics employed were varied. They did not adopt more traditional forms of 'protest', such as signing petitions or engaging in public demonstrations. Instead, they worked hard to develop a strong network with a consensus on the key aim of improving the representation of women in political office and in the operation of the new Scottish Parliament. They were successful in bringing together women of different political persuasions, party and non-party, in the trade unions, in the voluntary sector, in the churches, women in business and the professions, in different communities throughout Scotland. Attendance at the many events organised by the Scottish Women's Coordination Group demonstrated that this activity could not be dismissed as the indulgence of a few white, middle-class feminists. A second tactic was to produce materials accessible to different constituencies of women to be used in promoting their case. They kept up pressure on politicians

during local, general and European elections by distributing question-
naires seeking the views of candidates on equality issues; they lobbied
politicians behind the scenes, sharing their expertise and providing
information for sympathetic MPs. Unity across the party divide helped
put pressure on the parties. In this way, the representation of women
has become one of the issues on which they will be judged in the first
elections to the Scottish Parliament. Should they fail to field a significant
number of women candidates, the possibility of the creation of a
women's party cannot be ruled out.

One area where the campaigners have been less successful is in
obtaining media coverage for their activities, despite events and press
conferences. Coverage has generally been reserved for the few occasions
when there have been differences between women on the issue of
representation, or more recently, the dispute about amendments to the
Scotland Bill and the intervention of Lord Irvine. Failure to take the
issue seriously is a cause of ongoing frustration. It would have been
tempting to organise more overt public protests, even stunts, to gain the
media's attention. Instead, the decision was made to build a broad-
based consensus amongst women and to accept that equal representation will be a hard fought struggle. In a political and media culture that
is so male-dominated, it is perhaps surprising that women have managed
to make as much progress as they have and that, despite setbacks, they
have continued with a united campaign. Such activity, which does not
result in media headlines, may require a redefinition of the criteria that
are traditionally used to measure political protest.

Another way of interpreting the achievements of women activists in
Scotland is that they were in a sense pushing an open door and that the
parties have managed to incorporate their demands in a way that will
not result in a serious challenge to the sources of power. In this respect,
it is useful to recall Sarah Perrigo's account of the progress made by
women in the British Labour Party over the last twenty years. It
contends that the response of the party to pressures for change can only
be understood by exploring the dynamics of changes in the party itself.
'The culture and organisation of the Labour Party in 1979 provided an
inhospitable terrain for women to organise around gender issues, but
since that time women have been able to use the spaces created by other
agendas for party adaptation and change, particularly demands for
party democratisation and party modernisation, to develop a gender-
party dynamic which has allowed women to press their claims more
effectively, but only in ways that are congruent with the leadership's
modernisation strategy.'[11] Such an interpretation can perhaps provide a
partial explanation for the advances made by women in Scotland. In a
climate of decreasing public satisfaction with politicians and politics,
aggravated by revelations of sleaze and corruption, the involvement of
more women may be seen as part of a modernisation process, as well as
a way of appearing more representative and accountable.

Finally, it is necessary to consider what, if anything, this political activity tells us about the women's movement in Britain. Some commentators believe it has experienced something of a setback in the 1990s or is less easily identified than in the past.[12] This view does, of course, rest on how one defines the women's movement and the way in which one measures its impact. Analysis of what have been described as the first and second waves of feminism exist in numerous sources. In an attempt to understand contemporary conditions, some feminists have developed the proposition that we may be in a third wave.[13] In the wake of recent economic, social and political turmoil, feminism has been provided with fertile territory for radical alternatives and the political space to build alliances and coalitions of interest between women in order to effect change. Attention is drawn to the increased demands for women rights, their empowerment through women's groups, challenging institutions in which they work, highlighting the democratic deficit in representation, and proposals to change citizenship culture. To quote from the originators of this idea, 'Women in positions of power or within formal political structures are increasingly linking up with women in the wider community to form a powerful movement for women. The third wave is pluralist. It aims to work creatively with difference while forging a common agenda. It has the beginnings of a strategy and a historic opportunity to reshape a social, economic and political future which is literally up for grabs. The third wave of feminism has the potential to connect women's practical strengths with feminist ideas in ways which are truly transformative for democracy worldwide.' If they are correct, then it could be argued that the women's movement is beginning to overcome some of the past divisions between women, as well as the divisions between theory and practice, and is working towards a stronger movement as a result. The concept of the 'new suffragettes' in particular accords with the increased focus on representation in government, a focus not confined to Scotland or to the UK.

Conclusion

It is difficult to predict what would have happened if women in Scotland had not decided that equal representation was such an important issue for them to take up. After all, during the constitutional debate in the 1970s there is little evidence of their mobilising as women and across the political party divide on questions of equality. Since the 1970s a number of factors, examined above, have contributed to the politicisation of the demand for gender balance in the Scottish Parliament.

Protest has not taken the form of mass demonstrations. Nevertheless, the tactics employed to ensure that equal representation became a salient political issue have been varied. It has been argued here that they have also been effective. Although women political activists have not achieved all their aspirations, they have made significant advances. The establishment of a new political institution in Scotland has provided a real political opportunity to achieve much greater parity with men both in representation in political office and in representation of their interests through the policies of the new Parliament. They have been successful in bridging the ideological and political party divisions between them and in bringing together a wide range of women from different backgrounds and with different perspectives. After the elections for the Parliament are held in May 1999, we will be able to assess more accurately the outcome of their endeavours. Whether or not this period in the development of the women's movement can be classified as a new third wave will also require time before a firm conclusion can be reached.

1   See discussion in J. Lovenduski, 'Gender Politics: a Breakthrough for Women?', *Parliamentary Affairs*, 1997/4.

2   See R. Wilford, 'Women and Politics in Northern Ireland', *Parliamentary Affairs*, 1996/1.

3   See J. Osmond (ed.), *A Parliament for Wales* (Gomer, 1994), especially ch. 8.

4   See Lovenduski, loc. cit.

5   See A. Brown, 'Women and Politics in Scotland', *Parliamentary Affairs*, 1996/1.

6   See A. Brown, 'The Scotswoman's Parliament', *Parliamentary Brief*, April 1995.

7   A. Brown, 'Scotland: Paving the Way for Devolution?', *Parliamentary Affairs*, 1997/4.

8   Lovenduski, loc. cit., p. 713.

9   J. Lovenduski and P. Norris (eds), *Gender and Party Politics* (Sage, 1993).

10 A. Brown and Y. Galligan, 'Changing the Political Agenda for Women in the Republic of Ireland and in Scotland', *West European Politics*, 1993/2.

11 See S. Perrigo, 'Gender Struggles in the British Labour Party from 1979 to 1995', *Party Politics*, 1995/3.

12 See P. Byrne, 'The Politics of the Women's Movement', *Parliamentary Affairs*, 1996/4.

13 The Third Wave of Feminism was the intended title of a book to be edited by Helena Kennedy, Caroline Ellis, Yasmin Ali and Christine Jackson in 1995 but not published.

The Pro-Life Movement

BY MELVYN D. READ

THE law on abortion in England and Wales was reformed by the Abortion Act, 1967. It laid down that, subject to the agreement of two doctors, abortion would be legal if a continued pregnancy would produce a threat to the woman's life; a threat to her physical or mental health; injury to the physical or mental well-being of existing children; or a risk to the health of the unborn child. In addition, doctors were expected to take into account the pregnant woman's environment. The reforms came about, in part, to accommodate the increasingly influential Abortion Law Reform Association but, more importantly, to combat the serious medical complications resulting from women using unlicensed and illegal abortionists. Liberalisation has not resolved the issue to the satisfaction of anybody, in fact the abortion issue became more controversial thereafter. The continuing prominence of the abortion issue in Britain and, for that matter the world, is due to the activities of the pressure groups largely set up as a reaction to the reforms.[1] Indeed, several of the social issues addressed in the 1960s remained unresolved because legislation failed to meet the expectations of those expecting to benefit from it. Not surprisingly, supporters of the Abortion Act argued that it failed precisely those women most in need, while opponents maintained that it offered abortion on demand.

The division was mirrored by a clear distinction in organisation. The Abortion Law Reform Association was well organised and presented an effective case to support the cause of reform. Its opponents lacked the necessary organisation and coherent planning to influence the outcome of the bill, but this generated hostility against reform culminating in the launch of a campaign to reverse the 1967 Act. Here we look at the anti-abortion lobby to show how the core group, Society for the Protection of the Unborn Child (SPUC), has spawned a number of supporting, yet diverse anti-abortion groups which tend to operate at the margins of the controversy.

The 1967 reform

Before 1803 the law distinguished between abortion in the first stage of pregnancy and the second stage, when the pregnant woman first became aware of the foetal movement, known as 'quickening'. The Offences Against the Persons Act of 1803 enshrined the theological view that abortion was wrong in all cases but accepted the principle that termination after 'quickening' should be treated more harshly. More importantly, it was now punishable under criminal rather than common law. The Offences Against the Persons Act of 1861 removed all distinctions by making it a felony to procure an abortion or supply the means to bring one about. In 1869 Pope Pious IX declared that 'ensoulment' took place at conception and abortion at any time was declared a mortal sin. Ecclesiastical law and state law were united. Despite the 1861 Act, abortions continued to be performed if the woman's life was at risk even where this ran contrary to law. The Infant Life (Preservation) Act of 1929 dealt with this anomaly, allowing termination if 'such an act was done in good faith with the intention of saving the life of the mother'. This contradicted the 1861 Act which remained on the statute book. It was tested by the trial of a doctor who performed an abortion on a 14-year-old rape victim to preserve her physical and mental health. The judgment that this accorded with the 1929 legislation broadened the meaning of the Act to cover abortion on therapeutic grounds. By the 1960s, then, the law on abortion was in a state of confusion. The medical profession was divided between doctors who went beyond the statutory medical grounds and those who took a restrictive view of the law. Some women were denied the facility where they lived and sought help elsewhere. Reformers demanded change to improve public health and eliminate the abuses which seemed to be commonplace.

The 1967 Abortion Act was passed during a period often referred to as the 'age of liberal reform'. In hindsight, some of the laws were not liberal solutions to social problems. Capital punishment was abolished, in part, due to the disturbing number of executions following convictions over which doubt has raged for many years. Reforms to the laws on homosexuality simply defined the current situation and resulted in more prosecutions than before; the aim was to prevent the criminal abuse to which homosexuals were subject rather than to recognise homosexuality. Critics of the Abortion Act argued that it was a compromise which satisfied neither side. Closer examination of this liberalising legislation shows it to be an attempt to deal with social ills surrounding particular issues rather than helping those directly associated with the problems which these laws sought to correct. The same was true of the 1967 Abortion Act. Speaking on the bill, David Steel told the House of Commons that it was not advocating abortion: 'The main case for the bill and for clarifying the law rests on the grounds that we are hopeful that the scourge of criminal abortion will be substantially removed from our land.' The new Act resisted attempts to make abortion available on demand, simply extending the category under which abortion was allowed.

A major feature of the Steel bill was the lack of coordinated opposition. The Catholic Church's opposition to all abortion was clear. The medical professions were not subject to the same clear-cut values although a general unease about the ethical problems which abortion raised was felt amongst physicians. The Hippocratic Oath forbids them to 'give to a woman an instrument to produce abortion' and calls on them to 'maintain the utmost respect for human life from the time of conception'. Consequently, it was no surprise that the British Medical Association opposed motions widening the circumstances for abortion to include social grounds. In 1968, its Council refused to amend the ethical code to allow 'social abortion' even though this was then legal. The Royal College of Obstetricians and Gynaecology took the view that reform was unnecessary because the existing law worked well and argued that easy access to abortion would encourage promiscuity particularly among young women, while increased numbers of abortions placed additional pressures upon doctors who were already under strain. The Royal College of Nursing, also critically involved, did not formulate policy on what it saw as a medical issue; its concern was for its members' right to refuse to participate in abortions on the grounds of conscience; it also opposed 'abortion on demand' as a threat to both the conditions of its members and the resources of the National Health Service.

In effect, then, opposition to the 1967 Abortion Bill lacked coherence. The Catholic Church offered a moral dimension which opposed abortion in virtually all circumstances, compared to the medical professions which carried out abortions, under conditions defined as acceptable while maintaining restrictions in those cases where the definition of acceptability shifted to the patient. In January 1967 this simple and uncoordinated opposition to abortion was strengthened by the launch of the Society for the Protection of the Unborn Child (SPUC).

The anti-abortion lobby

Initially, opponents of abortion consisted of the Union of Catholic Mothers and the Catholic Women's League, underpinned by the professional support of the Catholic Doctors' Guild. In 1967, SPUC emerged ostensibly free of the Catholic Church but in practice sustained by it. In the wake of the 1967 legislation, the lobby was expanded to include the Festival of Light and various right-to-life groups. The most significant was SPUC, founded to oppose the bill, but its chances were slim. In its favour, it could boast of links with influential medical associations which, naturally maintained close connections with the Department of Health. Though useful in its early development, these links proved to be a liability because each of the associations had its own agenda which, once fulfilled by the 1967 Act, worked against the interests of SPUC. At the outset, its two principle founders, Phyllis Bowman and Elspeth Rhys Williams, received the endorsement of prominent gynaecologists who, along with the Bishops of Bath and Wells and of Exeter, forged the nucleus of its Council. The Catholic Church was excluded from the executive as the organisers wished to avoid being seen as a front organisation for it, though in practice, the Church sustained most of the campaign.[2] Initially, SPUC suffered from the independent activities of public figures promoting the anti-abortion cause by expounding views underpinned by hyperbole, often factually incorrect. Its representatives were circumspect in their approach but adopted a clear right-wing, conservative ideology that relied heavily upon clergy to promote the cause to their congregations.

A strategy which relied on over-stating the case in order to influence public opinion was fraught with danger because it would convince neither government nor decision-makers. Moreover, it alienated potential allies, for example, the British Council of Churches, which emphasised compassion over recrimination, acknowledging that some reform of the abortion laws was necessary. By fostering connections with the Churches, SPUC did little to dispel the accusation that it was a Catholic-inspired group even though its membership incorporated all faiths.[3] Despite the endorsement of prominent members of the medical professions and of right-wing politicians, it failed to convert this into effective pressure. This can be explained, in part, by the inability to attract a significant share of its potential constituency. A large section of the Catholic community opposed the more rigid demands of the Church's hierarchy. The strength of SPUC was found amongst active churchgoers, whatever their religion, rather than amongst those who simply identified with a religion.[4] Polls between 1965 and 1972 showed that public opinion favoured liberalising the abortion law, notably if the health of the woman or the child was involved. In the early years, then, SPUC failed to make significant progress within the population at large — a failing which would prove harmful to the future anti-abortion campaigning.

SPUC's methods of protest included using large public demonstrations, lobbying of political representatives, statements by leading clergy and, above all, propaganda. There were two elements to its strategy: political mobilisation within constituencies, through local groups, to encourage MPs to vote for amending legislation to the 1967 Act, and close contacts with sympathetic MPs who might introduce the necessary amending bill from the back-benches.[5] Although there was some success in the creation of links with people outside, SPUC failed in its objective to reverse the 1967 Act. The formation of LIFE in 1974 by dissident members, highlighted the difficulties of campaigning politically on an issue about which government did not hold a view one way or the other. While sharing similar long-term aims, LIFE set out to offer pregnant women an alternative to termination by providing both material and psychological help. Though organising at the national level, with the headquarters in Leamington Spa, it operates at local (regional) level.

LIFE supports 'total pro-life action' through four separate, though linked, agencies, three of which have charitable status. The National Pro-Life Pregnancy Care Service offers counselling, advice and support in 135 LIFE Care Centres and 40 LIFE Houses. They provide counselling for both men and women after abortions and offer modest financial support in cases of acute hardship. The National Pro-Life Education Service promotes awareness about abortion, with speakers for schools or local groups, accompanied by literature, posters and videos to underpin the message. The LIFE Health Centre in Liverpool, another registered charity, supplies free infertility treatment and well woman care (in addition, Zoe's Place is the first baby hospice in the world). LIFE Campaigns, which is non-charitable, is regarded as a pro-life political action group whose activities are determined not by the Charity Commission but by what its members want to do.

As a national charity LIFE is dedicated to caring for pregnant women and their children. It is non-political and non-denominational, although it does seek financial assistance from various denominations of which the Catholic Church is the most prominent (not unreasonably, since it is the most unequivocal on the issue). Its unpaid Trustees are the national officers and are elected at the national AGM. The policy-making body is the Central Committee, consisting of the trustees and elected representatives of LIFE Regions. Membership is open to anyone (16 years and over) committed to the utmost respect for human life from fertilisation, and members have an input through discussion with local (regional) representatives who communicate these to the Central Committee. Groups such as LIFE, which is a member-dependent organisation, experience periods of dynamism followed by intervals of relative inactivity. An additional contribution is made by specialist groups such as LIFE Nurses, LIFE Doctors, LIFE Anglicans, and Evangelists for LIFE. Run by volunteers in frameworks set by the main organisation, they coordinate education and support within their fields. The activity of such groups depends on individuals: when an organiser's situation changes, the fortunes of a specialist group may also change or it may cease to function. The central organisation remains constantly active, but subgroups are sustained by the emergence of volunteers.

The anti-abortion campaign

By the late 1970s opinion within the medical professions shifted in favour of the 1967 Act. In 1994 the Lane Committee identified 'some change of opinion within the medical profession towards a readier acceptance of abortion as a means of preserving health'. This was confirmed when the British Medical Association opposed White's Abortion (Amendment) Bill. The Royal College of Obstetricians and Gynaecology's position was simple: doctors were adhering to conditions which permitted abortion. The Royal College of Nursing also opposed abortion on demand but accepted that since this was not a serious problem, White's bill was unnecessary. This shift of medical opinion undermined the medical defence of the anti-abortion groups.

At about the same time, the Protestant Churches' view on abortion became less sure although the Catholic Church remained resolutely hostile. In 1975, a report from the Church of England, *Abortion Law Reform*, queried the number of abortions taking place and the effect that this was having on the sexual behaviour of young, unmarried people. Support for White's bill demonstrated the unease felt within the Anglican Church about the number of abortions rather than as an attempt to prohibit them. Its Board of Social Responsibility showed how some attitudes had hardened when it vetoed the publication of a report, written in association with Methodists, which favoured abortion on demand within the first 12 weeks of pregnancy. There followed a clash of theological views between the Family Life Division of the Methodist Church, which emphasised the importance of individual conscience, and the Anglican Church, which looked to moral teachings but which was also concerned that the Catholic Church should not 'stand out in this country for the sanctity of the life of the unborn child'. In 1975 the Family Life Division published a report rejecting the idea of abortion on demand while making it clear that this did not constitute the official view of the Methodist Church. Likewise, the Board of Social Responsibility stood firmly against abortion unless there was no other remedy, a position not acceptable to all clergy within the Anglican Church.

The second half of the 1970s was a period of consolidation for the anti-abortion lobby. Faced with desertion by the medical professions and splits within the Protestant Churches, it opted for a more aggressive approach. A major obstacle to its campaign was the ambivalent attitude of successive governments, even though most MPs, including party leaders, held firm personal views on this subject. It was difficult for anti-abortion groups to establish close links with either government departments or agencies within the decision-making process. Although pro-abortion groups were in a similar position generally, they formed closer contact with Department of Health which made small financial contributions to some of them.

In the wake of the 1967 Act, successive governments were criticised for failing to implement the legislation. Labour was criticised for its failure to provide adequate access to family planning information and contraception and adequate abortion facilities within the NHS (explained in part by the increase in the number of abortions requested). The shift in responsibility to the NHS from the Family Planning Association or privately-run clinics served the purposes of the pro-abortion groups. To coincide with International Women's Year (1975), the Abortion Law Reform Association launched a campaign to emphasise the central role that contraception played in family planning: with the inclusion of contraception in the NHS, it was argued, women should be entitled to an automatic termination for any pregnancy where contraception had failed. Changing attitudes within both the medical professions also paved the way for seeing abortion as a 'necessary evil' to prevent babies being born into unfortunate circumstances. In the late 1970s, then, the stage was set for a clash between pro-abortion groups defending existing legislation and anti-abortion groups seeking to reclaim public opinion.

The Lane Committee's endorsement of the 1967 Abortion Act and the method of implementation was a set-back for the anti-abortion campaign. This disappointment influenced its activities as a new phase of campaigning began. The objectives remained the same but recognised that they could be achieved only by influencing Parliament through back-bench MPs since the parties were determined to keep the issue off the party-political agenda. SPUC's success in organising within the Church was mirrored by some gains in Westminster. Between 1970 and 1975 there were four challenges to the 1967 Act. The first two failed to progress through lack of time. A third bill, introduced by Michael Grylls (Conservative) reached committee stage but went no further when four opponents refused to attend, making it inquorate. James White's bill received a second reading by 208 votes to 88, suggesting that the House of Commons was becoming more responsive to amending legislation on abortion. More importantly, there was a substantial shift towards the anti-abortion lobby amongst Labour MPs. Attempts to explain this were twofold: a rapid increase in the number of abortions performed after 1970 and the level of 'abuse' brought to light by anti-abortion propaganda (perceived rather than fact). SPUC's pro-active campaigning also played a role, as well as a general decline in public support for abortion.[6] The House of Commons stopped considering White's bill when a committee to review the workings of the 1967 Act was established. In 1977, William Benyon (Conservative) responded to the committee's first report with a Private Members' Bill to limit the role of charitable pregnancy advisory services. It received a second reading, by 170 votes to 132, and completed its standing committee stage, demonstrating how effective anti-abortion campaigners had become in servicing their parliamentary team.

In the next session, Sir Bernard Braine's Ten Minute Rule bill, informed by Benyon's bill, was introduced into the House of Commons by 181 votes to 175. Although such bills rarely succeed, and this one was no exception, they do provide some data on opinion in the House. As the decade progressed, the number of MPs voting on the abortion issue increased but with declining support for anti-abortion amendments. Whereas White's bill attracted 70% of votes cast, Braine's 1978 bill gained just over 50%. This can be explained by the fact that MPs' concerns about abuse of the abortion laws were laid to rest by the Lane Report and assurances from the Minister of State at the Department of Health. It was also apparent that pro-abortion groups had in turn become more adept at servicing their political allies.

The two sides of the controversy were pitched against each other again when John Corrie (Conservative) introduced a bill to amend the

1967 Act, a major assault on almost all its aspects (especially a reduction of the 28-week limit for termination to 20). The 1979 general election returned a Conservative government sympathetic to the anti-abortion cause and encouraged campaigners in the believe that their time had come. Confidence was boosted further when the bill received a second reading by 296 votes to 251. Subject to the difficulties of Private Members' Bills, however, opponents defeated it by tabling so many amendments that it was withdrawn. It was lost for several reasons. The medical professions now openly opposed amendments to the 1967 Act. The sponsors failed to win over enough Labour MPs to bolster their position: in fact, at the 1975 Labour Party conference delegates approved a resolution calling for abortion on demand to become party policy. The anti-abortion lobby was seeking change without a broad enough base of support. By relying on the Church for both financial and popular support, its campaign was too narrow in appeal. There was also the sponsors' tactical error in refusing any concessions to their opponents (e.g. for a 24-week limit). Inflexibility and the narrow social base of supporters are recurring characteristics of SPUC's campaigning style and have proved difficult to overcome. During the debate it alienated potential allies within various religious communities as well as politicians sympathetic to the cause but wary of being associated with such a strident group. This phase of the parliamentary campaign showed SPUC that legislative change would not be easily won. A different approach was required. The new strategy adopted recognised that the pro-abortion groups were less at ease when defending late abortions. This gave the anti-abortion lobby an opportunity to attack their opponents without compromising their views.

By concentrating on late abortions, it was possible to present these as typical of all abortions. Once established in the minds of the public, then, the whole concept of abortion would be open for attack. The 1980s witnessed a greater awareness about the rights of the foetus,[7] an argument sustained by advances in medical technology that could make an infant's life viable where previously this would have been impossible. It was clearly irrational for a doctor to perform an abortion after 23-weeks' gestation when other doctors were fighting to save babies born prematurely at that age or earlier. From here it was just a small step to argue that the foetus had rights. This view was tested in Parliament by Enoch Powell's Unborn Children (Protection) Bill. Despite a successful second reading, by 238 votes to 66 and a speedy passage through standing committee, the bill was defeated at report by 157 votes to 82.

Despite this, the issue of the foetus as a victimised 'person' had been raised. In 1987, David Alton (Liberal Democrat) introduced the Abortion (Amendment) Bill which questioned the morality of abortions after 18 weeks given the advances in intensive care for premature births. Concessions accepting that in some circumstances abortions at a later stage were permissible ensured a second reading by 295 votes to 251.

Supporters made strenuous efforts to stir up public opinion in Alton's favour by emphasising late abortions. Some distributed Lars Nilsson's photograph purporting to show a living 18-week old foetus in the womb. This propaganda was reported in the media as fact although later much of it was shown to lack substance. Misuse of evidence was another feature of SPUC's more emotive style of campaigning.

In the following parliamentary session six Private Members' Bills on abortion were introduced into the House, although only Ann Widde-combe's Abortion (Amendment) Bill had any chance of success and even this fell at second reading. In the meantime, the anti-abortion lobby's aspirations were boosted by news that the Conservative government favoured a reduction in the upper time limit for termination. Sir Geoffrey Howe, Leader of the House, allowed amendments to be attached to the Human Fertilisation and Embryology Bill and tabled a clause setting the new upper limit at 24 weeks, which was agreed by 409 votes to 152. Virginia Bottomley, the Minister of State in the Department of Health, said that this would bring existing law into line with medical recommendations. During report stage several amendments were accepted to reflect the views of both sides to the controversy but pro-life MPs failed to make significant gains.[8]

The government's legitimisation of a 24-week limit virtually ruled out further meaningful parliamentary discussion of abortion for several sessions. Subsequently, there was a shift away from trying to influence legislation in favour of direct action to influence public opinion. Anti-abortion groups looked to USA where Rescue America, an association of American Catholics and fundamentalist Protestants, had adopted a more violent side to their campaigning. Its counterpart in Britain, Rescue UK, was coordinated by an ex-Catholic priest, James Morrow, who proclaimed the direct action message favoured by his American colleagues, including, 'pavement counselling' and the disruption of abortion clinics. In November 1993, the fear of violence increased for a time when the founder of the American movement, Don Treshman, came to England, but he was arrested and deported under the Immigration Act on the ground that his presence in Britain was not conducive to the public good. A second American organisation, Rescue Outreach, sent representatives to encourage the use of direct action in the UK.

In the UK such violence was viewed with trepidation by most campaigners. In the first place, militancy is anathema to many within the pro-life campaign. Secondly, it alienated further potential supporters from outside the movement. It remained possible to muster sufficient sympathisers to campaign in a less aggressive manner, including marches and demonstrations in various cities throughout Britain. Although some accepted the use of a more belligerent style of protest, to protect the unborn child, this was frowned upon by others as an ideology based upon the values of the American organisation. Nuala Scarisbrick of LIFE said that the charity did not wish to do anything illegal or to be seen bullying women. Not surprisingly, then, anti-abortion groups like SPUC and LIFE make a public show of keeping more militant campaigners at arm's length. The Catholic Church maintains a discrete distance also.

The rejection of direct action placed the pro-life movement in something of a quandary as it could no longer rely on either of the main political parties to achieve its aims. The Conservative government legitimated abortion by setting an upper time limit of 24 weeks effectively ruling out any absolute prohibition of abortion on social grounds. The Labour Party was opposed to such a proposal, indeed many Labour MPs favoured abortion on demand. As the 1997 general election loomed and opinion polls showed Labour to have a good chance of replacing the Conservatives in office, the pro-life lobby came under pressure. The Catholic Church's stance was difficult because on the one hand it backed much of Labour's thinking on social justice, but on the other hand rejected its position on abortion. John Scarisbrick, chairman of LIFE, stated that since it was the only party to adopt a pro-choice consensus as party policy, all Catholic support at the coming election was forfeit. Emily's List, a charity supporting Labour women parliamentary candidates, underscored this problem by requiring members to make a pro-choice declaration as a precondition for receiving funding. Tony Blair tried to play down abortion as a political issue. Cardinal Thomas Winning, head of the Catholic Church in Scotland, accused Blair of washing his hands of the issue and New Labour of expounding Christian values while refusing to condemn abortion. Phyllis Bowman challenged Tony Blair for consistently voting in the Commons to liberalise abortion. For some, then, the fear was that this attack on the Labour leader was a further indication of the rise of single-issue politics associated with zealots who would create an American style campaign at the forthcoming general election.

Before the 1992 general election Mrs Bowman had been arrested under the Representation of the People Act (1983) for incurring unauthorised election expenses while promoting the election of a candidate (although the case never came to court). In 1996, the task of representing the anti-abortion/pro-life movement at elections became the responsibility of a new political party, the Pro-Life Alliance. Its immediate aim was to stand candidates against MPs from all parties, including senior members, who were seen as being pro-abortion. Launched by Bruno Quintavalle, son of Countess Josephine Quintavalle, a prominent LIFE member, it was initially funded by Mohammed Al Fayed of Harrods but this financial aid was soon withdrawn. The party took as its defining statement 'The mass destruction and trivialisation of human life — and its corrupting effect on society as a whole — is the supreme challenge of out time.' Its long-term aims were twofold; to oppose abortion, euthanasia and the destruction of human embryos, and to show absolute respect for human life from fertilisation until natural death. It gave priority to the human embryo since this was where all human life began but found it difficult to generate widespread public support for this cause. Consequently, abortion, which generated more public passion and emotion, was adopted as the central core of the party's campaign. In effect, the policies of the Pro-Life Alliance brought the aims and objectives of the various campaigning groups under one banner. The manifesto revealed that its main policies were to repeal the 1967 Abortion Act and the 1990 Human Fertilisation and Embryology Act; to outlaw euthanasia; to provide more maternity grants, child benefit, maternity leave, counselling and hospice facilities for the terminally ill.

The Pro-Life Alliance presents itself as an independent political organisation, but it is clear that the party is closely associated with the charity LIFE. As such, it undertakes a provocative campaigning style which charitable status prohibits. In early 1998 there were no members because there was no organisation to service a membership list, but its leaders envisage a large membership in the future—drawing, of course, heavily on individuals already committed to the cause through their association with other anti-abortion groups. In the meantime, funding for the party and its prospective parliamentary candidates is found locally and from willing sponsors—in 1997 many of the candidates paid their own election expenses.

At the 1997 general election, the Pro-Life Alliance fielded 53 candidates, sufficient to give them the right to a party political broadcast. This served its interest to prevent the depoliticisation of the abortion issue. In the run up to the election, it built upon Cardinal Hume's comments, on GMTV's Sunday programme, that abortion was 'unworthy of a civilised society'. The party used this to urge Anglican clergy to 'get off the fence' on this issue, but the Church of England was unimpressed. A week later, Cardinal Hume wrote to the Alliance saying that he did not want to be associated with or used by any political campaign. In a second move, the Alliance notoriously tried to show footage of a late pregnancy being terminated (a sequence taken from an American anti-abortion video called *The Hard Truth*) in its television broadcast. Both Janet Anderson, Labour's spokesperson for women, and Teresa Gorman, a Conservative MP, facing a Pro-Life candidate, complained about the proposed broadcast. In fact, the BBC banned the sequence because it did not comply with taste and decency guidelines. The Alliance applied for a judicial review of the decision but this was refused and that evening the political broadcast was transmitted cut (the Alliance then, took the matter to the Appeal Court which found in favour of the BBC).

At present, the pro-abortion/choice lobby maintains the upper-hand: abortion remains legal (but not on demand) and the time limit meets the guidelines of the medical professions. Pro-life groups have achieved little beyond marginal changes to the implementation of the 1967

Abortion Act, evidenced by the regional disparities in the unequal treatment of women seeking abortion within the UK. What seems clear, however, is that though it has not succeeded politically, the pro-life campaign has successfully promoted its case to ensure that the debate over abortion continues both in Parliament and in public. Of course, the issue is highly charged and methods used to ensure public recognition of the problem are often frowned upon by allies and opponents alike, but justified by those who use them in the cause of saving children.

Though the debate rages on it is possible to argue that the anti-abortion lobby has failed to gain significant support for its stance on abortion. In 1997, a Gallup poll revealed a growing concern over the time limit at which pregnancies could be legally terminated: 51% of respondents thought that the upper limit should be reduced to 10 weeks, but 89% accepted that abortion should be available, 26% on demand. The poll strengthened the resolve of the pro-life movement because it also showed that 58% of respondents thought that a pregnant woman who did not want her baby should continue with the pregnancy and offer the child up for adoption; only 28% thought that abortion was the answer while just 9% agreed that it was the woman's right to choose (*Sunday Telegraph*, 26.10.97). Whatever the views expressed, the number of abortions carried out each year show that women are still prepared to put themselves through this torment and, in some cases, abuse from pro-life campaigners. In 1996, 177,225 abortions were carried out in the UK (about 89% at less than 13 weeks and about 2% after 20 or more). This suggests that the annual rate of abortions in the UK exceeds the total membership of the pro-life movement given the high degree of cross-group membership. In effect, then, while anti-abortion protest may have had a significant impact on the parliamentary and public debates on abortion, it seems to have had little practical effect on women seeking termination of pregnancies.

Conclusion

This account has charted the progress of anti-abortion protest since the Abortion Act of 1967. At its inception, during the latter stages of the bill, the movement was little more than the public face of religious concerns, in particular of the Catholic Church, about legalising abortion. From this, it has grown into an effective lobbying organisation which has developed sufficient political acumen to ensure that abortion remains both on the political agenda and within the public domain. This is striking when one considers that it is challenged by a political process which would prefer to see the issue dropped. Often lobbies which attain a high public profile cannot translate this into legislative gain. The pro-life lobby is no exception. It cannot claim any major parliamentary success: the main achievement, reduction of the termination limit from 28 weeks to 24, was a recommendation of the Lane Committee and supported by medical professions.

The pro-life lobby's constant presence has been accomplished by adapting to changed circumstances and defending its case effectively on several fronts: aggressive public campaigning (Society for the Protection of the Unborn Child), compassionate campaigning (LIFE) and, more recently, political campaigning (Pro-Life Alliance). Such activity cannot stand alone; it must operate within a morality, in this case clearly defined by the Catholic Church. The Protestant Churches lack similar commitment. The medical professions also shifted their stance once it was demonstrated that termination, perhaps a 'necessary evil', was not available on demand as claimed by the pro-life lobby. In spite of this haemorrhage of support, the campaign distributed its resources sufficiently well to compete on several fronts.

The most striking feature, perhaps, is that what might be thought a broad-based, wide-ranging protest movement, something more than a group or a lobby certainly, is little more than an efficient use of limited human rather than financial resources. First, the movement is not so much a network of groups that have developed independently, though united by a shared interest, but it is a network of groups that have grown one from the other offering different approaches to reach the same goals. Their leadership has close ties and their membership overlaps. The strength of the anti-abortion movement can be found in this tight-knit relationship at the peak of each organisation as well as within the membership which, in effect, carries the fervour engendered by abortion from one group to another. Hence, it is possible to argue that it is the activity of zealots which makes the pro-life campaign so effective rather than the presentation of a clear argument. Of course, cross-membership also raises questions about the depth of support which the anti-abortion lobby can actually muster beyond the core of church-going activists. It is difficult, therefore, to argue that the pro-life organisation is much more than a central core, SPUC, funded by the Catholic Church — which has spawned several campaigning bodies with a joint leadership and common membership.

1   J. Lovenduski, 'Parliament, Pressure Groups, Networks and the Women's Movement; The Politics of Abortion Law Reform in Britain (1967–83)' in J. Lovenduski and J. Outshoorn, (eds) *The New politics of Abortion* (Sage, 1986).
2   M. Simms and K. Hindell, *Abortion Law Reformed* (Peter Owen, 1971), p. 182.
3   Lovenduski, loc. cit., p. 52.
4   Baker, *American Political Quarterly*, January 1981.
5   D. Marsh and J. Chambers, *Abortion Politics* (Junction Books, 1981), p. 58.
6   Ibid., p. 31.
7   J. Hadley, *Abortion: Between Freedom and Necessity* (Virago, 1997), p. 86.
8   J. Issac, 'Britain: The Politics of Morality', *Parliamentary Affairs*, April 1994.

Defending Animal Rights

BY ROBERT GARNER

IN the two decades after the second world war, animal welfare was largely absent from public discourse. Even the burgeoning environmental movement in the 1970s, in so far as it touched upon animals at all, focused upon wild species and, more specifically, the plight of whales. Many animal protection societies still existed but they tended to be dormant, engaging in little active campaigning and relying financially on bequests rather than subscriptions from an active membership. The position of the Royal Society for the Prevention of Cruelty to Animals (RSPCA) was a symbol of this inertia. Founded in 1824, it had by the 1960s become a respected charitable organisation, but it was inactive on most animal welfare issues, concentrating on pet animals and, in particular, the development of its inspectorate which polices existing legislation. The climate was summed up by the Littlewood Committee, set up by the Conservative government in 1962 to look into the case for reforming the law on animal experimentation, which found, in its 1965 report, no evidence of extensive public demands for reform, let alone pressure which might be electorally significant.

Animal rights and animal welfare

The revitalisation of the animal protection movement, which was well under way in Britain by the 1970s, can be measured in terms of new groups, increased membership of older organisations and, as both cause and effect, much greater public interest in animal protection issues.[1] It took on a radical hue. The previously dominant language of animal welfare, whereby animals were to be protected from unnecessary suffering, was challenged by the new language of animal rights or liberation.[2] Animal rights activists called for an end to, rather than the regulation of, the raising of animals for food and the use of animals for medical research and product testing.

The revitalisation of the animal protection movement has been partly due to the failure of the party system to address increasing public concern about the treatment of animals. No mainstream political party, concerned with building a coalition of support, can take on board the absolutist demands of the animal rights movement and, by itself, this helps to explain the attractiveness of belonging to a movement which can remain morally pure. (It might be argued in passing that the mainstream parties' focus on the traditional ideological battles centring on the economy now fails to encompass the values of a public increasingly concerned about moral issues and that the growth of the animal rights movement is one reflection of the moral vacuum in public policy discourse.)

A characteristic of the modern animal protection movement has been the growth of grass-roots activism. Traditional animal welfare groups, and in particular the RSPCA, tend to be elitist and cautious, relying on expert opinions and preferring to leave campaigning to their own paid staff. From the 1970s, local groups proliferated and, including college-based ones, about 300 now exist. A significant part in the development of local activism was played by Animal Aid, an animal rights organisation set up in 1977, who encouraged this development, as did the older anti-vivisection societies the National Anti-Vivisection Society and the British Union for the Abolition of Vivisection. While some local groups have been set up by a national organisation which provides logistical and, more rarely, financial assistance, more often than not they have emerged independently. The members may belong to one or more national organisation, which may seek to use them as a resource for particular campaigns, but most local groups remain autonomous deciding their own campaigning preferences and methods.

The growth of grass-roots activism is a product of the moral urgency engendered by animal rights. The present ways in which animals are treated — as commodities in factory farms and as our testers in laboratories — are regarded as so objectionable that those involved with animal rights actively seek to change society's views about the subject and show impatience with the failure of the political process to recognise the moral imperative. For some, this impatience has boiled over into a willingness to partake in various forms of direct action. The use of direct action dates back to the formation of the Hunt Saboteurs Association in 1963, but is particularly associated with the Animal Liberation Front formed in 1976 and, subsequently, various splinter groups.

The Hunt Saboteurs Association was formed when a number of activists left the League Against Cruel Sports as a result of the new chairman's success in steering the organisation towards less confrontational activities. Now based in Nottingham, it remains extremely active in the field during the hunting season, employing a variety of methods (e.g. diverting the attention of hounds through the use of horns or the masking of the quarry's scent) to disrupt hunts. Hunting was an ideal target for animal rights activists. Not only was it a minority pursuit for which there was little public support, but it was also relatively easy, as an outdoor activity, to disrupt.

By the late 1960s some Hunt Saboteurs activists, disillusioned with the limited impact of non-violent civil disobedience, formed a breakaway faction, which began by damaging the property of hunt participants and supporters before moving on to target research laboratories and factory farms. In 1972, this group renamed itself the Band of Mercy and four years later became the Animal Liberation Front (ALF). Since then, ALF 'cells' have been responsible for thousands of actions, ranging from small-scale damage inflicted on butchers, meat wholesalers and furriers to laboratory break-ins where equipment may be destroyed, information taken and the animals released. In the 1980s, direct action began to take a different and more dangerous form, with some activists prepared to target politicians and scientists with letter or car bombs and to plant incendiary devices in department stores selling fur. It was claimed in a *Brass Tacks* television programme shown in 1986 that annually since 1982 there had been 2,000 actions causing £6 million worth of damage.

Only a tiny proportion of activists are involved in the more extreme forms of direct action: this type of illegal activity should not be regarded as a characteristic of the animal rights movement. In the early 1990s, the Animal Liberation Front claimed that it had 2,500 members, although the police estimate that the hard-core number was only about 250. Some animal rights organisations, such as Animal Aid, are implacably opposed to it on both moral and tactical grounds, while the League Against Cruel Sports has always sought to distance itself from the Hunt Saboteurs Association. Even amongst direct actionists, there has been a running debate about the efficacy and morality of violence, particularly when it is directed at people rather than property.

Most animal rights activity is of the traditional law-abiding variety characteristic of outsider groups: the mass demonstration; the distribution of campaign literature setting out the animal rights position and often inviting the recipients to write to politicians or other interested parties; and the use of celebrities, such as Joanna Lumley or Paul and Linda McCartney, to promote the cause.

The key divide in the animal protection movement is not between advocates and opponents of direct action but is based around the ideological distinction between rights and welfare. Moderate welfare organisations still exist, of course, but the visibility of animal rights activist organisations has undoubtedly had the effect of radicalising the objectives and strategies of older established groups. A special case is the RSPCA which, as a charitable organisation, has to make provision for an elected ruling council. From the late 1960s, animal rights activists fought, with considerable success, to win seats on the council and, as a consequence, the society began to develop policy positions on most animal protection issues, including a commitment to the abolition of hunting.

The impact of protest

The renewed campaigning edge of the animal protection movement has had a considerable impact. Public opinion, for instance, is now much more favourably inclined towards the objectives of the animal rights movement. This has undoubtedly had a knock-on effect on government policy but its importance cannot be measured exclusively in these terms. Changing consumer patterns have had an impact on commercial enterprises which use animals. A social stigma is now attached to the wearing of fur; the number of vegetarians has increased markedly, creating a new marketing niche; the demand for 'cruelty free' cosmetic products has played an important role in the decision of many manufacturers to seek alternative testing methods.

Laboratory raids have forced research institutions to increase security: video surveillance and windowless buildings enable the animal rights movement to portray the research industry as anxious to hide its activities from public gaze. Given the secrecy, it is very difficult for animal rights groups to find out exactly what it done in laboratories and a great deal of the material used in anti-vivisection campaigns is gained through laboratory break-ins or undercover work by activists disguised as employees. The possibility of an Animal Liberation Front raid has probably made researchers treat their animals more carefully, in case their activities become subject to greater public scrutiny.

On occasions, protest can have a considerable impact, raising public awareness and sometimes leading to changes in government policy. In 1975, for instance, the *Sunday People* published an article, using information provided by an Animal Liberation Front raid, about beagle dogs being forced to smoke tobacco at the Imperial Chemical Industries laboratories in Cheshire. Such was the public outcry that the Home Secretary announced that dogs would no longer be used in smoking research. In 1985, to give another example, a raid on a laboratory run by the Royal College of Surgeons produced evidence of the maltreatment of monkeys (including a photograph of an animal with the name 'crap' tattooed on its forehead). This, and the subsequent conviction of the College for cruelty, was an enormous propaganda coup for the animal rights movement.

Cases like those mentioned above, together with incessant and wider anti-vivisection campaigns, contributed to the Conservative government's reform of the law on animal experimentation in the mid-1980s. The legislation provided for the creation of an Animal Procedures Committee, within the Home Office, which reviews its operation. Consisting of representatives from industry, academia and the animal protection community, it receives 'regular reports of campaigns mounted by anti-vivisection groups, together with copies of reports prepared by these groups about particular aspects of research'.[3] Information drawn to the attention of the Animal Procedures Committee can lead to significant action being taken.

One case in 1990 involved an 89-year-old researcher at the Medical Research Council's Institute for Medical Research. An undercover operation by activists produced evidence that he caused animals to suffer through, among other things, the incorrect application of anaesthetics. The publicity generated resulted in severe embarrassment for the government which subsequently acted to revoke the researcher's licence and initiated stricter rules for those over retirement age.

Campaigns by animal rights activists in the 1990s have also brought to the Committee's attention cases of illegal animal abuse at a number of animal supply and contract research establishments. Home Office investigations resulted in severe reprimands for these companies, the revoking of some licenses and compulsory training for staff. While the British Union for the Abolition of Vivisection, primarily responsible for the campaigns, argued that stronger action was necessary, it did have its first meeting with Home Office officials as a result of these cases. Furthermore, the companies 'have been deeply wounded by the whole affair, receiving widespread negative media coverage and losing business from a number of their client companies'.[4]

Protest against hunting has also had an impact. The disruption caused by Hunt Saboteurs Association activists has proved to be newsworthy and, coupled with the gathering of evidence revealing the suffering inflicted on the quarry, this has been crucial in raising public awareness of the issue. Public opinion has been against hunting for many years and this opposition has hardened. Gallup polls between 1972 and 1987, for instance, revealed that opposition to fox hunting had increased from 52% to 68%.[5]

The effectiveness of the campaign against hunting is reflected in the reputation the League Against Cruel Sports has among MPs. An Access opinion poll in 1994 revealed that 73% of MPs knew the League very well or fairly well, while over half had very favourable or favourable impressions of it.[6] An increasing number of MPs are prepared to support anti-hunting Private Members' Bills in the Commons. In the latest example, a bill introduced by the Labour backbencher Michael Foster in November 1997 (fulfilling Labour's manifesto promise of a free vote, which led to a £1 million donation from the International Fund for Animal Welfare) provoked high-profile campaigns by the animal protection movement and the hunting community. The bill received a massive 260-vote majority at second reading (this followed party lines, with 99% of Labour MPs for, 94% of Conservatives against), but it subsequently ran out of time as a result of filibustering by its opponents.

Labour's general antipathy to hunting undoubtedly reflects a percep-tion that it is the preserve of wealthy rural people; one might not expect much sympathy from a party steeped in the urban working class. This provides an interesting contrast with the first animal welfare campaigns in the nineteenth century which focused on middle-class efforts to outlaw working-class urban practices such as bear baiting and cock fighting.[7]

The impact of anti-hunting campaigns has also been felt outside of the conventional political system. Hunt 'sabbing' undoubtedly enables some animals to elude capture. The League Against Cruel Sports now owns about 2,000 acres of land in 30 separate sites in the West Country, strategically placed to hinder deer hunting. Not only does this prevent some animals from being killed by hunters, it also can lead to extensive publicity whenever a hunt trespasses on the land. In addition, the League provides legal assistance to those who have been affected by a hunt through the killing of a family pet or the destruction of private property.

Even more important has been the successful campaign to persuade the National Trust to ban deer hunting on its land. This decision, confirmed in April 1997, severely restricts most of the West Country deer hunts and puts their future in doubt. It was followed, in November 1997, by a similar decision from the Forestry Commission which owns land used for hunting in the West Country and the New Forest. For several years, so-called 'Hunt Monitors' from the League have been collecting footage from meets of the New Forest Buck Hounds. Some of this—film showing hounds attacking a live deer, hunters standing on a buck's neck and of hunters pushing the head of a buck under water before it was shot—was influential in the Forestry Commission's decision.

Another important impact of animal rights protest has been the reaction it has provoked from the movement's adversaries. Agribusiness interests often disguise the grim realities of factory farming and proclaim their concern for animal welfare in their sales promotion. The animal research community—including universities and the pharmaceutical industry—has also had to change its tactics. Rather than focusing on traditional lobbying, it now seeks to challenge the animal rights movement in the public arena. Organisations such as the Research Defence Society and the Animals in Medical Research Information Council now produce glossy information packs countering claims that their work is both immoral and ineffective. This battle is also fought in the classroom, where emotive anti-vivisection messages are now countered by heart-tugging cases of sick children kept alive by drugs developed and tested on animals.

Hunters have been organised for many years, the British Field Sports Society, formed in 1930. Faced with increasing public opposition to hunting and the election of a seemingly unsympathetic Labour government in 1997, it has sought to mobilise rural support for hunting. It played a leading role in the creation of the so-called Countryside Alliance which organised two major demonstrations in London. The second of these, on 1 March 1998, attracted an estimated quarter of a million people. While supposedly concerned with a whole range of rural issues—such as farming, the right to roam, the development of the green belt and the state of the rural infrastructure—opposition to Foster's anti-hunting bill was the primary objective.

The counter-mobilisation of agribusiness, the animal research community and hunting has probably reduced the effectiveness of animal rights campaigns. The publicity given to the Countryside Alliance demonstration, for instance, has made it less likely that the Labour government will introduce its own measure to abolish hunting. What the counter-mobilisation does reveal, however, is a recognition by vested interests that the politicisation of animal welfare issues threatens their ideological hegemony and their privileged position within decision-making arenas. Indeed, the animal protection movement (including both welfare and rights factions) has gradually become a valid spokesman for a legitimate set of interests, involving consultation, negotiation, formal recognition and inclusion.[8] Many MPs, who receive more mail from their constituents on animal issues than on almost any other subject, take the movement as an important player in the pressure group world. More significant is the greater access now accorded to animal protection lobbyists by the government, an access regularised by animal welfare participation on the Farm Animal Welfare Council (Ministry of Agriculture) and the Animal Procedures Committee (Home Office).

Surprisingly, perhaps, there is little evidence that even the most extreme forms of direct action have alienated public opinion or politicians. The campaign against fur in the 1980s, for instance, did not seem to be greatly damaged by incendiary devices in department stores. The tabloid press has generally found material revealing animal abuses more newsworthy than the methods by which it was obtained. It can also be argued that representation of the Animal Liberation Front activist as a dangerous urban terrorist has provided a much harder image for an issue which was once regarded as the preserve of eccentric old ladies. There are still widespread reservations about the objectives of the animal rights movement, but it is harder to ridicule it. An important caveat is that, so far, no innocent member of the public has been killed as a result of animal activism. This outcome, sometimes owing more to luck than judgement, has undoubtedly prevented a more hostile public reaction.

The limitations of protest

A key goal of protest, and the purpose of seeking access to decision-makers, is to influence public policy. From an animal rights perspective, this is the weak link in the chain. Since 1979, all of the major parties have included animal welfare commitments in their manifestos. However, these have rarely satisfied any but the most moderate animal welfare advocates, and even these limited concessions usually have a very low priority. As far as animal welfare has troubled decision-makers, it has traditionally, with the notable exception of hunting, been regarded as a cross-party issue. By and large, the policy commitments of the two main parties, and their actions when in government, have not differed much. There was cross-party support for the 1968 legislation on farm animal welfare, while both Labour and Conservative committed themselves in the 1980s to reform the law on animal experimentation. The Conservative government's eventual bill was not opposed by the Labour front-bench, nor by most Labour MPs.

As we saw, Labour has always been much more antagonistic towards hunting than the Conservatives and it is also true that the most committed supporters of animal welfare reform in the Commons also tend to come from the Labour benches. With the party's large majority after the 1997 election, the prospect of legislative progress looked bright. Successful legislative initiatives in farm and laboratory animal welfare are almost always executive-inspired, however, and none of the Labour MPs who have shown a past interest in animal welfare are in senior positions in the government. As a consequence, there is considerable doubt whether the government will introduce a bill to ban hunting—especially since the strength of opposition to such a measure was revealed—let alone take steps to improve the welfare of farm and laboratory animals significantly.

A number of the Labour MPs known for their interest in animal welfare are on the left and have little influence on the agenda of New Labour. The link between left-wing Labour and animal welfare is no coincidence. The representation of minority causes was reflected in much of the left's strategy in local government during the first half of the 1980s, particularly in London where a number of boroughs (such as Lambeth and Islington) adopted 'animal charters'.

It is questionable, anyway, how far elected politicians can alter the direction of long-standing and insulated policy communities within which those with vested interests in the use of animals are influential. The research community and pharmaceutical industry are an important influence on government policy on animal research. Likewise, the relationship between the National Farmers Union and the Ministry of Agriculture is usually regarded as the classic example of a closed policy-making network which excludes those (such as environmentalists, consumers and animal advocates) who challenge intensive agriculture.[9]

There are signs that the privileged position of these interests has begun to decline. Evidence may be legislative reforms. The passage of the Animals (Scientific Procedures) Act in 1986 has already been noted. In terms of farm animal welfare, the findings of a governmental committee in 1965 (the Brambell Report) led, in 1968, to a law which, for the first time, specifically protected farm animals from unnecessary suffering and established the Farm Animal Welfare Council, a committee, with representation from the animal protection community, which advises the Ministry of Agriculture on welfare matters. Moreover, it empowers the Secretary of State for Agriculture to make regulations for the welfare of farm animals, and most of the animal protection movement's successes in this area—such as the abolition of the veal crate or sow stalls and tethers—have come through this route.

While they should not be belittled, the improvements in farm and laboratory animal welfare that have occurred do look suspiciously like managed concessions. Few have seriously damaged agribusiness or research interests: no specific scientific procedures are outlawed and animal husbandry is still dominated by factory farming. Nevertheless, the need for government to demonstrate an interest in animal welfare, however superficial, is by itself an indication of the politicisation of the issue in recent years brought about largely by animal rights protest.

Recruiting activists

The difficulties of persuading decision-makers to adopt an animal rights agenda are acute. One only has to compare the feverish approach adopted by recent governments in the face of the BSE ('mad cow') crisis, where human interests were at stake, with the rather supine attitude to the controversy about the export of live calves and sheep. The recruitment of animal rights activists would also seem to be disadvantaged by the nature of the cause. Despite the growth of the animal rights movement over recent years, membership remains very small compared to animal welfare and wildlife conservation organisations (the Royal Society for the Protection of Birds and the World Wide Fund for Nature have 770,000 and 124,000 members). In terms of finance, the difference is as great.

That the animal rights movement has prospered in recent years, despite recruitment problems, is the result of various compensatory devices. There are many examples of individuals prepared to pay the costs, as well as playing a crucial role in launching organisations and keeping them going. Animal Aid was set up in the house of a Kent housewife; LYNX, the anti-fur group, was almost entirely the responsibility of Mark Glover who paid a heavy financial cost when his organisation was successfully sued by a furrier; the International Fund for Animal Welfare is inextricably linked with Bryan Davies.

It remains the case that a fair number of people have been recruited by animal rights organisations and a proportion of them are prepared to protest actively against the exploitation of animals. This can involve considerable costs in time and money, as well as emotional pain for those who have to confront the often grim reality of animal exploitation. At the extremes, the cost can be a lengthy prison sentence. An exploration of the motives of such individuals reveals that animal rights ideology performs a useful recruitment and mobilisation function. The goal of animal rights and the identity activists gain through belonging to a movement espousing it are undoubtedly linked. The ideology of animal rights is also central to organisational maintenance, uniting activists and separating them from others. The development of such an exclusive collective identity is important for movements with no common geographical, social or occupational base. The 'them' becomes the 'sadistic' scientist and the 'money-grabbing' farmer common in animal rights literature but can also include those members of the public who refuse to accept the ideology.

This collective identity can, however, be dysfunctional for the achievement of movement goals. It is difficult enough to generate concerted opposition to abuses of factory farming or animal research, let alone concerted demands for a complete prohibition of raising animals for food and the use of animals for medical research. There are, on the other hand, welfare goals—such as the prohibition of particular practices or the tightening up of enforcement—which have potential public support and therefore a greater likelihood of acceptance by decision-makers. The ability of reformist national groups to pursue their more moderate goals successfully can be hindered by the organisational need of animal rights groups to maintain an uncompromising position, since any dilution of that reduces their exclusiveness.

The literature of the animal rights movement is hard-hitting, condemning those directly concerned but also, by default, the politicians who allow it and the public who accept it. There is a tendency to pillory humans for unnecessarily causing animal exploitation. Anti-vivisectionists regularly argue that animal research is only necessary because of the need to cure diseases caused by easily avoidable human life-styles—poor diet, smoking and drinking. Activists often leave themselves open to the charge of being 'people haters'. There have also been elements of sexism in some campaigns (the poster labelling the fur wearer a 'rich bitch' was not designed to please feminists, nor were the female models in the 'I'd rather go naked than wear fur' campaign). Such strategies may be useful recruiting and fund-raising devices since they provide the moral shocks which motivate activists and help set them apart. They may also make it more difficult to generate a dialogue with decision-makers and build a coalition of public support behind achievable objectives.

The dysfunctional role sometimes performed by animal rights campaigns, should not be exaggerated: they are tendencies, the worse-case scenarios of what can happen. Some activists, of course, are more pragmatic than others. However, the movement does face a severe problem because of its non-human focus, and alliances with other social movements for specific short-term ends are essential. There are many opportunities. Factory farming, for instance, has environmental and public health implications, while there is a strong case against the reliability of animal experimentation which puts it at odds with consumer and public health interests. The benefits of a broad and all-inclusive strategy were clearly seen in the campaign against live exports. Although animal rights activists were centrally involved in the Colchester campaign, the language of animal rights was conspicuous by its absence. Indeed, a large poster outside a pub read 'You Don't Have to Stop Eating Meat to Care—Ban Live Exports'. Moreover, some of the participants did not see animal welfare as the major issue at stake and few saw it as the only one. The campaign also drew in those concerned about local democracy, civil liberties and police powers.

Conclusion

Over the past twenty years or so, the animal protection movement has made considerable progress. The institutional exploitation of animals — on factory farms and in laboratories — has become an important political issue. Many animal protection organisations, including some which would regard themselves as animal rights groups, have become recognised by decision-makers as speakers for a legitimate set of interests. In addition, some public policy goals, albeit of a moderate nature, have been achieved. Much of the credit for this progress must be accorded to the reorientation of the movement, which has produced a harder campaigning edge and a greater willingness to engage in grass-roots activism.

It has also been argued, however, that the animal protection movement faces severe political and organisational problems. In the first place, vested interests stand to lose a great deal as a result of extensive animal welfare reforms, let alone the more far-reaching objectives of animal rights. Animal exploitation is central to many important public policy areas, in particular food and health policy. As a result, established government-centred policy networks, within which vested interests are extremely influential, have evolved. There is evidence that the political and social influence of agribusiness, pharmaceutical and scientific interests has begun to wane, and public protest has played no small role in this. It is doubtful, however, that this marks a decisive shift towards an alternative policy paradigm which takes much greater account of the interests of animals. A more persuasive explanation is that it represents a spoiling tactic by existing power structures to co-opt the moderate wing of the animal protection movement and to satisfy public pressure for reform, thereby avoiding the need for more far-reaching change in the future.

It is a truism that a public protest movement is strengthened by unity and an ability to forge alliances with other causes. The animal rights movement has problems on both counts. Animal rights is unique for the altruism required of its adherents, an altruism which limits its ability to attract widespread public support. Moreover, the process by which individuals are recruited into the animal rights movement and mobilised to act appears to be related to the exclusivity that membership provides. This, in turn, tends to produce an unwillingness to build bridges with other social movements, even when such coalition building increases the prospects of achieving particular objectives. There are, nevertheless, great potential benefits to be had in the forging of alliances between animal rights advocates and environmentalists, consumer groups and public health interests.

1 For this and other matters discussed here see R. Garner, *Animals, Politics and Morality* (Manchester University Press, 1993) and *Political Animals: Animal Protection Politics in Britain and the United States* (Macmillan, 1998).

2 The best known academic exponent of animal rights is T. Regan, *The Case for Animal Rights* (Routledge, 1984), while P. Singer, *Animal Liberation* (Cape, 2e, 1990) provides a utilitarian challenge to animal welfare.

3 *Report of the Animal Procedures Committee for 1994*, p. 5.

4 British Union for the Abolition of Vivisection, *Campaign Report*, Autumn 1993.

5 'Hunting and Public Opinion', League Against Cruel Sports leaflet.

6 *Blood Sports, Lobby Groups and the Criminal Justice Bill: A Survey of MPs* (Access Opinion Limited, 1994).

7 H. Ritvo, *The Animal Estate* (Harvard University Press, 1987).

8 W. Gamson, *The Strategy of Social Protest* (Dorsey Press, 1975), p. 28.

9 See M. Smith, *The Politics of Agricultural Support in Britain: The Development of the Agricultural Policy Community* (Dartmouth, 1990).

Europe, Goldsmith and the Referendum Party

BY NEIL CARTER, MARK EVANS, KEITH ALDERMAN AND SIMON
GORHAM

JAMES GOLDSMITH announced in November 1994 that he would be forming a Referendum Party aimed at securing a referendum on Britain's future in Europe. When the party's *Statement of Aims* was launched in October 1995, he declared: 'This is a single-issue biodegradable party which will be dissolved once we have achieved our aim' (*The Times*, 25.10.95). Parties campaigning on a single issue are not unknown in British politics: the Pro-Life Alliance, campaigning to tighten the law on abortion and human embryo experimentation, put up 53 candidates in the 1997 election. More unusual is the phenomenon of a very rich businessman seeking to 'buy' influence — Goldsmith committed £20 million to the party. The most notable example was the unsuccessful launch, by the newspaper barons Beaverbrook and Rothermere, of an Empire Free Trade Crusade in the 1930s. Goldsmith's intervention may be better compared to the contemporary cases of Ross Perot in the USA and Silvio Berlusconi in Italy, both of whom tapped a widespread alienation from the political system with their personal brands of authoritarian-populism. But perhaps the most unusual feature of the Referendum Party — in the context of British politics — is that it had a modicum of success: it played a not inconsiderable agenda-setting role and it achieved the best ever performance by a 'minor' party in a general election.

Goldsmith was the architect and benefactor of the Referendum Party. He had previously been very sympathetic to the European idea, but by the early 1990s several factors had combined to give him serious doubts about the inexorable drive towards political and economic integration. Vehemently opposed to the Maastricht Treaty, he regarded it as a step too far towards a European superstate in which power would increasingly reside in centralised, bureaucratic, supranational Brussels-based institutions. His objections also contained a degree of anti-German sentiment, for he firmly believed that Maastricht contributed to German hegemony over a federal Europe. Goldsmith was also a strong protectionist and opposed the GATT negotiations in 1992, believing that the prosperity of the EU in general, and his personal business portfolio in particular, would suffer from global free trade.

The son of a Conservative MP, Goldsmith had always harboured political aspirations and, having been elected as a French MEP in 1994 as part of an anti-Maastricht coalition, he evidently believed that he could influence the European debate in Britain. But despite his close relationship with the Conservative Party (particularly during the Thatcher years) Goldsmith rejected attempting to direct his campaign through that party. Its leadership would simply have absorbed the issue into its own agenda on European integration in an intra-party compromise. Goldsmith judged his campaign would be more influential if launched from outside the Conservative Party, drawing on cross-party concern about European integration.

As a high-profile entrepreneur who had changed his views on Europe and was prepared to stump up £20 million to support his creation, Goldsmith's venture into British politics attracted extensive media interest. Not surprisingly for a successful businessman, he was highly opportunistic and took advantage of a situation in which other factors had already conspired to give Europe prominence on the political agenda. The Labour and Liberal Democrat parties were not immune from disagreement over Europe, but the Conservative Party was particularly vulnerable to internal dissension on the issue. Opposition to Margaret Thatcher's position on Europe had played an important part in her enforced resignation as Prime Minister in 1990. British ratification of the Maastricht Treaty in 1992 provoked a damaging wave of internecine warfare within the Conservative Party.[1] The fragile truce that followed was again shattered by the passage of the European Communities (Finance) Act during the 1994–95 session of Parliament which led directly to the withdrawal of the Conservative whip from eight backbench rebels and, indirectly, to Major's decision to force a fresh leadership election in 1995 to reassert his authority.[2] The intensity of these long-established Conservative divisions over Europe was exacerbated by the wider political context. The popularity of the Major government plummeted after the Black Wednesday ERM crisis in September 1992 and never recovered. By-election defeats and defections meant that its narrow majority of 21 after the 1992 election declined steadily throughout the Parliament, disappearing altogether in November 1996. The timetable for further European integration via the 1996 intergovernmental conference and the forthcoming 1998 deadline for governments to express intent to join the European Monetary Union offered opportunities for Eurosceptics to exploit. Many Conservative Eurosceptics also genuinely believed that a firm 'anti-Europe' position might save the party from electoral defeat. This hope was fuelled by opinion polls indicating growing public discontent with aspects of EU membership and the fervently anti-Europe tone of such newspapers as *The Times*, *Sun* and *Daily Telegraph*.

By the time of Goldsmith's arrival on the scene, the Conservatives were thus already deeply divided over Europe and apparently shifting steadily towards a more Eurosceptic stance. Goldsmith was, however, keen to stress that the Referendum Party was not explicitly anti-Europe. Admitting his personal desire for a return to a Europe of Nations, he asserted that the Referendum Party was 'wholly agnostic' and 'just wants a referendum on the fundamental issues and the fundamental relationship between Britain and Europe' (BBC, *On the Record*, 13.10.96). But with such a mixed message coming from the party's architect and benefactor, there was inevitably some confusion over exactly what it stood for. Even its 'single issue' was malleable. Goldsmith had always declared that it would campaign for a referendum on Britain's future relations with Europe. But for a long time there was uncertainty over precisely what this meant. The question for which the party would campaign was eventually announced on 28 November 1996: 'Do you want the UK to be part of a Federal Europe? Or do you want the UK to return to an association of sovereign nations that are part of a common trading market?' This convoluted and ambiguous wording clearly revealed Goldsmith's Eurosceptic colours. As the election approached, the Referendum Party's public utterings became increasingly Eurosceptic in tone. It was an ideological shift which helped shape the party's organisational development, campaign strategy and, ultimately, its impact.

Organisational development

It is possible to identify two phases in the organisational development of the Referendum Party: (1) the rise of the Party as an Idea (November 1994–October 1995); (2) the Party as a single-issue movement (October 1995–May 1997).[3]

For its first year, the Referendum Party was less an organisational entity than an attractive — if still somewhat inchoate — idea. Goldsmith's political enterprise struck a chord with several groups of people. His Eurosceptic leanings clearly found resonance with individuals, from all parts of the political spectrum, who were unhappy with what they regarded as the Major government's soft attitude towards European integration (and the even more pro-Europe sympathies of the opposition parties). The Referendum Party also offered a safe port of call for disaffected Tory voters unwilling to shift to Labour or the Liberal Democrats. Finally, the project had a democratic dimension, providing a potential source of popular legitimation. For some sympathisers, the party's clarion call 'Let the People Decide' reflected the argument that the British electorate had been disenfranchised on the European issue. It is apparent that not all of the Referendum Party's supporters, or its elite activists, were rabid Eurosceptics. As one regional organiser, a small businessman, put it: 'The two major parties were making vital decisions about the future of the country without consulting those whom the decisions would affect . . . no one appeared to be championing the cause of the little guy . . . the small village shop keeper, the local farmer, small businessmen. I was really drawn to the Referendum Party because I saw the issue of Europe as a vital issue of democracy.' The campaign's non-partisan character enabled the Referendum Party to attract three types of supporter: Eurosceptics, disaffected Conservatives and democrats. It was a coalition of interests which appeared to pose a particular electoral threat to a Conservative Party experiencing unprecedented levels of mid-term unpopularity.

Most pressure groups start modestly, hoping to grow as public opinion is mobilised; the Referendum Party's experience was quite different. The absence of financial constraints enabled it to start with a bang, attracting massive publicity. But it had no ready-made organisation. It was launched on a false premise: the self-styled party lacked the machinery of a party. Goldsmith could call on management expertise from his business empire, but he lacked both politically experienced personnel and a mass membership. The party was thus unable to organise itself quickly and efficiently into a cohesive campaigning machine. Goldsmith's response to this problem was to develop a relatively sophisticated administrative centre and to secure the expertise he required to coordinate central campaigning. By October 1995, the party had established a hierarchical, three-tiered (centre, region and constituency) organisational structure. It was tightly coordinated from the centre by Goldsmith, assisted by a kitchen cabinet, which included two former Conservative Central Office staff and Lord MacAlpine, a former Conservative Party Treasurer. Although his subordinates had operational autonomy, the organisational design placed much power in Goldsmith's hands: 'Goldsmith really ran the show—it was his party in all senses of the word. He provided the majority of the capital and directed its activities.' (A Referendum Party candidate). His instructions were carried out through a hierarchical chain of command from the centre (which had around 50 staff) through the ten regional coordinators to agents and prospective parliamentary candidates in the constituencies. The regional offices varied widely in size and efficiency: while some had proper offices, others operated out of private houses. In determining campaign strategy, 'The regions very much played second fiddle to the central structure and at the end of the day it was Goldsmith who called the shots' (regional coordinator). Constituency offices were instructed to plan their activities around national party campaigns.

There was no attempt to give the party a democratic structure. Rather than members, it had 'supporters' who had no rights or powers. There was no subscription fee, though sympathisers could donate money. There is controversy about the exact level of support. By February 1997 the party claimed 160,000 registered supporters, but that figure apparently included many who had simply requested information about it. A division of labour was deliberately established between the elite activists at the centre and grassroots activists. A top-down organisational structure concentrated decision-making at the centre and devolved only minimal discretionary powers to the regions and constituencies. Participation by supporters was regarded as both inefficient and undesirable. This hierarchical, undemocratic organisational design was seen as providing the flexibility and efficiency deemed crucial to the strategy of electoral pragmatism.

Candidate selection, a relatively laborious process in Britain's established political parties, was a hurried affair in the Referendum Party. Candidates were subjected to no refereeing or screening and only single interview. As one candidate put it: 'the aim was purely to get a candidate in every English, Scottish and Welsh constituency. It didn't matter one iota who it was. In fact in the run-up to the deadline we were literally grabbing people off the streets to stand.' Each constituency organisation was encouraged to raise a £1,000 contribution towards the pre-election campaign, the Centre then provided matching funds of up to £1,000. The funding for each candidate's official campaign, including the deposit, was then paid entirely by the centre.

The training given to constituency agents and prospective candidates was exiguous. A Regional Training and Information Day was organised at a Manchester hotel in February 1997. Three party officers gave short presentations on aspects of campaigning in a morning session which lasted less than two hours. Two candidates recall the event: 'I'd never been involved in an election campaign before and was expecting to receive some real instruction. It was interesting and the food was great but it hardly provided us with training for what was to come' — 'It was a party not a training day. Only my palate was educated by the experience of drinking expensive champagne and nothing else.' It was clear to all involved that this was a public relations rather than a training event. Another candidate remembered: 'I got on the train home feeling slightly merry and stinking of cigar smoke then it suddenly hit me that I still didn't have a clue what to do.' Nevertheless, all candidates were issued with a handbook, a substantial section of which was devoted to dealing with the media, since that would 'inevitably be a significant component of your campaign'. Detailed information was provided on handling interviews, press releases and press conferences as well as the differing approaches required for local newspapers as opposed to the national press.

Campaign strategy and political activities

The party's campaigning was focused primarily on its relations with and influence upon the Conservative Party. It had three broad aims. It focused on getting European issues onto the agenda, encouraging debate on the subject and then winning the war of ideas. Elites were targeted both for donations and expertise. An important tactic was to attract well-known personalities from business, the arts and academia to its major events. The party also pursued a more broadly-based mass mobilisation strategy through the distribution of a party newspaper, *News from the Referendum Party*, advertising and the organisation of set-piece events such as conferences. These broad aims remained in place, although the balance of activities altered as the party organisation took shape, for the emergence of a cadre of parliamentary candidates and agents in the run-up to the general election brought a greater emphasis on constituency servicing.

A national conference in October 1996 was intended to attract potential supporters and the press. The 5,000-plus in attendance were addressed by forty speakers drawn from a variety of backgrounds. Many were household names, including the actor Edward Fox, the former Speaker Lord Tonypandy, the ecologist David Bellamy and the millionaire zookeeper John Aspinall. The press were particularly well looked after, as one journalist recalled: 'huge amounts of money were spent on courting the press, no expense was spared—we had excellent champagne and quality buffets.' The Conference established two specific objectives for the Referendum Party: to get as many votes as possible and to influence the number of votes in the marginals. Goldsmith's declaration that 'the success of the Referendum Party would be judged solely by its total number of votes', effectively conceded that it was unlikely to win any seats.

This conference also indicated the growing shift in a Eurosceptic direction. As one constituency agent recalled: 'Prior to the conference the tenor of the campaign was based on informing the public about the issues both pertaining to the European debate and to the referendum as a mechanism for gauging the public's attitude. The emphasis was on informing the public about the European situation and explaining the history of the referendum device in Britain and other European countries. However, as the campaign progressed, tactics and attitudes changed. The party became more Eurosceptic. This was reflected in the propaganda of 'No Surrender to Brussels' and in Goldsmith's speeches. Moreover, reporting of the party in the media concentrated overwhelmingly on its Eurosceptic credentials and the party did nothing to refute this image. This was demoralising for those of us who were in it for the democratic issue.' As the election approached, the message became more simplistic. A regional organiser observed: 'Whereas at the conference many of the arguments drew on intellectual and historical dimensions (Sir James Goldsmith for example, frequently quoted from Hegel!) the final stage of the campaign relied on tabloid-style tactics. This was particularly reflected in the campaign literature.' One explanation for this shift in the final months was the intervention of a new personality, Paul Sykes, a Yorkshire millionaire businessman. Fearful of the damage that the Referendum Party might inflict on the Conservative Party, he offered financial support to any Conservative candidate who publicly opposed a single currency. As backbenchers swarmed to take up his offer, the Referendum Party adopted a more trenchant, purist Eurosceptic position. The regional organiser quoted above argues that 'Sykes had changed the stakes of the European debate on the sceptical wing and there was a need to change tactics in order to counteract the damage which he ultimately inflicted on the Referendum Party's campaign'. A rally, entitled Our Right to Decide on Europe, was held two weeks prior to polling day at Alexandra Palace. It received a fair amount of media coverage but disappointed some activists who saw it as insufficiently close to polling day and too Eurosceptical, running directly counter to the initial all-party character of the campaign.

The Referendum Party made little attempt to develop ties with other organisations. Supporter networks are of crucial importance for many pressure groups and small parties because they provide resources and political opportunities that may be vital if the group is to survive and to have impact. One measure of a group's success is therefore whether or not it has engaged in bargaining relationships. A supporters' network might have included a range of research bodies, single issue groups, broad campaign groups or political parties, sympathetic to the Referendum Party's ideas. Yet it developed very few formal links with other organisations in similar issue networks. Other than a few business contacts, the only formal political link before the election was with the Ulster Unionists. This single example entailed Goldsmith brokering a formal deal under which he agreed not to put up Referendum Party candidates in Ulster and to provide around £250,000 campaign funds in exchange for the sole Unionist MEP joining his Europe of Nations grouping in the European Parliament (this additional member enabled the group to retain its funding from the Parliament!). Goldsmith personally had a formal financial connection with a political think-tank, the European Movement, headed by the Conservative MP Bill Cash, which was the subject of some controversy in June 1996, as it appeared that Goldsmith was directly funding Tory Eurosceptics. Otherwise, the absence of the financial difficulties that plague most campaigning movements and, probably, Goldsmith's reluctance to share the limelight with anyone else, seems to explain this lack of interest in forging links with other movements.

Media relations

It was essential for the Referendum Party to build up a strong media presence. As a very recent arrival on the political scene, it needed to raise its public profile rapidly in preparation for a general election which many expected to be held in 1996. There was also no possibility of creating a constituency-level organisation to rival the long-established machines of the major parties, a weakness compounded by the lack of political experience of the great majority of its candidates. The inescapable consequence was that despite Goldsmith's well-known contempt for the media—he was on record as having declared that 'reporting in England is a load of filth' (*Financial Times*, 19.10.96)—the party had no option but to concentrate heavily upon projecting itself through the media. In this respect, Ian Beaumont, a former press officer at Downing Street under both Margaret Thatcher and John Major, who was appointed head of the Referendum Party's public relations team in

August 1996, had the great advantage of having a multi-million pound budget to help buy the Referendum Party access to the press.

One very visible manifestation of the party's exploitation of the press was a series of 13 single-page and one double-page advertisements in all the national broadsheets. The first of these appeared in October 1995. They were, of course, extremely expensive — one seasoned commentator described them as 'a boon to the newspaper industry' (*Financial Times*, 19.10.96). They attracted considerable criticism from his opponents as an exercise in cheque book politics of the sort associated with Ross Perot in the USA, and were clearly an important influence upon another commentator's depiction of the party as 'a well-publicised nuisance' (*The Times*, 24.10.96). A number were strategically timed to coincide with pronouncements by one or other of the major parties — especially the Conservatives — such as the publication of the White Paper on Europe in March 1996. These newspaper advertisements were paralleled by a range of other, expensive, forms of publicity. The most ambitious advertising project was the publication of what the party described as 'Britain's biggest mass-circulation tabloid newspaper'. A single issue of the eight-page *News from the Referendum Party*, edited by a former editor of the *News of the World*, was distributed to 24 million households at the beginning of February at an estimated cost of £2 million. A national poster campaign using some 1,500 separate sites was launched in January 1997. In total, the party spent £7,208,000 on press advertising during 1996–97. Two cinema advertisements were also produced. During the official election campaign mass leafleting was also employed (over one million leaflets were delivered in total) and 100,000 copies of a 20-minute promotional video were sent to private households.

The heavy emphasis on paid advertising was made all the more necessary by the party's failure to secure some other forms of media exposure. It experienced a major setback on the issue of its coverage by the broadcast media. In February 1997 a leaked internal BBC memorandum revealed that the Referendum Party would be treated somewhat more favourably than other 'minor' parties during the election campaign, because it had 'a distinctive stance on one of the major issues of the campaign'. But it was also made clear that there was no likelihood of it being treated on a par with other parties which had MPs at Westminster on programmes such as *Question Time* and *Election Call*. The party was, initially, more successful over party election broadcasts. The Committee on Party Broadcasting, having first proposed to allow broadcasts only to parties which could demonstrate 'proven electoral support', subsequently relented (under pressure in which Goldsmith played a significant part) and agreed to abide by the rules which had applied in 1992. These enabled any party with more than 50 candidates to have at least one broadcast. But having yielded on this point, the Committee went on to determine that the Referendum Party would be given only the one broadcast allowed to several other minor parties (Labour and the Conservatives each received five.) The party applied for a judicial review against the BBC and the Independent Broadcasting Commission on the grounds that, since it had 547 candidates standing, it was 'grotesque' that it should be put in the same category as other minor parties fielding far fewer candidates. The application was, however, rejected by the High Court, the BBC having argued that the decision was fair 'because the Referendum Party cannot seriously claim to have any realistic prospect of any seat in Parliament' (*Guardian*, 12.4.97). The significance of this reverse was underlined when polls indicated that Referendum Party support appeared to double after its sole five-minute television broadcast (*Irish Times*, 28.4.97).

Although the party (or, more especially, Goldsmith himself) received a good deal of coverage in the press, much of it was less than favourable. It often tended to focus as much upon Goldsmith's and the party's 'curiosity value' as its political arguments. The party issued numerous press releases but held only one national-level press conference — and that was at the very end of the election campaign. One manifestation of the frequently-present disharmony between Goldsmith and certain sections of the press occurred on the occasion of the party's national conference, at Brighton, in October 1996. Coverage of this one-day event — which appears to have been staged (at a cost of some £750,000) primarily to cultivate the media — included reports that 'journalists who had been critical of the party had been barred' (*The Times*, 19.10.96). Goldsmith's action, in March 1997, of issuing a writ for libel against the *Daily Express*, for its comments on the conduct of his own campaign against David Mellor at Putney, was further evidence of strained relations. Inevitably, it also served to attract further adverse press comment.

Yet compared to most pressure groups, the Referendum Party had heavy media exposure. It is frequently claimed that the most common reason for the failure of a movement or pressure group is a negative media image: 'The media generally present images of movement protest without elaboration of the substantive issues involved.'[4] But the upmarket and tabloid media played a crucial role in linking the Referendum Party's demands with both political elites and the wider public. Crucially, with significant elements of the press already sympathetic to the Eurosceptic cause, its campaign benefited unusually from strong issue-oriented reporting. While Goldsmith and his party may have suffered criticism and mockery, the issue they wished to proselytise was widely debated.

Impact on the European debate

'The Referendum Party has been created for one reason only: to obtain a fair referendum on Europe' (Referendum Party, *Statement of Aims*). If the success of the Referendum Party is to be judged solely by this single stated aim, then it clearly failed. In 1998 the possibility of a referendum on the broad question of Britain's future role within the European Union looks even more remote than it did when the party was formed in late 1995. The election of the Labour government brought a more positive attitude towards Britain's membership of the EU. Yet it would be wrong wholly to dismiss the impact of the Referendum Party—which may be seen in two ways. First, it helped promote Europe on the political agenda and added to the pressure which eventuated in the three major parties promising a referendum on the specific issue of EMU membership. Second, although the party had no effect on the outcome of the election, it did attract a respectable level of support and its presence contributed to the Conservative's dismal electoral performance.

It is very difficult to quantify the significance of the agenda-setting role played by the Referendum Party in the run-up to the general election. There were certainly several important developments in the European debate following the party's formation in November 1995. There was a distinct hardening of the Conservative government's official position towards Europe from early 1996. The most important manifestation of this changing attitude was the Cabinet decision, in April 1996, to include in the Conservative election manifesto a promise to hold a referendum on EMU if Parliament decided to recommend entry. The Liberal Democrats had already made a similar promise and the Labour Party eventually followed suit in November 1996. Yet the Cabinet compromise around this wait and see position, failed to satisfy the Eurosceptics, whose opposition to it repeatedly bobbed to the surface over the next twelve months and culminated in approximately half the Conservative candidates fighting the election with personal manifestos opposing a single currency.

The significance of the Referendum Party's contribution to these developments needs to be established, since the issue of European integration had been a problem for the Conservatives throughout the Parliament. Its formation does seem to have played an important role in bringing about the Cabinet rethink on an EMU referendum after a series of heated Cabinet discussions between February and April 1996. The idea of pledging a referendum on the single currency had been suggested by the then Foreign Secretary, Douglas Hurd, in late 1994, but although the Prime Minister approved of the idea, he was unable to get it through Cabinet. Major hinted publicly that he would be willing to consider a referendum in a television interview with David Frost in January 1996. The following month his formal proposal attracted the support of a majority of the Cabinet, but several powerful individuals blocked it. In particular, Kenneth Clarke and Michael Heseltine, who were both pro-Europe, fiercely rejected it—and it was made widely known that Clarke had threatened to resign over the issue. The leading Eurosceptic, Michael Portillo, was also against it at this stage on the grounds that he opposed referenda on principle. After growing back-bench and media pressure on the leadership to concede a referendum pledge, and much Cabinet wrangling, the objectors were finally talked round and the new position was announced on 3 April. To win over Clarke and Heseltine, the Prime Minister agreed that the pledge would be binding for one Parliament only and that there would be no further shifts in a Eurosceptic direction before the election.

Despite Clarke's explicit denial that the Cabinet's decision was a response to the Referendum Party, the view was widely held in the press that Goldsmith's presence had influenced the decision. The leading political correspondents George Jones and Robert Shrimsley claimed that Goldsmith's 'intervention is one of the major factors that have forced the Prime Minister to seek Cabinet backing for a manifesto commitment to a referendum' (*Daily Telegraph*, 9.3.96). Robert Peston, political editor at the *Financial Times*, also argued that Goldsmith 'played a role in bringing the issue to the fore' (3.4.96). The consensus view was that Major returned to the referendum issue because he had been 'motivated by warnings from Conservative Central Office that Sir James Goldsmith's Referendum Party could take vital votes away from Tory candidates fighting marginal seats at the general election' (*Financial Times*, 14.3.96). From the moment of its official formation in October 1995 senior Conservative circles had been reported to be worried by the potential electoral threat. These concerns were exacerbated after Gold-smith's February 1996 announcement that all candidates at the forth-coming election would be asked for copies of speeches or press releases concerning a referendum on Europe. This announcement put the Con-servative leadership on the defensive. Backbenchers began clamouring for 'guidance' on how they should respond. Anxiety became more acute after publication of a leaked memorandum based on a report by a party researcher which suggested that the Referendum Party could cost the Tories 25 seats and 'make the difference between winning or losing the next election' (*Financial Times*, 12.3.96). In public the Party Chairman, Brian Mawhinney, maintained that 'The Conservative Party will not change its views on these matters as a result of the interventions of any fringe party ... no parliamentary seat will change hands at the next election due to the activities of any or all fringe parties.' But concern over the electoral threat in marginal constituencies led him to push for some concession behind the scenes. Several newspapers reported that Major had approached Goldsmith via an intermediary to determine what he would have to do to persuade Goldsmith to disband the Referendum Party. The feverish atmosphere gradually won over the doubters in the Cabinet until an increasingly isolated Clarke was eventu-ally persuaded to drop his opposition to a referendum pledge.

Unfortunately for the Conservative leadership, the pledge to hold a referendum on EMU, dismissed by Goldsmith as an 'empty gesture', did nothing to deter the Referendum Party. The pressures that had contributed to the Cabinet decision did not suddenly disappear. The Government tried to draw a line at its 'wait and see' position, but Eurosceptic sniping continued. Two votes on European issues—an attempt to curb the powers of the European Court of Justice in April and a Private Member's Bill calling for a referendum on Britain's future in Europe introduced by Bill Cash in June—attracted the support of 66 and 78 Tory backbenchers respectively. Some were undoubtedly persuaded to rebel by the hope that such a public display might dissuade Goldsmith from putting up Referendum Party candidates in their constituencies. The 3.5% share of the vote obtained by the UK Independence Party in the Staffordshire S.E. by-election in April 1996 was disturbing: if an impecunious party with no national figurehead could gain this result, what might be achieved by the Referendum Party, with its massive war chest and publicity? Although a MORI poll in late April found only six Referendum Party voters in a sample of 1947 voters, Major continued to come under pressure to talk to Goldsmith. John Redwood (defeated in the Eurosceptic leadership challenge to Major in 1995) did meet Goldsmith, but was rebuffed. Major was no doubt wise to reject such a formal dialogue, for he had no further concessions to offer. Nor was it at all clear, by this stage, that Goldsmith would have been prepared to disband the Referendum Party: he was clearly enjoying the enterprise.

Senior Tories therefore went on the offensive with a series of vitriolic and often personal attacks. In the space of a few days in late April, speeches by Major, Clarke, Mawhinney and Hurd directly attacked the Referendum Party and Goldsmith. Hurd argued that 'The government's policy must not be put at the mercy of millionaires who play with British politics as a hobby or as a boost to newspaper sales.' At the Conservative annual conference in October, Michael Heseltine, in a bizarre example of a millionaire's envy of a billionaire, expressed his fear that the Referendum Party could let Labour into power and personally attacked Goldsmith: 'As you commute between the luxury of your hacienda in Mexico, your chateau in France and your palazzo in Venice, just remember the rest of us. We would have to stay here. We would have to suffer them.' Even when ministers adopted a more subtle approach, as with Mawhinney's attempt to play down the threat from the Referendum Party by claiming that it would take votes equally from all parties, or his assertion that the Tories were the true 'referendum party', there can be little doubt that the Referendum Party was taken very seriously by the Conservative leadership. Nevertheless, with the exception of a few defections, notably McAlpine and George Gardiner (deselected Conservative MP for Reigate), backbench discontent was contained until the election campaign really took off early in 1997.

Impact on the election

Goldsmith had kept a relatively low profile during the winter of 1996–97. The Referendum Party had chosen not to contest by-elections, judging the risk of a derisory vote to outweigh the advantages of an opportunity for considerable publicity. Indeed, opinion polls during this period (doubtless in part because of this low profile) put its support at no more than 1%; only in the final two months leading up to the election did they start regularly to register support at 2–3%. The party launched its campaign on 9 April in the port of Newlyn in Cornwall, where Goldsmith sought to whip up anti-Europe sentiments amongst fishermen. By delaying the announcement of the list of seats that the party would contest until mid-April, he was able to maintain pressure on worried Conservative MPs to the last moment. Conservative MPs' fears had not been assuaged by Major's wait and see policy, or his recent tough line on various European matters, notably EU fishing quotas. With polls still showing no swing towards the Tories, the increasingly febrile atmosphere enabled Eurosceptics to stir up opposition throughout the parliamentary party against the leadership's position. This discontent was given a focus by Sykes's undertaking in early April to contribute to the campaign costs of all Conservative candidates who explicitly rejected monetary union in their manifestos. This intervention and the imminent publication of the list of Referendum Party candidates brought the simmering disagreement amongst Conservatives into the open. Rumours circulated that more than 150 backbench MPs would issue election addresses stating their opposition to a single currency. Richard Body, a long-standing Eurosceptic, announced his intention to stand as a 'Conservative against a federal Europe' candidate. Major's plan to downplay this turmoil by turning a blind eye was quickly undermined by declarations from Angela Rumbold, Conservative Party vice-chairman in charge of candidates, and two junior ministers that they, too, would reject the official line in favour of a firm 'no' vote in a referendum on a single currency. These announcements coincided with a Gallup poll putting support for the Referendum Party at 3% which, although probably influenced by the furore over fishing quotas, was its highest so far. Clearly worried, the Prime Minister used a party political broadcast to appeal to be allowed to keep open his negotiating position on Europe. It was, in effect, a presidential appeal over the head of his party for the public to trust him, personally, to deliver the best deal for Britain. But it failed to stem the panic among Tory candidates, 317 of whom eventually pledged their opposition to a single currency.

In the event, this rebellion did nothing to dissuade the Referendum Party from standing candidates against particular individuals; Goldsmith had previously declared that he would judge them by actions not words alone (BBC, *On the Record*, 13.10.96). Its 547 candidates made it the largest minor party ever to contest a general election. In addition to the Speaker's seat and the Ulster seats, 'The Referendum Party chose not to fight 93 seats where the leading candidate is considered to be in sympathy with our objective of obtaining a referendum to allow the whole electorate to decide Britain's future in Europe' (*Referendum Party Press Release*, 16.4.97). The 65 Conservative MPs, 26 Labour MPs (mostly Campaign Group left-wingers) and two Liberal Democrats whom the Referendum Party did not oppose were all incumbent members with long-standing records of hostility to Europe: not recent recruits to EMU scepticism.

But while Europe was a central issue for the Tories, it failed to ignite commensurate interest amongst the electorate. Although several opinion polls revealed considerable opposition to membership of the EMU in particular or the EU in general, it was not a salient issue on election day; indeed, according to MORI, it was ranked only as the eighth most important issue determining voting preferences. The Referendum Party helped focus Tory attention on Europe. The *Spectator* suggested that, 'By frightening so many Tory candidates into coming out against the single currency — as he certainly has — Sir James may have saved them from defeat by winning them anti-single currency votes' (19.4.97). But others were motivated by the same mistaken belief that Euroscepticism was a vote-winner. A hard core of Eurosceptics backbenchers had always been expected to 'create mischief'. The presence of the Referendum Party merely strengthened their hand, as did the Eurosceptic press — notably *The Times*, *Daily Mail* and *Daily Telegraph* which published daily lists of candidates planning to reject the official position. *The Times* eschewed declaring a preference for any one party, instead urging its readers to support the most Eurosceptic candidate. Xenophobic sentiments were further excited on 21 April by the President of the European Commission, Jacques Santer, in an ill-timed speech condemning the widespread expression of anti-European sentiments. Indeed, several surveys show that the press published more stories, articles and editorials on Europe than on any other issue during the campaign, although the vast majority of this coverage, particularly that concerning the Conservatives, was negative.[5] The Referendum Party played its small part in placing Europe at the top of the media's agenda during the campaign.

In the event, the scale of the Labour landslide rendered the Referendum Party's part irrelevant to the outcome of the election. Its performance was, nevertheless very impressive in several respects. Its 547 candidates attracted 811,827 votes — an average of 3.1% in those seats it contested (2.6% overall); 42 saved their deposits.[6] It was the best ever performance by a minor party in a general election. (It clearly outperformed the UK Independence Party which averaged 1.2% in the 194 constituencies it contested and trailed the Referendum Party in all but two of the seats in which both stood.) It polled particularly strongly in Southern England and East Anglia — averaging 3.9% in this region. It did best in seats with large agricultural, fishing or elderly populations, such as Harwich 9.2%, Folkstone & Hythe 8.0%, West Suffolk 7.6%, St Ives 6.9% and Falmouth & Cambourne 6.6%.

Despite the worst fears of many Conservative MPs, the Referendum Party had only a marginal direct impact on Conservative fortunes, although, at first glance, this claim appears to do it an injustice. For it performed better in seats defended by Conservatives (3.6%) than by Labour (2.5%), and there were 19 seats in which the Referendum Party vote exceeded the Conservative candidate's margin of defeat. But by no means all Referendum Party voters were drawn from Conservative ranks and some, disillusioned with the government, might have supported another party in its absence. MORI polls suggested that just over half of Referendum Party voters had voted for the Tories in 1992, the remainder being drawn roughly equally from Labour, Liberal Democrat and non-voters. On the basis of this data it is estimated that, at most, Referendum Party candidates cost the Conservatives six seats.[7] Using a different approach, Curtice and Steed suggest that where the Referendum Party attracted its average vote of around 3%, about two-thirds of that probably came from former Tory voters. However, where its vote was higher than average, the Liberal Democrats appear to have been the main losers—suggesting that the Referendum Party was the preferred party of protest in these constituencies. They identify six seats in which the presence of an anti-European candidate (two UKIP) probably cost the Conservatives the seat; conversely, in up to three seats a narrow Conservative victory coincided with a very strong anti-European vote which might have come disproportionately from the opposition. Whichever estimate is accepted, it is clear that the direct impact of the Referendum Party on individual contests was minuscule.

The indirect electoral impact of the Referendum Party on the Conservatives was probably more significant, though unquantifiable. By fuelling Eurosceptic opposition to the Conservative leadership, it certainly contributed to the Conservative obsession with Europe. And there can be little doubt that by engaging in a very public internal conflict over Europe, the Conservatives reinforced the widely-held and electorally-damaging perception of a weakly-led, divided party.

Political party or pressure group?

The Referendum Party was a single-issue movement which exhibited some of the characteristics of a pressure group and some of a political party. Like many pressure groups it was organised to achieve a specific collective political end—in this case a referendum on Britain's future within Europe. But, like a party, it sought to achieve this objective by presenting candidates for election to Parliament (although Goldsmith initially hoped that a mere threat to contest the election might induce other parties to concede all or part of this objective). However, if elected, the sole responsibility of the party's MPs would be to vote in Parliament for a referendum. Once that referendum had been held, the party would dissolve itself. In this respect, it bore a closer resemblance to a pressure group than a political party, the latter having goals that are ongoing and, in most cases, seeking to form a government. Thus the Referendum Party shared several characteristics of each type of organisation and is best viewed as a single-issue 'interest-party'.[8] Its organisational distinctiveness lay in the absence either of dependence on a membership for funding (due to Goldsmith's wealth) or, indeed, possession of any formal membership structure. While new social movements may also share these characteristics, they usually do so because their supporters express an ideological preference for participatory democratic structures. The Referendum Party, by contrast, was Goldsmith's personal creation and his autocratic style precluded internal power-sharing.

The Referendum Party may be seen as indicative of a broader trend in western democracies towards a new politics in which citizens have shifted from traditional methods of representation to new styles of political action. The emergence of libertarian new social movements and political parties has been well documented as one manifestation of this development. Goldsmith's Referendum Party, like Ross Perot's United We Stand/Reform Party, offers a rather different manifestation in which entrepreneurial elites have set up independent political parties in an attempt to challenge the established political order and force through new political agendas at the heart of governing structures. But, unlike Perot, the Referendum Party was not seeking to govern the country. Instead, voting for it could be interpreted as similar to the much more conventional protest activity of signing a petition. For all its lack of resemblance to traditional conceptions of protest, functionally, the Referendum Party was an attempt to alter policy on a single issue through non-conventional methods. In this respect, it achieved a small degree of success. Although the 1997 general election produced a Labour government that was more sympathetic towards Europe than its predecessor, it was also, as a result, in part, of the impact of the Referendum Party, committed to holding a referendum before Britain joined the EMU.

In addition to the sources cited, this article draws upon a number of unattributable interviews with Referendum Party activists. For further information about Goldsmith's views on economics and politics, see his two books: *The Trap* (Macmillan, 1993) and *The Response* (Macmillan, 1995).

1   See K. Alderman, 'Legislating on Maastricht', *Contemporary Record*, Winter 1993.
2   See K. Alderman, 'The Conservative Leadership Election of 1995', *Parliamentary Affairs*, April 1996.
3   This article does not deal with the party's relaunch as the Referendum Movement after the 1997 general election.
4   T. Rochon, 'The West European Peace Movement and the Theory of New Social Movements' in R. Dalton and M. Kuechler (eds), *Challenging the Political Order* (Polity, 1990), p. 108.
5   See D. Butler and D Kavanagh, *The British General Election of 1997* (Macmillan, 1997), p. 175 and T. Burns, *The Impact of the National Press on Voters in 1997* (Test Research, 1997).
6   The electoral analysis is drawn from J Curtice and M Steed, Appendix 2, in D. Butler and D. Kavanagh, op. cit.
7   R. Worcester and R. Mortimore, *The Impact of the European Issue on the Election Outcome* (MORI, 1997).
8   Y. Yishai, 'The Thin Line between Groups and Parties in the Israeli Electoral Process' in K. Lawson (ed.), *How Political Parties Work* (Praeger, 1994).

NAME INDEX

—A—

Alderman, K. 177n
Al Fayed, Mohammed 146
Ali, Yasmin 136n
Allen, George 115n
Alton, David 144
Ames, Fisher 13
Anderson, A. 102n
Anderson, Janet 147
Apter, D.E. 61n
Arnold, Edward 115n
Ashdown, Paddy 24
Aspinall, John 167

—B—

Baggott, R. 31, 36n
Baker, S. 49n
Beaumont, Ian 168
Beck, U. 115n
Beith, Alan 79, 85
Bell, Martin 2, 58
Bellamy, David 167
Benewick, Robert 13, 20n
Bennie, Lynn 16, 17, 31, 102n
Benson, Matt 58
Benton, T. 49n
Benyon, William 143
Berlusconi, Silvio 162
Bevan, Aneurin 123
Blain, J. 102n
Blair, Cherie 32
Blair, Tony 3, 24, 32, 146
Body, Richard 174
Borre, O. 12, 20n
Bosso, C.J. 97, 102n, 115n
Bottomley, Virginia 145
Bowman, Phyllis 139, 146
Braine, Sir Bernard 143
Brier, A. 88n
Brook, L. 88n
Brown, Alice 132, 136n
Brown, Lord Justice Simon 42
Burns, T. 177n
Burstein, P. 9, 20n
Butler, D. 177n
Byrne, Paul 7, 9, 12, 20n, 88n, 115n, 126n, 136n

—C—

Callaghan, James 119
Carson, Rachel 103
Carter, Jimmy 17
Cash, Bill 168, 173
Chambers, J. 149n
Cigler, A. 6, 19n, 36n
Clark, J. 115n

Clarke, Kenneth 171, 172, 173
Coe, Sebastian 33
Colvin, Michael 24
Connery, Sean 32
Cooper, Jilly 42
Corrie, John 143
Corston, Jean 107
Crozier, John 33
Cullen, Lord 26, 28, 35
Cunningham, Roseanna 131
Curtice, J. 176, 177n

—D—

Dafis, Cynog 67
Dalton, R. 9, 10, 14, 20n, 177n
Davies, Bryan 158
Dewar, Donald 32, 133
Diana, Princess of Wales 1, 2, 3
Dickson, L. 102n
Dowse, R. 88n
Dunleavy, P. 11, 20n
Duyvendak, J.W. 20n

—E—

Eggar, Tim 17
Einwohner, R. 20n
Ellis, Caroline 136n
Euchner, Charles 6, 19n
Evans, K. 61n
Eyerman, R. 102n

—F—

Fay, Chris 95
Foot, Michael 119
Forsyth, Michael 24, 27, 33, 34
Foster, Michael 154
Foulkes, George 24
Fox, Edward 167
Fraser, P. 61n
Freedman, E.J. 61n
Frost, David 171

—G—

Gaitskell, Hugh 117
Galligan, Yvonne 132, 136n
Gamson, W.A. 9, 75n, 161n
Gardiner, George 173
Garner, Robert 10, 160n
Gazzard, Jeff 61
Gerlach, L. 75n
Gilje, Paul 13
Giugni, M. 20n
Glover, Mark 158
Goggins, Paul 57
Goldsmith, Sir James 162, 163, 164,

165, 167, 168, 169, 170, 172, 173, 174, 175, 176, 177
Goodwin, Barbara 46, 49n
Gorman, D.G. 102n
Gorman, Teresa 147
Goyder, J. 115n
Grant, W. 36n
Grylls, Michael 143
Gubbins, Bridget 84
Gummer, John 54
Gundelach, Peter 6

—H—
Hadley, J. 149n
Hamilton, Neil 2, 57, 58
Hamilton, Thomas 21, 24
Havel, Vaclav 6
Healey, Denis 119
Hershey, M. 36n
Herzog, H. 49n
Heseltine, Michael 171, 172, 173
Hill, Julia 2
Hill, R. 88n
Hindell, K. 149n
Hine, V. 75n
Hollander, J. 20n
Hooper, Daniel ('Swampy') 1, 3, 50, 56, 57, 61, 65, 121
Howe, Sir Geoffrey 145
HRH, Duke of Edinburgh 34
HRH, Queen Elizabeth II 2
Hughes, J. 88n
Hughes, Robert 29
Hume, Cardinal 147
Hurd, Douglas 171, 173

—I—
Inglehart, R. 7, 20n
Irvine, Lord 132, 134
Irwin, A. 115n
Issac, J. 149n

—J—
Jackson, Christine 136n
Jamison, A. 102n
Jamison, W. 49n
Jasanoff, S. 114n
Jenkins, J.C. 20n
Jones, George 172
Jordan, Grant 2, 3, 7, 20n, 36n, 88n, 92, 99
Jowell, R. 75n, 88n

—K—
Kavanagh, D. 177n
Keith, Penelope 42
Kennedy, Helena 136n

Kent, Bruce 124
Kiernan, Victor 13
King, Tom 107
Klandermans, B. 20n
Koopmans, R. 13, 20n
Kraft, M.E. 102n
Kriesi, H.P. 13, 20n, 75n
Kuechler, M. 177n

—L—
Lash, S. 115n
Lawrence, Philip 34
Lawson, K. 20n, 177n
Lees, Andrew 64
Lessnoff, M. 12, 20n
Lewis, Terry 25
Loomis, B. 6, 19n, 36n
Lovenduski, Joni 129, 132, 136n, 149n
Lowe, P. 115n
Lumley, Joanna 42, 152
Lunch, W. 49n

—M—
MacAlpine, Lord 165, 173
Major, John 23, 163, 168, 171, 172, 173, 174
Maloney, W. 7, 20n, 36n, 88n, 102n
Mar, Countess of 107
Marsh, David 13, 25, 36n, 149n
Mawhinney, Brian 172, 173
May, James 97
Mazmanian, D.A. 102n
McCarthy, Michael 13
McCartney, Linda 152
McCartney, Paul 152
McCulloch, A. 102n
McGuire, Anne 32, 33
McKenna, Rosemary 131
McKie, D. 61n
McLaren, Marilyn 131
McLeish, Henry 130
McLeod, Rhoda 8, 17
McMaster, Gordon 103, 107
Meenan, P.A. 102n
Melchett, Lord 95
Mellor, David 24, 170
Milch, J. 61n
Miller, W. 12, 20n
Monbiot, George 67, 72
Moore, N.W. 114n
Morely, Elliot 37
Morrow, James 145
Mortimore, R. 177n
Mowlam, Marjorie 34

—N—

Neilson, J. 102n
Nelkin, D. 61n
Nilsson, Lars 145
Norris, Pippa 132, 136n
Norris, Steven 65
North, Mick 22
Norton-Taylor, R. 114n
Nownes, A. 115n

—O—

O'Brien, Lord 39, 40
O'Neil, Martin 21
Osmond, J. 136n
O'Sullevan, Sir Peter 37, 42
Outshoorn, J. 149n

—P—

Parkin, F. 125n
Pearce, F. 102n
Pearston, Anne 21, 22, 23, 25, 26, 31, 32,
    33, 34
Penman, Danny 43
Perman, D. 61n
Perot, Ross 162, 169, 177
Perrigo, Sarah 134, 136n
Peston, Robert 172
Pious IX, Pope 138
Pollak, M. 61n
Popplewell, Justice 42
Portillo, Michael 171
Powell, Enoch 144
Prescott, John 58
Press, D. 102n
Pritchard, C. 125n
Purdey, Mark 107, 113

—Q—

Quintavalle, Bruno 146
Quintavalle, Countess Josephine 146

—R—

Redfearn, S. 49n
Redwood, John 173
Rees-Mogg, William 17
Regan, T. 161n
Rhys Williams, Elspeth 139
Ritvo, H. 161n
Roberts, Peter 41
Robertson, George 24, 26, 34
Robins, L. 88n
Rochon, T. 177n
Rose, Chris 92
Rotherman, Heinz 95
Rothermere, Lord 162
Rucht, D. 102n

Rudig, W. 102n
Rumbold, Angela 174
Ryan, Michael 21, 24

—S—

Santer, Jacques 175
Sawa, N. 61n
Scarbrough, E. 20n
Scarisbrick, John 146
Scarisbrick, Nuala 145
Secrett, Charles 67
Serpell, J. 49n
Seyd, P. 10, 20n
Shrimsley, Robert 172
Simms, M. 149n
Singer, P. 161n
Smith, M. 161n
Smith, Trevor 9, 13, 20n
Snook, Liz 50, 58
Solesbury, W. 102n
Steed, M. 176, 177n
Steel, David 138
Stevenson, Peter 39, 40, 41, 47, 49n
Strachan Yvonne 133
Straw, Jack 32
Stringer, Graham 56
Sykes, Paul 167, 174
Szerszynski, B. 115n

—T—

Tannenbaum, E. 49n
Tarrow, S. 75n
Taylor, B. 75n, 88n
Taylor, I. 61n
Taylor, R. 125n
Thatcher, Margaret 163, 168
Thompson, Jack 79, 85
Timpson, A. 12, 20n
Tonypandy, Lord 167
Townsend, Peter 13
Treshman, Don 145
Trotter, Neville 86
Tyme, John 62

—U—

Upsall, D. 102n

—V—

Van Deth, J.W. 19n
Vig, N.J. 102n

—W—

Waite, Terry 50, 58, 60
Waldegrave, William 111
Wall, D. 75n

Watkins, George 98
Watterson, A. 115n
Weale, A. 115n
West, D. 36n
Westminster, Duke of 8
White, James 143
Whiteley, P. 10, 20n
Widdecombe, Ann 145
Wilford, R. 136n

Winning, Cardinal Thomas 146
Wolfsfeld, G. 75n
Worcester, R. 102n, 177n
Wynne, B. 115n

—Y—

Yishai, Yael 10, 20n, 177n
Young, Hugo 16, 99
Young, K. 88n